W9-BWF-125

Where the
Money Is

Where the Money Is

<hr/>

Advancement Research for Nonprofit Associations

by

Helen Bergan

BioGuide Press

Copyright ©2001 by Helen Bergan
Printed in the United States of America

All rights reserved under International and Pan-American Copyright
Conventions. For information contact:

BioGuide Press
P.O.Box 42005
Arlington,VA 22204
(703) 820-9045
E-mail: hbergan@cs.com
www.bioguidepress.com

Other books by the author:
  Where the Money Is: A Fund Raiser's Guide to the Rich
  Where the Information Is: A Guide to Electronic Research
      for Nonprofit Organizations
  Climbing Kilimanjaro: An African Odyssey

Publisher's Cataloging-in-Publication Data

Bergan, Helen.
Where the Money Is: Advancement Research
for Nonprofit Organizations/Helen Bergan.
        p.   cm.
Includes bibliographic references and index.
ISBN 0-9615277-7-3
1. Bergan, Helen. 2. Fund Raising – Research.
3. Millionaires – Research.
4. Philanthropy. 5. Nonprofit Organizations. I. Title.
HG177.B48   361.7   2001
Library of Congress Card Number: 2001117951

Contents

➤ Preface ❖

Has any other profession changed as drastically in the last few years as nonprofit prospect and donor research? I doubt it. The profession even has a new name—development or advancement research—indicating its new role in the entire fundraising process.

This change is shown most dramatically in the resources used by researchers to find information on their prospects and donors. My first book on the subject came out in 1985. *Where the Money Is: A Fund Raiser's Guide to the Rich* almost exclusively described print resources found in public and academic libraries. The second edition of that book in 1992 included those resources, but also introduced online databases available on *Dialog* and the newspaper and magazine indexes *Datatimes* and *InfoTrac*. I hinted at what electronic resources were to come, but most of us were clueless as to where this new technology might take nonprofit prospect research.

When my book, *Where the Information Is: A Guide to Electronic Research for Nonprofit Organizations,* came out in 1996, the Internet was just then becoming a useful tool. Some databases had to be accessed via Gopher. When was the last time you heard that word when it didn't pertain to the University of Minnesota football team?

During the first years of the Internet era, it was reported even Bill Gates was slow to acknowledge the significance of that technology. Since then, the Internet has become the *most* useful tool for nonprofit prospect and donor research. Much information that previously was available only for a price became available free on the Internet.

While the Internet is a wonderful way to find information about prospects and donors, it can be a gigantic time-eater. When we get thousands of hits to a search query, we are forced to check only the first few or forget the whole thing in frustration. Knowing where to look is the magic key to the Internet. We also need to realize that everything about a person is not on the Internet, and as we become more concerned about privacy, I hope it never will be.

After my earlier prospect research books were written, advancement research has become even more indispensable to the funding process in nonprofit offices. Researchers are better trained and have faster tools that access more and improved databases. Using a profile gleaned from electronic resources, development officers and agency executives can approach potential donors with the confidence they have the necessary information to facilitate the solicitation.

For those beginning a career in nonprofit research, this book tells how to establish and organize a research office. Those who have done research for years will find resources and information in this book to enable them to carry on special assignments. This book highlights the important role research plays in rating prospects, selecting board members, naming facilities, and finding alumni addresses. It can truly be said: Without research there is no development.

Information for this book came from many sources:

- My personal experience as a librarian and researcher

- Internet listservs where seasoned researchers answer questions

- My continuing contact with nonprofit researchers

- Articles in newspapers and magazines

- Little bits of paper on which I scribbled notes when I heard of a new Web site or other useful resource

Throughout this book sidebars relevant to the topic being discussed are included. Some mention gifts that reflect a simpatico relationship between the donor and the nonprofit institution. Others are tidbits I thought were interesting or amusing, my attempt to lighten a subject that sometimes became quite serious.

I would like to thank Pat Feistritzer for editing this book and Bob Rand for design and typesetting. Clarence Mundy drew the cartoons. Many friends offered encouragement and ideas. They convinced me that, even in these days of the Internet, nonprofit researchers could still use a print book. I appreciated their help.

Helen Bergan
July 2001

What Is Advancement Research?

"The low-hanging fruit has been picked.
We've got to go higher in the tree."
—Brad Freeman
George W. Bush's
California finance chairman

I t is tempting to think of ours as a modern-day gilded age, like the time at the beginning of the last century when the simply rich became extremely rich. In the late 1990s, every day almost we heard of a new group of multi-millionaires, or even multi-billionaires, who were big winners in the stock market sweepstakes with controlling shares in unfamiliar companies. All around we saw evidence of CEOs with appreciated stock holdings and large salaries that turned into golden parachutes, with stock options thrown into the mix. Real estate values soared ever higher.

According to some estimates, four to five million millionaires live in the United States. Using U.S. Census Bureau statistics in 1999, one in fourteen households has a net worth that tops seven figures—that's four times as many households as a decade ago. This could be the time when those with extreme riches could become modern-day benefactors such as John D. Rockefeller and Andrew Carnegie, who laid the groundwork for philanthropy by using their vast wealth for civic purposes. Happily, the concept of charitable gifts from wealthy individuals continues.

With the robust economy and increasing evidences of wealth, it was not surprising that individuals gave 82.8 percent of the $203.5 billion given to charities in 2000. That figure, which includes bequests, surpassed the 5.3 percent of that total given by corporations and the 12 percent given by foundations. Within that $203.5 billion, individual charitable gifts are described as the "largest ever" to this or that type of institution. It could be the largest from a woman, the largest from a faculty member, the most from an anonymous donor, the most received from a non-alumnus, or the biggest gift from an athlete. Most such gifts made newspaper headlines.

Perhaps it is significant that during this gilded age, wealthiest American Bill Gates gave millions to wire libraries to 21st century broadband standards in some of the same buildings that Andrew Carnegie's donated wealth built in the early 1900s.

In this era, many fundraising campaigns were better than ever could be imagined. When Johns Hopkins University kicked off a major campaign in 1994, it hoped to raise $900 million. After passing that mark in less than four years, the institution raised its goal. At campaign end, the university had raised $1.5 billion, 65% more than initially expected. That sum included five of their largest-ever gifts, one for $100 million from alumnus Michael R. Bloomberg, founder of the business news service that bears his name.

The University of Virginia topped $1.5 billion in a five-year campaign that aimed for $1 billion. Five other colleges have raised more than $1.5 billion: Harvard, Yale, Columbia, Cornell, and the University of Southern California.

Research comes before development

For those universities, it must seem this is a gilded age of philanthropy. But is it the gilded age for all nonprofits? Probably not. It sounds so easy when a large gift is reported in the press. Seldom does the newspaper story tell what led to the donation. It doesn't mention the contact that identified the prospect, the research process that analyzed the giving potential and determined links between the prospect and the organization, the long cultivation process, and finally the solicitation by a top development officer or institution president. Without the necessary research and the steps leading up to it, would there have been a gift?

It is no accident that research comes before development. In the same way that corporations have research and development departments, academic and nonprofit institutions have development departments. At some point in the institution's development or advancement history, the question may have been raised: Do we need a research component in our development office? That question has been answered in the affirmative in most academic institutions and large nonprofit organizations. Now even small nonprofits are concluding that the answer must be yes.

Most organizations that raise funds have staff members responsible for the funding process. Whether called fundraisers, development officers, or advancement officers, they are the ones who actually solicit contributions, often with the assistance of the college president or the organization's head executive, especially if the hoped-for gift is large. The more background information those fundraisers have on the prospective donor, the more likely their success. That's why development research is essential.

Although most people understand the difference between a nonprofit organization and a for-profit enterprise, many still do not understand the ways a nonprofit institution gets funding. The development researcher has a crucial role in that process. The main purpose of the research office is to assist grant seekers and development officers in their search for funds to carry out the mission of the institution or organization.

Advancement officers may be seeking contributions from individuals, foundations, corporations, the government—or all of the above. The researcher is required to gather information to determine the most likely donors from a database of thousands of individuals or from directories of thousands of corporations or foundations. It's not an easy task, but it is essential. An organization must use its resources where they can do the most good. Development officers must spend their time cultivating donors who are the most likely to have the interest and ability to give to the organization.

Finding likely prospects

While researching individuals, the task is to help identify prospects, gather biographical and financial information on prospects and current donors, and analyze the giving potential of those persons. This may include researching a prospects' stock and real estate holdings, discovering contributions made to other organizations, and finding a person's main interests, as well as his or her connection to the organization's mission. The researcher wants to determine why the prospect should want to give here. It is not a question of just listing and researching wealthy persons (anyone can do that), but of finding those most likely to contribute, then providing an opportunity to match their interests with the institution's needs.

The researcher will want to identify relationships among donors and prospects to determine the right person to cultivate and to solicit the gift.

Part of the research responsibilities will be looking for clues leading to potential conflict of interest. Avoiding public relations disasters by the development office may be as important as raising funds.

As there is a limit to an organization's staff time and resources, it is pragmatic to rate prospects not only by their ability to give, but also by their inclination. Some refer to this as the LAI principle: linkage, ability, and interest. Others define the task as finding persons with 3 Cs: capacity, concern, and care. Researching wealth (or "wealth chasing") without researching connections and interests will be of little benefit.

Seeking foundation funds, the researcher may be asked to determine which foundations give to what type of organization and how much they give. Does the organization have some connection with the foundation, perhaps through the board of directors? What are the foundation's criteria for making grants and what is the application process? Are there grant deadlines or are applications accepted at any time? Who established the foundation? What was that person or that family's philanthropic philosophy? How can one get a list of other organizations that have received grants from that foundation?

Similar information may be needed when searching for corporation grants. Many corporations have established foundations for their philanthropic endeavors. What can be discovered about the company? Does it have a geographical or board connection with your type of organization? Which of your organization's programs are best suited to which corporation? The researcher needs to determine that one of the company's "politically incorrect" products won't surprise the funded organization. The researcher may need to follow the company's financial history to determine when it is most apt to be generous.

Too often nonprofit organizations overlook funding possibilities from government grants. How can you find out what grants the federal, state, or local governments have to offer institutions? What are the procedures for applications? Where can you find a good index to the federal assistance available? Do any Internet or online resources identify government grants?

Information is available

Welcome to the world of prospect research. Once a researcher realizes that information in all those categories is readily available, the research task is not as daunting. This book will deal with the position of the development or prospect researcher within a nonprofit organization or institution, and tell where to find answers to the questions asked about individuals, foundations, and government grants.

Thanks to the present information age, a researcher can get most answers without even leaving the office. Keep reading for research techniques and resources. Throughout this book, the research function will be referred to as prospect research, nonprofit research, and development or advancement research. In short, researchers are the behind-the-scenes folks who can lead to the success of the development or advancement office.

But, first, how did prospect research get started?

The beginning of development research

Even though the techniques have changed dramatically, the reasons for doing nonprofit prospect research remain the same since John D. Rockefeller, Jr. stated:

> It is a great help to know something about the person whom you are approaching. You cannot deal successfully with all people the same way. Therefore, it is desirable to find out something about the person you are going to—what his interests are, whether you have any friends in common, whether he gave last year, if so, how much he gave, what he might be able to give this year, etc. Information such as this puts you more closely in touch with him and makes the approach easier.

The executives who heard Rockefeller's speech in 1933 to the Citizen's Welfare Committee in New York may have taken the need for research seriously and gone back to the office to command someone, probably a secretary, to make a file of newspaper clippings on wealthy persons. Thus began the process known as prospect research.

The tools used to find information on generous donors such as John D. Rockefeller, Jr., were limited in 1933. If he expected those who approached him for a contribution to do their homework first, that task was not easy. Back then, the person doing research on a wealthy donor could hope the person was in *Who's Who in America*, a reference volume first published in 1899. Another venerable biographical set, *National Cyclopedia of American Biography (NCAB)*, started in 1898. If researchers from the Rockefeller era had access to that resource, they were fortunate. It gave a lot of Rockefeller family history and details about their business.

Using its index that began in 1913, early prospect researchers could find articles on potential philanthropists in *The New York Times* at a good public library. Hunting for the exact issue in those massive bound news-

Lives of the rich and famous in the 19th century

Evidence that people were interested in the lives of the wealthy in the 19th century is a publication entitled *Wealth and Biography of the Wealthy Citizens of New York City, Comprising an Alphabetical Arrangement of Persons Estimated to be Worth $100,000, and Upwards.* Published in 1845, it gave information on the well-known wealthy such as John Jacob Astor and Cornelius Vanderbilt. Interesting details were provided for some who have faded from the history books. There was Henry J. Sanford (rated at $100,000), a wood dealer, who "made his own money but was an adventurer in matrimony," and George Douglas, whose "wine cellar was more extensive than his library."

Thanks to the *Internet Prospector* for that clue to a resource a prospect researcher (if they had existed) might have used in mid-19th century.

papers in the library stacks wasn't easy, but there were few alternatives until microfilm made research somewhat easier. With the hope of finding periodical articles about the rich prospect, the researcher could refer to *Readers' Guide to Periodical Literature,* dating back to 1905. In that same New York library, the librarian may have established a collection of individual files on important or wealthy persons.

When it was acknowledged that research had an important role in the solicitation of donations, institutions and organizations formalized the prospect research function by spelling out what they hoped to accomplish with research.

Research was done to identify potential donors; compile and analyze biographical, financial, and professional data; determine relationships and donation history to the organization or institution; interpret charitable interests and giving inclination; and compile the information in profile reports to be used as part of the development process.

One of the many reasons for research was to target an appropriate "ask" during a solicitation. The more information the development officer has about the donor's financial status, the more precise the solicitation can be. Those who solicit contributions do not want to ask for an amount much too high—it might embarrass and alienate the prospect if the amount is higher than possible. Too low an amount would be a missed opportunity.

Books on prospect research written in the 1980s and early 1990s, including my own, listed print resources and a few fee-based services such as *Dialog*. Along came the Internet in the mid-1990s. It changed almost everything about development research. Who could ever have imagined, just a few years ago, the resource riches available now for the nonprofit researcher? Now researchers gather needed information from their internal files, from print directories and indexed publications, and from CD-ROM databases. Then they go online for a vast array of Internet Web sites, professional and business directories, and public records. It's even possible to skip looking at print resources and head straight for the Internet to get all that is needed.

Those resources don't mean research is necessarily easier; it's just different. A researcher needs to know which Web sites are the best or spend time wandering aimlessly through cyberspace. Once found, the wealth of data on a prospect still has to be analyzed and evaluated in the context of an individual's relationship to the organization and his or her inclination to give.

Gradually the research function evolved to include the proactive identification and management tracking of individual, foundation, and corporate prospects. In most offices the researcher was responsible for not only gathering the data but also for maintaining the information library in paper and electronic files.

The history of the Association of Professional Researchers for Advancement

As the importance of nonprofit research became more apparent to colleges, universities, and many nonprofit organizations, a group calling themselves "Fund-Raising Researchers" met at Augsburg College in Minnesota to organize a local group to discuss common concerns. The group met twice a year and in 1983 formalized under the name Minnesota Prospect Research Association. From that beginning, members expanded the range of the association from a local to a national organization. The American Prospect Research Association (APRA) was officially incorporated in January 1988, and its first truly national board of directors was elected in 1989.

That board affirmed that the chief goal of the association "is to raise the stature of researchers, both in terms of professional training and in terms of our position in the development profession as a whole." Realizing the importance of ethical conduct in research work, a subcommittee on ethics was charged with the formation of a code of research ethics. An APRA Statement of Ethics and A Donor Bill of Rights, developed by other fundraising associations, were adopted.

The organization began to get members from other countries and, in 1995, the APRA board voted to accept the results of a membership referendum to change APRA's name to the Association of Professional Researchers for Advancement. The new name reflects the current thinking that nonprofit research is more than just researching prospective donors, and it avoids a potential misinterpretation about what type of personal information is sought.

Recognized as a premier international professional association, its vision is to address "the changing needs and wide scope of skills required of advancement researchers and advancement service professionals within the non-profit community." APRA established a Basic Skills Set and an Advanced Skills Set that outlined what is expected of nonprofit researchers at both levels. With its Web site, APRA now offers JobQuest, a posting of career positions for advancement professionals.

Membership has grown to almost 2000 members with 25 regional chapters in more than half the states and several foreign countries, indicating that APRA is a thriving organization, geared to meeting the changing role of nonprofit researchers in the 21st century.

Staffing for advancement research

Nonprofit researchers have a variety of titles, depending on the organization's structure. As a relatively new profession, it is not surprising that the position title has evolved along with the position duties.

Here are some titles that appear on business cards of advancement researchers.

- Advancement Associate
- Advancement Research Manager or Officer
- Advancement Researcher
- Development Associate
- Development Officer for Research
- Development Research Analyst
- Development Researcher
- Director of Prospect Research
- Donor Information Manager
- Donor Information Specialist
- Nonprofit Researcher

- Prospect Management and Tracking System Coordinator
- Prospect Researcher
- Prospect Tracking Specialist
- Research Assistant
- Research Strategist

Most researchers have bachelor's degrees and many have master's degrees. A few have a Ph.D. Many in nonprofit research positions enter the field with degrees and experience in library and information science. Most researchers come with a liberal arts background, but almost every academic study can be good preparation for research work. Some researchers come to the profession from other areas of development and learn research on the job.

In a perfect world there would be enough staff to do what needs to be done in the research office and a sufficient budget to pay for all the needed resources—electronic and print. Wouldn't that be lovely? Research takes both time and money; good research takes even more time and even more money!

One often-asked question when researchers get together or communicate at APRA meetings or on PRSPCT-L, a listserv for nonprofit researchers, is the average ratio of research staff to development and major gifts officers. Answers indicate a 1:5 ratio is healthy—one researcher for five development officers. This assumes a good working relationship where the officers are specific about their needs and consider the researcher an important partner in the fundraising process.

To whom does the nonprofit researcher report? Ideally the head of the research office reports to the same person to whom the development officers report. That could be the director of development, vice president for advancement, director of major gifts, director of advancement services, or someone with a similar title. Assistant or associate researchers report to the director of advancement research or whatever the title.

In some research offices, individuals responsible for database management of the main contact records for the organization are a part of the research office. Ideally in-house databases should be linked electronically, or at least available to the research and development staff. That doesn't mean everyone can add, correct, or delete anything from the record. That should be highly controlled and the responsibility given only to designated staff members.

How much the researchers are involved in the entire fundraising process may depend on the physical arrangement of the development offices. Are the researchers out-of-the way, off in a corner somewhere or isolated in a distant office? Or are they centrally located and accessible to the entire development staff? Obviously, the latter arrangement is more desirable, depending on available office space.

Staff meetings

Researchers should use staff meetings as a public relations opportunity to promote the value of research to the organization. As crucial members of the development staff, researchers should be included in scheduled department meetings. They should be involved in discussions of development strategies, prospect tracking, donor recognition, policy decisions, office procedures, and ethical issues.

Productive meetings most often deal with a specific topic. Then the research staff has the opportunity to reinforce their own position by providing pre-meeting research on issues or prospects to be discussed. By attending meetings, researchers are not left in the dark and will know who are the active prospects and donors and which need more research and cultivation.

The largest so far

It's hard to maintain the *largest ever* label in these days of huge pledges and gifts, but the William and Flora Hewlett Foundation holds that title for now. The foundation made a $400 million pledge to Stanford University to support undergraduate education and add to an endowment for the humanities and sciences. The gift is a tribute to his father, said Walter Hewlett, foundation chairman and son of the electronics pioneer, who died in January 2001.

William Hewlett, along with fellow Stanford alumnus David Packard, founded the Hewlett-Packard Company in 1936. Together, and with their foundations, the two men have contributed almost $400 million to Stanford, in addition to this *largest ever* gift. Before then, the Annenberg Foundation's gift of $125 million to the University of Pennsylvania was the largest amount given by a private foundation to a single American college or university. (*The Chronicle of Philanthropy,* May 17, 2001)

Proactive researchers may suggest names of new prospects to be researched. Ideally the researcher will have both formal and informal methods of insuring that the officers follow up on such suggestions and leads. When the researcher is responsible for providing the name of a person who becomes a major donor, the researcher's contribution should be acknowledged. It's a morale booster in the research office when that happens.

Many development offices hold annual training meetings, or perhaps even off-site retreats, so all staff members can understand the mission and goals of the department. Those offer excellent opportunities to educate, review policies, and to develop a team approach to the task at hand. Researchers might consider asking to be on the program schedule to promote the research office by offering some dramatic contribution of that office.

An orientation session with research staff for new officers and administrative staff can let them know about reference services, available resources, office procedures, and research policies. Because many new development officers have a limited knowledge of the Internet this is a chance for researchers to show off some of its most exciting and useful Web sites, relating them to the information the officers will need. Such a meeting is an opportunity to explain why the often-requested, up-to-the minute statement of a prospect's total net worth is something even the best researchers cannot provide.

Often new board members need to be educated to understand the function of the organization's development or advancement office. Researchers should ask to be a part of orientation sessions for new board or trustee members. This will show board members the vast amount and variety of data now available on Web sites on the Internet. Explaining the research function should eliminate the possibility of an incorrect assumption that the research staff is being too nosey or intrusive when some facts become part of a prospect profile. Seeing what public information is available on the Internet and from fee-based databases may give board members ideas about how to use these resources to add new names as prospective donors.

On a regular basis, the research office may send out memos or e-mail messages to inform about an interesting Internet site, for example, or to inform others about a fee-based service now available. These notices may be about a resource to which the research office subscribes or to let development staff members know that such a service exists. By mentioning a desired new service a few times and pointing out its value, when the researcher's budget request goes up the chain of command, it may have a good chance of being accepted.

It may take awhile, but development and major gift officers may need to be nudged towards realizing the importance of research so it becomes part of their mindset. They will then be less apt to forget, or ignore, the researched profile that took time and crucial financial resources to develop.

"You know, Pete, being a millionaire just isn't as much fun as it used to be."

Organizing the Research Office

"Research is formalized curiosity.
It is poking and prying with a purpose."
—Anonymous

Perhaps you have worked in a nonprofit office for a while and now have a new title with the responsibility of setting up and managing research operations. Or perhaps you have been doing research for a while, but now are thinking your office techniques need a complete overhaul. There must be a more systematic way to do things, but what is it?

As many ways to organize nonprofit research offices exist as there are nonprofit research offices. This chapter will give ideas. You can pick and choose what will work for you. Don't change everything at once. It would be like cleaning out all your closets on the same day. You will never find anything and it might lead to psychological collapse. Take it easy and make changes as necessary. Soon the office will be organized or reorganized. At least, you can hope so.

It is first necessary to determine how you will organize and store prospect and donor information. Will you maintain any paper files or will everything be stored electronically? The day of the 3 x 5-inch box of alphabetized donor cards is gone. Thank goodness! You can only marvel how a research office could operate before the computer era. Still, the concept of the paperless office is not yet here. More than likely, your office will maintain both paper and electronic files.

Donor tracking software

Whether you are starting from scratch or upgrading an outdated system, it is important to investigate a variety of donor management and fundraising software to chose the one that meets current and future needs. This decision will be one of the most important investments a nonprofit organization can make. Making the wrong choice may cause years of agony.

The terms "donor management system" and "fundraising software" may have the same end result but are not necessarily the same. Donor management applications help to keep track of the complete fundraising process, beginning with the first prospect contact. Look for a system that lets you record all data from the prospect/donor profile. The system should be able to record donations and generate pledge reminders; separate gifts by planned, annual, and campaign pledges; find a specific donor by name and gift category; include notes about when to solicit and who knows the prospect; and include information from call reports.

The term "fundraising software" is sometimes used interchangeably with "donor management system," but it usually incorporates more extensive tools for making and managing the initial contact. This software is more into marketing, with connections to telephone directories, screening databases, and prospect research resources. When talking to vendors about software, regardless into which category it may fall, be sure the software completely does what you need.

Be aware that, like everything else electronic, donor and fundraising products are evolving products. Earlier, many such products operated with MS-DOS. Now most operate with Windows or at least Pentium PCs. If yours doesn't, the sooner it is converted to Windows, the better. With the change to Windows, it is inconceivable that a vendor for this type of software does not have an Internet presence. It must have a Web site—for marketing, if nothing else—and to provide prospective customers with product information.

Some companies provide donor-tracking services so their nonprofit clients can gain access over the Internet and store their records off-site with the vendor rather than by installing software on their own system. Look for software products designed for change and updating, so you can add prospect-tracking modules and other capabilities.

Once committed to a particular company, customers can expect their vendor to use the Internet for customer service. Vendors can post FAQs (Frequently Asked Questions), newsletters, software patches, and downloads of new versions. More and more, these software vendors are linking their products to the Internet and offering sophisticated features. Payment through EFT (electronic fund transfers) and credit card processing are becoming usual features in this software as organizations see the Internet as a fundraising tool.

Many software companies establish listservs so their clients can communicate among themselves. Software companies Millennium and Blackbaud both have listservs for subscribers. CharitySoft is a listserv that discusses development-related software, including research databases. Check this Web site for a long list of other nonprofit related listservs and information on how to join them.

http://CharityChannel.com/Forums/

Many recently developed software programs coordinate all phases of the development office. Not only are they depositories for storing data, they can link to screening and electronic research databases. How well the fundraising software links together will determine how successfully the research office will function within the development process.

Most software packages provide several ways to manage a database, and they can be interfaced with programs like Microsoft Access or dBase. At least, the better ones do. Some development offices use Access as their main prospect/donor database. Users like the way they can manipulate the system to their own needs. Access allows a great deal of flexibility and it can be expanded as tracking needs increase. Users can add new forms and then do various queries to find which prospects fit into which categories and are thus ready for the next step in the development process.

Where do you find the vendors who provide donor management or fundraising software? It's a competitive and growing market. Most newspapers and periodicals that cater to nonprofit administrators are filled with product advertisements. Look for them in *The Chronicle of Philanthropy, The NonProfit Times, Contributions,* and *CASE Currents.* (See the appendix of this book for a list of several fundraising software companies with their addresses.)

A small organization with few names on its donor list may be able to find either free or inexpensive software. As announced in July 2000, eTapestry, an Indianapolis software company, was offering its Web-based software free to charities with fewer than 1,000 donor records. (*The Chronicle of Philanthropy,* July 13, 2000) This marketing technique will, the company hopes, hook charities on eTapestry software as their donor list grows and they are able to pay for services. For details and a full demo, check the Web site:

http://www.etapestry.com

Another software program offered free to small nonprofits is eBase. Thousands of copies have been given away, either by downloading it from the Internet or requesting the software by mail. Look for details at

http://www.ebase.org/

If after researching all the Web sites and direct mail pieces on non-profit software, an office still can't decide which to purchase, contact the IT Resource Center in Chicago. That organization either helps nonprofits choose the best fundraising software or assists them in building their own donor management software. Annual membership fees depend on an organization's budget. Call 1-312-372-4872 or take a look at the Web site at

http://itresourcecenter.org

Another source of software information is PRSPCT-L, the listserv most used by nonprofit researchers. Researchers on PRSPCT-L often ask each other for opinions on specific fundraising software. Check PRSPCT-L archives to find recent answers.

Assume the research is done and, after some agonizing, your organization has decided on a software package. Now your office has a fundraising database to electronically store the information you gather. You have attended the vendor's training session and have a good working relationship with the company's support staff. Now what?

One question that must be resolved is who will be in charge of entering basic information into the database? Who will enter contact or trip reports into the database? That may be the head of development research or the head of data management, depending on what title is used. That person should have some control over what is entered.

Many development offices have found it is advisable for officers to enter their own contact reports, using e-mail from laptops while on trips or submitted when the officer is back in the office. Getting these reports filed in a timely manner is not always easy. In some offices, the filing of contact reports is expected within 10 days. In others, the status reports are discussed at monthly meetings. If the report is not finished by then, it may be a bit embarrassing for the officer and may prompt compliance. Some institutions tie reimbursement of travel expenses to submission of the contact reports. That may be the most effective way to achieve the goal of rapid contact reporting.

Guidelines for entry of reports should be established, keeping in mind that many institutions have open-file policies where donors may see their own files. It is better to edit out unfortunate comments from contact reports than face embarrassment later. At least one other person beside the one who wrote the report should review a report before or after it is entered into the database to prevent something insensitive from getting into the database.

Paper files

Even after you have chosen a fundraising software and have learned to use it to its fullest advantage, you'll probably still need paper files. Although many offices are using scanning or document imaging to reduce or eliminate some paper files, it hasn't yet eliminated the need for paper files. Realizing that, it is useful to note in the computer database where to find hardcopy material on the prospect/donor.

An organization must decide what level of giving makes a major donor. That individual requires a separate folder. Perhaps it is $1,000, $5,000, $10,000, or $100,000, or—lucky you—$1 million. Information on donors who give less may originally be filed alphabetically by last name. You can always hope donors in that file will someday get a folder of their own by making a sizable gift.

What should you keep in those hardcopy files? (Remember when the term *paper* became *hardcopy*?) It may vary by type of organization, but generally, details are kept about the prospect: correspondence to and from the person; donation records with photocopies of checks; news clippings, press releases, and photographs; contact reports, the dated research profile; bequests and planned giving requests. If it is an alumni file, include records

Flushed with money

Thomas J. Stanley, author of the best-selling *The Millionaire Next Door*, offers his own experience to show that, in his opinion, fundraisers waste their time trying to divine the complex psychological factors that prompt donors to give. He says donor motivation is not so complicated. "I went to three colleges and taught at four colleges and I have been on the best-seller list for 43 weeks straight, and I haven't gotten a note from any one of them. It's astonishing to me. Don't you think people are more likely to give when they are flush with money?"

relevant to the college years. For corporation files, keep annual reports, pertinent information on mergers and acquisitions, philanthropy records and whatever information links it or its executives to your organization. In foundation files, keep your grant proposals to it, their responses, plus funding information from and about the foundation.

Keep in mind that less is often more. After saying what to keep in prospect/donor paper files, I must caution researchers to resist the temptation to think that every mention of the donor in print and every scrap of information must be kept. Don't fill your files with meaningless clutter. Recognize what is vital information that will lead to finding why the person may be interested in your organization, what projects might interest him or her, and what will help determine the potential for a significant gift. Toss out the rest.

It's not enough to know where to find information on prospects. Once found, you need to organize it so you, or someone else, can find it again when needed. Remember, you are setting up a filing system that can be used by staff years after you have left the organization.

Deciding to include the paper background material when submitting a profile to a development officer will depend on whether there are things on paper that are difficult to summarize but will add significantly to a solicitation. Sometimes a newspaper or magazine article includes human-interest stories or photographs, added benefits for the officer who is soliciting a contribution.

File management

Be consistent. That's the first rule for managing both paper and electronic data. Without consistency, you will have alphabet soup instead of retrievable information. Forget the promise made several years ago that by the end of the last century—the 1900s, not the 1800s!—you would have a paperless office. If it happens in your lifetime, you can always act surprised.

Here are suggested principles of paper file management:

- Keep all files relating to prospect and donor fundraising and grant seeking in one place in a central file rather than scattered around in many offices within an organization. This may be easier in a small organization than in a large one, where some staff members may feel territorial about their own files. Nevertheless, it is best to keep things together in one alphabetical arrangement, with controls about who can use the files or take items from it. If, perhaps at a staff meeting, the nonprofit researcher can describe the benefit of having one central file, compliance may be better.

- If all files are centrally located, one person should be in charge of the files. That person is the responsible person—responsible for security, accuracy, accessibility, and consistency. If a file is out, the file manager will know where it is because he or she checked it out and kept a record of its destination. Try to make a rule saying no files, or parts thereof, can leave the building. (If it is necessary for someone to take a file from the building, state that the director of development must sign the request.) Set a limit to the time a folder can be out of the file.

- Because some files may contain confidential material, it is crucial that each office establish a strict security system with access limited only to those who need the material. That probably eliminates access by volunteers and students. (See the APRA Statement of Ethics.)

- Files should be in alphabetical order, barring a very good reason not to. Most people find it easy and quick to use an alpha file. After all, the alphabet is one of the first things we learned in grade school and it hasn't changed, even in our electronic world. Some offices use numerical files, but that requires an extra step to find a multi-digit number as an "address" to the needed file. Alphabetical paper files can easily be coordinated with prospect and donor computer files.

- Putting files into alphabetical order can be a bit tricky. Does MacDonald come before or after McDonald? Here's a clue. Historically, librarians have filed all names with mc and mac as if they were mac. So, one need only know the person's first name and alphabetize by that within the macs. With library online catalogs, the computers make some alphabetizing decisions. Well, not quite, it's up to the humans who program the computers. Consistency may have fallen by the wayside.

- To get file organization off to a good start, or to clean up a messy file, check the American Library Association Web site for information on ordering a booklet on alphabetizing rules used in libraries.

http://www.ala.org

- Consider color coding your paper file. Use the basics: red, yellow, green, and blue. Colored file folders or just simple colored dots or colored end tabs can be used. Consider your prospects. They are individuals (perhaps with special notations or colors for board and trustee members), foundations, corporations, and perhaps government grant-making agencies. Each group gets a different file color available at any office supply store.

- Setting up and maintaining a good paper file is important until that magic moment when everything is electronic. If you can get it right from the beginning, you will avoid headaches later. You may need to use SEE and SEE ALSO cross-referencing as used in library card or online catalogs. Use such references to connect couples with different last names or to identify family members with different names. Use these to connect individuals with their companies or corporations, if they are both individual and corporate donations.

- When setting up paper donor files, or finally getting them into top-notch order, consider how long you will keep the files. If your office

"Let me see, I know I have information on Jack Smith here someplace."

becomes too crowded, decide if non-current files should be archived into a storage area after a certain number of years. Should the file for a deceased donor be sent to an archival area immediately after the will is settled? Before doing that, determine if other family members might become donors. If so, information on the deceased donor is useful.

Scanning and/or document imaging

Keep in mind that technology is changing how development research files are kept. Scanning print information into a computer file may be the space-saving method of choice. This imaging of documents is a means of storing information in a digital format rather than on paper. It can provide better access to stored data and allow searching of all databases in one pass. By using keywords to search by category, it may be possible to find appropriate prospects within your own database that might have been missed in a paper file. Imaging can improve security by limiting access to only those staff members with password control.

At the same time, in a large university with development offices spread around campus, access to scanned documents in a central file and available in each office will make it unnecessary for each office to keep their own files. To get compliance with this concept, the highest ranking officer must require that all documents be kept in one central file, paper or imaged. Reports and documents for imaging can be sent via e-mail, fax, CD-ROM, or floppy disc. (See the appendix of this book for a list of some companies that do document management by optical imaging.)

Before deciding to scan all paper files, consider the decision very carefully. What may sound like a great move towards achieving that mythical paperless office may not work that way. In principle, paper documents are scanned and stored in a virtual library within a Local Area Network (LAN). When setting up the system, work out a strategy to identify each item as it is scanned, besides just the batch number and date scanned. Once a subject is identified for file retrieval, it takes a while for the file to appear on the screen. Then, most often, the person needing the information will make a hardcopy of it—making it no longer a paperless transaction!

For a good summary of how optical imaging works, the advantages of it for your office, and to see how much it might cost, see the following Web site from a presentation on the topic at the 2000 APRA conference by staff at the USC Development Research Office. Click Staff Presentations, then look under 2000 for "Implementing a Document Imaging System."

http://www.usc.edu/source/

❊ 3 ❊

Procedures and Profiles

*"The amount of electronic information is doubling
every 60 minutes. How do you decide what to
keep and what not to keep?
What is the value of information?"*
—John L. King, Dean
University of Michigan
School of Information

Even the smallest research office—perhaps especially a small office—will benefit by establishing specific procedures and using forms both to request research and to report back the results.

Using "Request for Research" forms enables those who need the information (development officers, major gift officers, or administration officers) to focus on and explain exactly what they need and when they need it.

Does she or he need just a contact address plus phone number or a complete financial and biographical profile? The researcher should make sure what is needed before spending hours on a wild goose chase.

The best way to control that is to require written requests for research. If you find a name scribbled on a Post-It note stuck to your desk, return it to the requester with the required form. Soon development officers will get the point and realize it helps to let the researcher know what specific information is needed.

A request form should specify levels of research. Accepting the request "Everything you can find" means giving the rest of the week to find it. Ideally the requester and the researcher can discuss the request. The more the development officer understands the research process, including its limitations, the better your working relationship will be.

It's a known fact that it takes as long to find nothing as to find something. You need to check the same resources. Some requests will be a cinch; others will be impossible, especially if the officer spelled the prospect's name incorrectly. Consider putting a line for variant spelling of the surname on the request form. (And be a bit sympathetic to the person who gives you the wrong spelling. Perhaps a board or trustee member passed along poor information.) If you find nothing about the person with the requested spelling, try other possibilities. Might Smith be Schmidt or Schmid?

To provide research when needed, it is useful to divide prospects into categories depending on where they are in the cultivation process. For example, to determine if a prospect is capable of becoming a major donor, a quick assets check may drop the name completely or move the person into a category for further contact. Only then will the officer ask for more details so the new prospect can be cultivated. Before a prospect is to be solicited for a major donation, a complete updated profile can be done.

A "Request for Research" form could look something like these examples. They should be adapted for your office situation. Each form will depend on such things as access to electronic resources, resources in a print library, whether constituents are local or national, and the number of researchers in the office. (See Form 1)

Individual research

The person making the request should supply as much basic information as is known and be specific about what is needed. Sometimes an officer may not want to fill out the form and would rather discuss the request with a researcher. That's fine, but the researcher should fill out a form for each request to return the information and record as research work completed.

Your use of a research request form will help eliminate impossible (or, at least, difficult) requests like these:

- "Give me all details on the 50 most wealthy persons in this city."

- "Who is that electronic businessman from Korea named Kim?"

- "What's the name of that woman who is head of that company?"

You will, no doubt, be called on occasionally to research the impossible, or nearly impossible. Use tact when deflecting these requests, but use the opportunity to explain research resources and their limitations.

Research Request Form   Date: _____

Requested by: _____

Phone/ext._____ E-mail _____

Prospect name: _____

Variant spelling of surname or nickname_____

Please add what information is known.

Address: _____

_____

Phone: Home _____ Business _____

Where employed: _____

Title: _____

Spouse's name: (and maiden name) _____

Where employed _____

Connection to this organization:_____

Or year of graduation: _____

Major gifts:_____

Who knows this prospect? _____

Level of research:

____ Basic: Address, phone numbers, biographical, employment, history, real estate holdings, general financial, interests or hobbies

____ Complete: Detailed financial data, indications of wealth, board or professional memberships, family history, court house records, second residences

_____ Update: Recent news articles, current stock and real estate values, job promotion or change

When needed?

____ Routine (two weeks, but longer for detailed financials)

____ ASAP (within one week)

____ Urgent (within 48 hours)

What specific information are you looking for? _____

Are you meeting the prospect? _____ When? _____

Return research as a paper copy_____ e-mail attachment _____

Please bring or send this request form to the Research Office.

Form 1

Prospect/Donor Profile

Name: _____

Place and date of birth: _____

Home address: _____

   Second home address: _____

Home phone numbers: _____

Business phone number: _____

E-mail address: _____

Education: _____

Where employed: _____

   Title: _____

Description of the business and/or ticker symbol: _____

Career history: _____

Religious affiliation: _____

Political affiliation: _____

Professional memberships: _____

Social/civic club memberships: _____

Corporate/ foundation board member: _____

Honors, awards, publications: _____

Personal interests/hobbies: _____

Affiliation with this institution (or others): _____

Spouse's name: _____

Spouse's maiden name: _____

Spouse's place and date of birth: _____

Spouse's e-mail address: _____

Spouse's education: _____

Spouse's business: _____

Spouse's business phone number: _____

Description of the business and/or ticker symbol: _____

Spouse's career history: _____

Form 2

Spouse's professional membership: _____

Social/civic club membership: _____

Spouse's corporate/foundation board member: _____

Spouse's honors, awards, publications: _____

Spouse's personal interests/hobbies: _____

Affiliation with this institution (or other): _____

Family history: _____

Parent's name, including mother's maiden name: _____

Spouse's parents, including mother's maiden name: _____

Children: _____

Where children are/were educated: _____

Their addresses: _____

Family wealth indicators: _____

Prospect/Donor: _____

  Salary/fees/ bonuses: _____

  Major stock holdings, options, pension benefits: _____

  Inheritance: _____

Spouse: _____

  Salary/fees/bonuses: _____

  Major stock holdings, options, pension benefits: _____

  Inheritance: _____

Real estate holdings: _____

Lifestyle "big ticket" items: _____

Estimate of family wealth, if possible: _____

Family philanthropic history: _____

  To this institution/organization: _____

  To other institutions/organizations: _____

Friends, peers, or contacts at this institution/organization: _____

_____

Profile prepared by _____

Date prepared _____

Form 2, Continued

Use this discussion as an opportunity to suggest electronic resources your office does not have that may provide the needed answers.

Once gathered, the information on the individual or corporate prospect should be analyzed and presented in a succinct, easy-to-read format. Rather than clutter the report with everything you found, pick out the crucial facts that answer the questions asked on the request form. For example, don't include the whole proxy statement, just show the prospect's salary and/or stock ownership.

Use good judgment. The more you do this research, the better you can highlight details in an appropriate manner. You are creating a written picture of a person who may become an important donor to your institution. Your report may show the prospect's interests that may link to a specific project that needs funding. Research is an important part of the funding process, and you should not be reluctant to emphasize, when appropriate, its value.

Individual research profile template

Using a Prospect/Donor Profile sheet (See Form 2) for each completed research request will help both you and the person who requested the profile. With it, you can see at a glance what information has been found and what is still lacking. As with the other forms, make one to meet your needs. This example is a suggestion of the answers you may be asked to locate.

Foundation and corporate research

The nonprofit development researcher may be asked to find funding possibilities from foundations and corporations. (See Forms 3 and 4)

Checklist of resources

Consider having a resource checklist on the reverse side of each research request form. This will show the thoroughness of your search, although some items may remain unanswered. In fact, in most profiles, there will be unanswered items. Your checklist will depend on the available reference tools, either print or electronic, in your office. A copy of the checklist can be put into the paper file so future researchers will know what was originally checked. Sometimes while doing research on a person, foundation or corporation, something unexpected, but significant for the funding process, turns up. By all means, pass it along!

Foundation Research Request Form

Date: _____

Requested by: _____

Phone/ext._____ E-mail _____

Name of foundation: _____

What information do you want?

_____ Address and phone number

_____ Web site

_____ Contact person

_____ Donor/family

_____ When established

_____ Philanthropic philosophy

_____ Average amount of grants

_____ Principal officers

_____ Grant application information

_____ Connection or previous grants to this organization

_____ Other, describe _____

When needed?

_____ Routine (two weeks)

_____ ASAP (within one week)

_____ Urgent (within 48 hours)

Return research as paper copy_____e-mail attachment _____

Form 3

Depending on when a profile is needed, some researchers group their requests and check the resources for several names at once. Once you are online at a particular Web site, it is easy to type in other names. Others feel it is easier to research one name at a time, giving it their full attention before moving on to another name.

Answers to items on the profile may need to be backed up with paper documents in the file. For example, if some bit of information is from a newspaper article, the article should be filed in the prospect/ donor folder if it includes things not in the profile, such as pictures or human-interest details. Data retrieved online should have the printout in

---

Corporate Research Request Form

Date: _____

Requested by: _____

Phone/ext._____ E-mail _____

Corporation name: _____

Address: _____

_____

What information do you want?

_____ Headquarters address

_____ Type of business

_____ Number of employees

_____ Local address

_____ Annual sales/revenue

_____ Philanthropic policy

_____ Matching gift policy

_____ Principal officers

_____ Major stockholders

_____ Connections or previous contributions here

_____ Other. Describe_____

When needed?

_____ Routine (two weeks)

_____ ASAP (within one week)

_____ Urgent (within 48 hours)

Return research as paper copy _____ e-mail attachment _____

Form 4

the file. It may seem cumbersome, but it may prevent headaches if you are asked to verify something. It is difficult to retrace the trail to a specific Web site. Keep in mind what you put into the file may be used 5, 10, or even more years later. Date everything.

Some development officers prefer the researched profile, whether on an individual, foundation, or corporation, to be returned in narrative format. That profile should be concise but should include all pertinent details. Veritas Information Services, for training purposes only, has placed a sample prospect profile on its Web site that also includes useful guidelines for new researchers.

http://www.veritasinfo.com

How long does it take?

Although there is no accurate answer to the question about how long it takes to complete a profile, new researchers, and sometimes supervisors, want to know. Because each person researched is different from the one before and because some profiles are easy and others almost impossible, there are only estimates. As researchers are quick to point out, "It depends on how many interruptions we have."

A bare-boned profile may take two-three hours, but a complete profile, including financial and property details will take longer. Some say five to seven hours is more accurate, depending on what electronic resources are available. Also, is the researcher expected to analyze the data or just turn over computer printouts?

Updating profiles

A person's life may change quickly. For a profile to be relevant, it must be current. However, with hundreds or thousands of donors, the research staff would go crazy doing continual updates for every file. Most offices have basic contact information in a main database, so it is easy to print off that information as part of the profile. Keeping that database up to date with new addresses and phone numbers is a continuing process, probably done by someone for whom this is his or her main job. Most research offices do more thorough profile updating only "as needed."

"As needed" may be when a development officer has a meeting with the prospect and needs current information. It can be when the college president is visiting a distant city and wishes to hold a reception for prospects there. Development officers may request profiles on selected donors as part of a major campaign. Most organizations have a handful of major donors, trustees, and board members. As these are people in close contact with the organization, their profiles should be kept as current as possible.

Daily reading for researchers

Good researchers keep their eyes open for news about the organization's top prospects and donors in newspapers and magazines. Reading local publications should be a part of their daily tasks. Keep your ears open at meetings when names are mentioned and new facts about a prospect are presented.

You can win points by bringing new information to the officer who mentioned the name. Depending on when the original profile was compiled, check for a new address and telephone number, new employment and promotion, or a major life change. That can be almost anything—a birth or death in the family, an employment change, a best-selling book, an IPO (initial public offering), a bankruptcy, an inheritance, or perhaps a major illness. Remember to date this information.

Confidentiality

Most of what happens in a nonprofit research office should be considered confidential and treated as such by the entire development staff. That includes everything from the initial request for research to the completed prospect profile, including memos, contact reports, correspondence, and all materials gathered.

Each office should establish rules on donor confidentiality that include keeping paper information in a locked file cabinet. Computer files and database records must be password restricted. Because e-mail can be easily intercepted, some offices prohibit sending confidential information that way. The same is true for cellular and cordless telephones—not a good way to discuss any confidential item.

No prospect or donor information should be checked out of the file by anyone outside the development office without written approval by the director of development. Paper documents no longer needed should be disposed of using a mechanical shredder.

The manager of prospect research, or the person in that position no matter the title, should establish procedures to protect confidential information. This includes explaining procedures to each new employee who will have access to confidential data, however slight. Having the employee sign a Confidentiality Statement reinforces the importance of this directive. (See Form 5)

Early in its history, APRA realized a potential problem as employees left one development office to work in another, especially in the same geographical region. Can they take information on prospects to their new employees? The answer is no. APRA's Statement of Ethics reads, "Constituent information is the property of the institution for which it was collected. (It) shall not be taken to another institution."

Sample confidentiality statement

I understand information pertaining to the prospects and donors of this institution is confidential and should be protected so the relationship of trust between that person and _____is upheld. This means all files in the development office will be treated with discretion. I shall not release or discuss this information in any way outside the development office either during or after my employment at _____. I understand that adherence to this agreement is fundamental to my continued employment here and that any breach of this confidentiality agreement by me may result in disciplinary action or dismissal.

Signature:_____ Date: _____

Form 5

Inform student assistants and volunteers doing data entry or basic research they must be aware the names being researched are not to be discussed outside the office.

Some institutions require an exit interview with employees during which they are asked to sign a written document, in the presence of a third employee as witness, acknowledging they have worked with confidential information and it is to remain with the institution.

"*Only you development people ask to see a prospect-research report on the other passengers before upgrading to first class.*"

Reprinted with permission from Mark Litzler

⋙ 4 ⋘

Who's Rich and Who's Generous?

"Very rich people should start recycling their wealth.
Many rich people say they plan on giving away their money
when they die. Of course they will, what choice will they have?"
—Ted Turner

No one really knows how many Americans are millionaires. According to one estimate in 2000, 2.5 million Americans were millionaires; 267 were billionaires. (*Time,* July 24, 2000) About the same time the *Wall Street Journal* thought this country had 4 million millionaires. Merrill Lynch reported in May 2000 that the number of millionaires in the United States and Canada has risen almost 40 percent since 1997. (*The Washington Post,* May 10, 2000) Figures vary about how many millionaire families exist, but the undeniable fact is the number increased quickly. The high-technology boom made more people rich faster than at any other time in history.

Introducing its listing of the *Forbes* 400, that magazine stated the obvious: The new wealthy class is far bigger and more broadly based than in previous gilded ages. *Forbes* counted 400 Americans worth upwards to $725 million. Lower the yardstick to $100 million and the number might reach 4,000. Lower it to $5 million and 596,000 American families could make the cut. "Does $5 million make you rich?" asked the Forbes writer who then answered his own question. "Maybe not, but it certainly enables you to buy luxuries." (*Forbes,* October 9, 2000)

New York has the highest number of millionaires. Los Angeles is second; Chicago is third. Checking in with 158,000 millionaires, the Greater Washington area now ranks fourth. At America Online, in suburban Virginia, a thousand employees passed the magic million dollar mark—depending how AOL stock is going. (*The Washington Post,* December 2,

---

Even *after* the market crashed

"The very rich simply want to not leave their money to the federal government. It's a huge looming thing," said Tom Riley about the many billions, if not trillions, that are expected to be funneled into philanthropy in coming years. "I don't think most people have really grasped how consequential and transformative that money is going to be. My God, there's so much money out there that even if the market crashes, it's still a fantastic amount."

—Tom Riley of the Philanthropy Roundtable (*The Washington Post*, March 15, 2000)

1999) Unfortunately, things change quickly. That figure was given before the April NASDAQ stock plunge and now no one is guessing how many millionaires there are.

In 1999, for the first time since *Forbes* began to compile its list of 400 wealthiest Americans, more than half of those listed—268—were worth $1 billion or more. (*Forbes,* October 11, 1999) It probably came as no surprise to those who have been at least a little interested in such news. Surely, fundraisers for all kinds of organizations fit into that interested group. Recently they heard the good news that within the next several years, $10.4 trillion will be transferred as the parents of baby boomers die and dispose of their assets. (*Smart Money,* October 1999) That's the figure used in 1999; in 2000, *Time* magazine reported $41 trillion would be left to heirs and charities.

Both those $10.4 and $41 trillion figures are guesses. No one knows. Regardless of which figure you want to use, it is an amazing amount of money. Much of that money transfer is expected to go to charity. At least, everyone hopes so, although a study done by the Treasury Department notes that most wealthy people bequeath nothing to charity. Of 60,082 federal tax returns filed for people with an estate valued at more than $600,000 who died in 1992, only 19 percent of the returns reported a bequest to charity. Estates under that amount were not required to file an estate tax return. While those statistics are interesting, they do not explain the many creative ways the very wealthy develop to avoid estate tax.

Historically the greatest portion of millionaires inherited their wealth. In recent years, many billionaires built their fortunes without any significant inheritance. Now, based on the above estimate of wealth transfer, sons and daughters of the wealthy will inherit their wealth, as happened historically.

The U.S. Trust Corporation periodically tracks the top 1 percent wealthiest Americans from IRS and federal statistics based on their having an adjusted gross income of more than $225,000 annually or a net worth greater than $3 million. These affluent people are surveyed about financial issues in reports done since 1993. Many have a different figure about how much money will change hands during the next 20 years. U.S. Trust tells us it will be $5 trillion! Unfortunately, only 8 percent of estate planning is headed to charities.

Results of surveys are on this Web site. Click on Knowledge Center at the top, then find the surveys for Charitable Giving.

http://www.ustrust.com/

Another factor that may influence contributions from the wealthy is the democratization of assets. This means the basis for a contribution is no longer annual income, but is instead a prospect and donor's total assets. With the explosion of interest in the stock market, business owners and executives no longer are the only ones capable of making large gifts. Now literally tens of millions of Americans have financial assets worthy of note. Most often those assets are in stocks and mutual funds. Recent research showed that 48 percent of the nation's wealth is held by people who started their own business, compared with 33 percent held by corporate executives, and just 10 percent by people whose wealth is inherited.

That's a recent change. Fundraisers are advised to drop their focus on traditional-style donors and look to the new entrepreneurs. Start by taking a look at *Fortune's* "40 Wealthiest Americans Under 40" in the September 18, 2000 issue. That short list will give ideas about how to look for the newly rich among an organization's prospects. Click on the Frequently Asked Questions (FAQ) to read how the list was prepared. It gives hints about how to do a similar analysis on young and wealthy prospects. The best way to find articles within the *Fortune* homepage is to type keywords or article title in the search area. Type in Philanthropists for Fortune's list of the top givers.

http://www.fortune.com

According to statistics put out by the Internal Revenue Service, those with estates of $600,000 or more, who died between 1995 and 1997, had 18.8 percent of their assets in real estate and 33.6 percent in stocks. Cash made up 9 percent and the rest was scattered among other investments.

A Seiko watch and a chevy?

In their book *The Millionaire Next Door,* William D. Danko and Thomas J. Stanley debunked many theories we have about the wealthy. They wrote that one in twenty American households has a net worth of over $1 million. Realizing that, we should not be surprised to also be told that the average millionaire lives in a house worth $196,000, wears a Seiko watch for which he paid $235, and drives a $29,000 car. That leaves quite a bit for charity, if they are so inclined.

(Statistics of Income Bulletin, Summer 1999) No one knows how those figures will change when young entrepreneurs in the new economy reach the average age of death.

So, where do you find those wealthy—or wealthiest—Americans? Thomas J. Stanley, the author of *The Millionaire Next Door,* said they are everywhere. Although the book he wrote with William D. Danko was not specifically written for fundraisers, Stanley thinks fundraisers could glean much useful information from the findings.

Danko suggests it is a mistake for fundraisers to go after those on the *Forbes* 400 and similar lists because, he feels, it is much more important to look for people who have strong relationships with the cause or organization. That is not a new concept. Most fundraisers agree. Danko further suggests that "frugal" is the term that best describes millionaires. More of them drive Fords than any other car and only a fourth of the men ever paid over $600 for a suit.

Although those listed on the *Forbes* 400 may not be their best prospects, most fundraisers look at lists of the wealthiest as great spectator sport. Unless your organization is national, you may not have any reason to contact any of the 400, except those already known by and involved with your organization. As one researcher said, don't waste time chasing an unknown fish in the vast and remote ocean when there are ponds stocked with known fish swimming nearby. Nonetheless, many wealth lists are put on the Internet as they are issued so fundraisers can use them to identify the rich and wealth trends.

In 1982, the *Forbes* 400 list was the first scientifically compiled list of the wealthiest Americans, although the same magazine back in 1938 did a listing of America's 40 richest families or individuals. It was harder to put together such a list back then, before the Securities and Exchange

Commission made disclosure of stock ownership a necessity for public companies. When *Forbes* chose to include the 400 wealthiest, this number probably refers back to the gilded age of the Vanderbilts when the New York elite was dubbed "The Four Hundred"—the number of guests able to be accommodated in Mrs. William Astor's ballroom.

Look for the list of America's wealthiest in an October *Forbes* issue each year. An article preceding the list tells how the information was gathered to determine the wealthiest Americans. Prospect researchers can use those tips in their own research and, on the Internet, search the *Forbes* 400 list by location, marital status, and type of assets. Click on People for many other *Forbes'* lists.

http://www.forbes.com/
http://www.forbes.com/people

Just as a curiosity, the 40 richest Americans of all time were listed by *American Heritage* (October 12, 1998) in an article, "Worth a mere $62 billion." You can always hope to find names you recognize. Perhaps their children or grandchildren are on your donor list.

Who's rich in the world?

As it does for the wealthiest Americans, *Forbes* lists the World's Richest People annually. Click on People on the homepage.

http://www.forbes.com

EuroBusiness magazine published a list of the 200 wealthiest women in the world in August 2000. Look for it at this Web site.

http://eurobusiness.uk.com/

Newly rich entrepreneurs

A problem researchers have in finding newly wealthy entrepreneurs is the lack of broad documentation in biographical reference directories. But, thanks to the Internet and its wealth of Web sites, including directories, and its ability to ferret out data through a multitude of search engines, the task is becoming easier.

Not all companies that have recently gone public have made their executives millions, but many have, at least for a while. It's been surmised that many of these new entrepreneurs want to make sure their charitable investments benefit those in need and don't get lost in red tape and bureaucracy.

Entrepreneur magazine on occasion lists the 75 top entrepreneurs by state. At their site you can also search the *Thomas Register,* an old favorite in print format, and a list of franchise opportunities.

http://www.entrepreneurmag.com

Attendees at the 1999 conference of the National Society of Fund Raising Executives (NSFRE) were advised to "Put the Rockefellers in the philanthropy museum" and look for new models. They were cautioned that some of the new entrepreneurs are so busy building their companies they have little time for the special events and other efforts charities have traditionally used to establish relationships with prospects. Some charity fundraisers have found these young and rich prospects have little patience for long visits and presentations. A better way, it was suggested, is for nonprofit executives to get themselves invited to business meetings or recreational activities that the entrepreneurs attend. Consider getting an invitation to the corporate-owned "sky boxes" at sports arenas and stadiums.

Regional wealthiest lists

Following the popularity of the *Forbes* 400, many regional magazines and newspapers make their own annual list of the wealthiest, the highest paid, the biggest companies, and even the most generous local folks. An example is *Boston* magazine that includes Boston's 100 Richest People in its May issue. Examples of newspapers that do annual rich lists are *The Washington Post* and the *Chicago Sun-Times.*

In the Washington, D.C., area, *Regardie's Magazine* comes and goes— and now seems gone. With the title, *Regardie's Power,* it listed the 100 wealthiest in that area in its November/December issue. Some, but not all, profiles are on its Web site.

http://www.regardiespower.com/archives

Business publications often list the top companies in their region and the highest paid executives. Some even extend their coverage, as *Virginia Business* did in their December 2000 issue, to the legal profession, listing the The Legal Elite from that state. Click for the contents of past issues.

http://www.virginiabusiness.com/

Check regional magazines and newspapers in your region for similar profiles of potential prospects and donors. If you live in a large metropolitan area it is easy to identify some of the wealthy by newspaper and magazine reports of their activities. Each Sunday the *The New York Times* gives a whole page to showcase pictures of people attending social and charity functions, with enough names of those pictured to keep proactive researchers busy all week. *Quest* magazine covers the social scene for the "New York power elite," as do *New York* magazine, *Avenue*, and *Town and Country.*

City magazines, most often named after the city they cover, are published throughout the country. Look for the one in your city that compares to *Washingtonian, Dallas, Chicago, Dallas* or *Philadelphia.* Most report on charity fundraisers and prime social events attended by the elite of each city. An example is the Washington Social List published in *Washington Life* magazine each December. The 2001 list includes 550 persons "compiled over the past year by a secret panel of Washington insiders," according to the introduction. It continues, "All those listed have at least one thing in common—they are among the Capital's most socially active or desirable."

If you are wondering if a regional or society magazine in your area is online, check this list of magazines with hyperlinks to the magazines.

http://www.refdesk.com/

Because many prospective donors are business owners, *Business Journals* in many cities provide in-depth articles on movers and shakers. To see if a *Biz Journal* exists for the area of your research, check this Web site. Each year Entrepreneur of the Year awards are made and the journals often list the area's wealthiest residents. Click on Book of Lists to see what they offer.

http://www.bizjournals.com

Add the name of a city to that Web site to get the site for a particular city or regional paper. For example,

http://www.bizjournals.com/charlotte/

Gary Price's List of Lists includes links to several regional wealthiest lists. New items are being added continually, so see what other useful links are offered.

http://gwis2.circ.gwu.edu/~gprice/listof.htm

Print volumes

Who's Wealthy in America, a two-volume set from Taft, lists persons with "an inferred net worth of at least $1 million." The 1999 edition contains listing on more than 112,690 individuals with basic contact information and indicators of wealth in volume one. Volume two gives insider stock holding for those listed. Some of your wealthy prospects may be listed in that set, but if there are over 4 million millionaires in this country, why aren't more listed? I have the same concern about *The Rich Register.* (See the listing in this book's Bibliography.)

With the wonderful Internet resources now available free or for a fee, I believe the almost $500 price for the Taft set can be better spent for better resources. (Actually, the publishers came to the same conclusion. The 2000 edition will probably be the last.)

Who are the most generous?

More important than knowing who is rich is knowing who is both rich and philanthropic. Each year since 1996 the online magazine, *Slate,* lists the 60 most generous Americans. For several years, the late Ann Castle, a well-known prospect researcher, helped compile the list that appears each spring. Michael Kinsley, publisher of *Slate,* said he is hoping the kind of people who have made large sums of money and are competitive will bring the same competitive zeal to giving it away. By listing the most generous, Kinsley hopes others will aspire to get on the list. From the homepage, search for *Slate* 600.

http://www.slate.msn.com

Collaborating with *Slate* to compile and list the 60 biggest donors for 2000, *The Chronicle of Philanthropy* stated that Bill and Melinda Gates's donation of $5 billion to their foundation in 2000 put them at the top of the list. Their gift also was more than twice as much as the combined total given by the 59 other people who made the list. The *Chronicle's* list of the 60 most generous was in the January 25, 2001 issue and on its Web site for subscribers.

http://philanthropy.com

In its December issue, *Town & Country* magazine lists a dozen people considered "Earth Angels." The 1997 list included Ted Turner's gift of $1 billion to the United Nations—probably the largest single donation in history. At least, up until now. He challenged other wealthy persons to follow his example.

Worth magazine ranks those with highest lifetime donations to form The Benefactor 100. In sections categorized on its Web site as Wealth, Living, and Giving, *Worth* provides an ongoing look at those with money and how they got it. The site makes it easy to keep track of a prospect's stock profile—or your own.

http://www.worth.com

It is great sport to read the lists of the wealthiest and the most generous, but for most prospect research and fundraising purposes, it is just fun. Most prospects and donors won't be on those lists. Sorry! Perhaps just as interesting is reading how rich Americans still fit into some old stereotypes. Search *American Demographics/Marketing Tools* magazine for statistical characteristics of adults in affluent households. "Life on Easy Street" in the April 1997 issue includes a table showing their professions, age, and education status.

"Why Donors Give" from the June 1996 issue of *American Demographics* answers the question: What motivates people to contribute to fundraising organizations? The answer includes some basics: 1) Donors make their largest gifts to the groups where they spend volunteer time—or to their friends' favorite causes. 2) The biggest motivating factor is being asked to give, especially by someone they know and trust. 3) Donors often see philanthropy as "an obligation that is part of their privileged position."

Search *American Demographics* on the Internet for those two articles, then browse for other pertinent topics.

http://www.marketingtools.com

Where else do your wealthy donors give?

One question often asked on PRSPCT-L is how to tell if one's prospects and donors have given to other organizations, and if so, how much. Unfortunately, there is no easy answer to that question, only several suggestions.

Start by checking basic who's who type biographical and corporate directories that may give a person's alma mater, organizations the person is associated with, and sometimes even the person's interests. Then do a name search on an Internet search engine such as Google. I'm always amazed at what Google finds.

http://www.google.com

If the researched person is local, your best sources of donation information are your regional newspapers and magazines. If the person lives elsewhere, check online archives for newspapers where your prospect lives. (Don't forget summer or winter second residences.) Most newspapers have society pages showing pictures from fund-raising galas, indicating some level of support by those participating. Several Web sites list all newspapers and media sources in an area with links to the newspaper archives. The search is usually free, but there is a small fee for retrieved articles.

http://www.newslibrary.com
http://www.abyznewslinks.com

Annual reports from organizations reflecting a person's interests most often list the major donors, as do local hospitals, museums, zoos, theatres, symphony orchestras, and civic associations. Don't forget to check listings of donors in public radio/television guide magazines. All of those sources are useful not only for researching a specific person, but also for adding new names to a prospect list.

If you find indications of a donor's interest in other organizations, check those Web sites for donor lists or call to ask that your organization

"Have it your way, John, but reading every single word of 'Who's Wealthy in America' is not MY idea of relaxation."

be put on their mailing list to receive annual reports or published lists of donors. Offer to reciprocate with your reports. Some regional APRA chapter members get together once a year to swap annual reports.

It is possible to make an educated guess about other organizations that a donor may be supporting. It can be as easy as knowing the alma mater of the donor and spouse. Philanthropy often begins right there. Most college and university alumni magazines list donors segmented by amount given. Next, look into the possibility a couple may be supporting their children's private schools or colleges.

If a prospect or donor is from the corporate world, check the company's proxy statement that may list charitable interests of officers and directors. With *FC Search* from the Foundation Center, type in the prospect's name to see if he or she is a trustee of a foundation. Check the Foundation Center home page that links to the *Philanthropy News Digest* where major gifts are recorded. Subscribers to *The Chronicle of Philanthropy* can search online for names listed there after a major donation.

With Taft's *Prospector's Choice* on CD-ROM, researchers can search for foundation and corporate officers and find information on those listed. Taft's *Major Donors* reference book was last published in 1995, and its *Boardlink* is also no longer published. If it is possible to guess why those books are no longer published, it may be that gathering this donor information is difficult, labor intensive, and most often incomplete. If a major publishing company can't document philanthropy well, it is no surprise that many prospect researchers have difficulty doing the same, no matter how much their development officers would like that information.

Directories of Directors are available for New York City, the nearby tri-state area, and Boston and vicinity. Use it to find connections between corporate boards.

Waltman Associates in Minneapolis publishes the *2000 Donor Series* databases on CD-ROMs available in national or regional versions. These directories show names of major donors compiled from nonprofit annual reports, but does not include corporate or foundation gifts. Although some data may now be outdated and not all annual reports are indexed, the resource provides names not found elsewhere and shows indications of the person's interests.

Waltman Associates publishes an index to *Town and Country* magazine with references to thousands of personal names as the magazine chronicles social events of the wealthy. As stated above, each December *Town and Country* lists donors of more than $1 million, so these are picked up by the index. To see what is available, check this Web site or e-mail Inez Bergquist at *bergq003@tc.umn.edu* or call 1-612-338-0772. The Web site includes links to many popular prospect research resources.

http://www.waltmanassociates.com

Some fee-based services give charitable contributions for those listed. One such service is *WealthEngine.*

http://www.wealthengine.com

Prospect Research Online is another fee-based service that includes donor lists.

http://www.iwave.com

Even with some of the services and resources listed above, finding a person's total charitable contributions to other organizations and institutions is a hit and miss proposition. Information on all major contributions will not be available, but with some perseverance you may find enough information to make an assumption about the giving potential of a prospect.

It would be so simple if an organization's prospect list could be separated into three categories. The first are those who have a lot of money and *are* willing to give some. Second, are those who have a lot of money and *might* be willing to give some. Third, the rest of your names, with some very good prospects, if you only knew which ones. It's the task of a nonprofit researcher to find more information about persons in each category and determine those with wealth who might become major donors. It's not simple, but it is the challenge of prospect research in a development office.

❖

⇻ 5 ⇺

Demographics of Wealth

"I skate where I think the puck will be."
—Wayne Gretzky

Demographics is the study of the human population as it relates to size, density, distribution, and vital statistics. For the development office, demographics means using census and population figures to determine areas where wealthy prospects are most apt to live. Whether adding new names to a prospect list or determining the potential wealth of a prospect being researched, there are demographic clues that are helpful.

Fundraisers in Fairfax County, Virginia, may have cheered when they read in June 2000 their county was the first in the nation to achieve a $90,000 median household income, meaning half earn more and half less. The average household income in Fairfax is $123,028. Those figures, determined by Claritas Inc., a marketing information firm, used a variety of economic data to come up with the median household income for 2000. The figures reflected the Fairfax County Economic Development Authority's efforts to recruit high tech and other companies that pay their employees well. In fact, they had attracted so many high-tech companies the area is called Silicon East.

While the median income rose, so did the median net worth of the county residents. Of more than 48,000 households, almost 14 percent had net worth of more than $500,000. Fairfax County has fewer super-wealthy residents than affluent suburban enclaves near other cities, such as Westchester County near New York City, or Marin County outside San Francisco. Fairfax also lacks large numbers of poorer residents, bringing the median up. It's grist for the marketers' and fundraisers' mill.

Worth magazine lists the country's wealthiest counties each year with the list for the previous three years available online. It also includes articles on charitable giving.

**Percentage of households with
$500,000 net worth, by rank**

1.	Somerset County, New Jersey	14.04%
2.	Fairfax County, Virginia	13.86
3.	Morris County, New Jersey	13.85
4.	Nassau County, New York	13.77
5.	Fairfield County, Connecticut	13.58
6.	Montgomery County, Maryland	12.90
7.	Hunterdon County, New Jersey	12.89
8.	Los Alamos County, New Mexico	12.88
9.	Westchester County, New York	12.87
10.	Falls Church City, Virginia	12.51

Source: Claritas Inc. Reported in the *The Washington Post*, June 10, 2000

http://www.worth.com/
http://www.worth.com/articles/richdex.html

Worth's list of the 250 wealthiest towns is online at:

http://www.worth.com/articles/20006F01.html

Using names on a prospect list, a lot can be learned by knowing nothing more than a person's address. It's not foolproof, of course, but it is a start in the development research process. For a long time direct marketers have used nothing else to determine who gets what mailings and catalogs. It didn't take long, as geo-demographic screening became more accurate, for nonprofit organizations to begin using the same techniques. Using a computerized process, mixing many demographic elements, the zip code is often used as a dividing marker to determine buying power.

The United States has approximately 42,000 zip codes, with an average of 2,150 households per zip, although urban zips may contain more than 6,000 households. Manipulating zip code data is known as market research and it is a $6 billion-a-year business. Often it leads to some intriguing facts. Demographers are the folks who divided neighborhoods in the Washington, D.C., area according to whether the residents ate Velveeta or Brie cheese and reported it in *American Demographics*. They wrote, "Velveeta, mocked as Spam for vegetarians, is a mild processed brick that's been on the market for 60 years. Brie, the creamy cholesterol from France,

Median household income, by Rank

1.	Fairfax County, Virginia	$90,937
2.	Somerset County, New Jersey	89,581
3.	Morris County, New Jersey	83,773
4.	Hunterdon County, New Jersey	83,749
5.	Fairfield County, Connecticut	82,716
6.	Falls Church City, Virginia	80,562
7.	Douglas County, Colorado	79,313
8.	Santa Clara, California	78,057
9.	Montgomery County, Maryland	77,774
10.	Chester County, Pennsylvania	77,643

Source: Claritas Inc. Reported in *The Washington Post*, June 10, 2000

has an indelible association with overly earnest wine-and-cheese parties."
(The Washington Post, February 17, 1998) Income has a lot to do with one's tastes in cheese, the report concluded, and most of us knew all along that income is highest where the most Brie is sold.

Nonprofit organizations are using the same data, not to sell cheese, but to determine giving potential. One factor used to screen lists of potential donors into giving potential is nothing more than the person's address, based on demographic statistics for that zip code.

A word of caution is appropriate when dealing with demographics. Most data are from the U.S. census conducted at 10-year intervals. Except for the grand population total, what was discovered in the 2000 census won't be analyzed and available for some time. Communities are not static and during years of a robust economy, they change quickly. The same warning holds when using real estate figures by zip code. The house next door to your prospect may be the most expensive in the area, or it might be the least expensive. Checking the value of a neighbor's house may tell nothing about the owner of the house you are researching; then again, it might.

CACI, a marketing systems firm that has produced demographic analysis since 1977, provides *The Sourcebook of ZIP Code Demographics* and *The Sourcebook of County Demographics*. Both *Sourcebooks* are combined in *Sourcebook.America on CD-ROM*. Of most interest to development officials is the household income statistics: median household income and average disposable income by age of householder and spending potential.

But was it a wealthy zip code?

Before her death at 94, Olive Swindells lived in a run-down, trash-filled Victorian house in Baltimore, but owned shares in more than 50 companies after shrewdly playing the stock market for decades.

She bequested $3 million to Gallaudet college, the world's only four-year university for deaf and hearing-impaired students. "It's not unusual for the university to receive bequests," said Margarete R.Hall, Gallaudet vice president for institutional advancement, "but these gifts are for the most part from people we know well—alumni or long-time supporters of Gallaudet. Olive Swindell's gift was a complete surprise. A very pleasant surprise, I might add." Neither Swindelle nor her husband had attended the college, but he had been born deaf and she had become deaf late in life.

The man hired to liquidate the estate said it took a month to clear out the house. "There were no Tiffany lamps, no paintings by Van Gogh," but a lot of old bottles, old newspapers, and food containers. For months following her death, the mailbox was packed with prospectuses she had ordered from various firms. (*The Washington Post,* January 1, 1996)

Call 1-800-292-2224 for ordering information or check this Web site.

http://www.demographics.caci.com

CACI provides limited free information on its Web site. Enter a zip code and get a capsule demographic profile.

http://www.demographics.caci.com/Free/data.html

Because it's filled with interesting facts gleaned from the marketplace and applicable to nonprofit development, you don't have to be a statistician or a demographer to enjoy reading *American Demographics* magazine. It describes consumer trends and predicts the future—all based on demographics. Pick up a copy at the newsstand, call for subscription information at 1-800-529-7502, or check this site.

http://www.demographics.com

❖

✦ 6 ✦

Moves Management:
From Reactive to Proactive Research

In his will, a man in Wisconsin left $300,000
to a church he never attended, to a medical center
where he was never treated, and to a country fair
where he never went. No one knew why.

Most nonprofit prospect researchers consider themselves either a reactive or a proactive researcher. Reactive researchers think development officers have the responsibility to find prospects and submit new names for research. Others consider it their responsibility to take a proactive stance and vigorously search for new prospects to feed the insatiable appetite of development officers for new names. The lines between these two stances frequently become blurred. A reactive researcher may slide into proactive activity, even in the same position in the same institution.

In most development offices the need is evident for a systematic method, whether or not formalized, to identify new prospects and move them along the path toward the hoped-for large contribution. That process may be called prospect management, moves management, prospect tracking, or something else. It is a way to keep all development staff members focused and accountable. The researcher must be a part of that process.

Moves management

In this chapter, we'll call the process *moves management* and explain what it is. That term is often used, but not always understood. Moves management probably was coined at a major gift fundraising seminar and toted as

51

Please use the side door—or the Internet

Just when it seems that you're finally making some serious cash, Goldman Sachs comes along and does this. The investment bank is considering a new definition of true richness: $250 million. . . . That is what it may soon take to get the level of personal money-management offered to the firm's wealthiest clients. It used to be $100 million. . . . You don't have that much cash? Well don't worry, investors with between $1 million and $25 million will soon be able to come on board—but will be asked to do most of their business online." (*Money* magazine, February 2001)

a method for revolutionizing the field of fundraising and the art of major gifts. Called an organized and structured fail-proof system to assure the gift—at the proper level—it is used mostly for top prospects. Whether or not a gift happens depends on several persons who will be involved along the path.

For the purpose of this book, let's concentrate on the role of the researcher in the moves management process, which is defined as a series of steps, or moves, to get a prospect into an ever-increasing cycle of involvement with the institution. All along the way, each contact with the organization is plotted, weighed, and evaluated as to its effectiveness. The researcher's involvement will be that of a proactive researcher.

The steps involved in the moves management procedure are identified and detailed below.

Identify top prospects. If these names are already in the institution's prospect and donor system, so much the better. Using your office tracking software, do a sweep through those records to bring up:

- Persons with executive titles already in institution databases or files
- Persons who consistently have made contributions of a few thousand dollars over a long period of time
- Persons who live in wealthy zip codes or areas
- Persons over a certain age, perhaps without children, who have a strong connection to the institution

For new names, the proactive researcher may be asked to do some data mining of fee-based databases to identify candidates who may not yet have a relationship with the institution but are, for example,

- Executives with corporations in your city or state

- Individuals living close by in areas considered to be wealthy zip codes

- Persons who are connected through corporate or nonprofit board membership

Once identified, the prospect is assigned to the specific development officer who has the most compelling connection to the prospect. He or she will function as the prospect manager.

Deeper research. The researcher then may be asked to find more detailed information on the new names to determine their capability to be considered major donor candidates. Now is the time for electronic research for financial information such as a salary range, amount of stock ownership by corporate directors and insiders, and value of homes and commercial real estate.

For those candidates, the researcher should find biographical and personal information, including academic background, number and ages of children, interests, and contributions to political candidates and other organizations. In short, all information should be collected that is useful when the person is cultivated as someone who is or may become interested in the institution.

Make connections. Who knows this person? Are there connections to other donors or board members? Might he or she have neighbors known to your organization? If you find connections, a moves management step might be a development officer discretely approaching someone who knows the person being researched to gather additional comments. That contact person may become a very useful partner in the cultivation process.

As this new information is gathered by a development officer, it will, hopefully, be given to the researcher as a call report so it can become part of the development file. A moves management plan implies a team spirit with all players working towards the end result.

Cultivate the prospect. If the new prospect seems to have the qualities of interest, connection, capacity or inclination, the next step is to develop a strategy and plan the next series of moves. These can involve the major gift officer or development officer (or top executive) getting to know the prospect. Brainstorm to think of events to foster involvement, including invitations to luncheons, dinners, sporting events, seminars, lectures, and alumni gatherings—all within a time schedule. Those attending should be able to think of other events during the next 6 to 12 months that the prospect might enjoy.

By putting a definite time element into the planning, the strategy can be evaluated as you go along. Those who are getting to know the prospect—and providing ways for the prospect to know the institution—can note how well those events are bringing the prospect closer to the goal.

Summing up. Is the plan working? Have the steps been methodically documented to predict future contacts with this prospect, and with other prospects in the future? Should the development staff consider a different approach? Is there a way to speed up the process? Perhaps it is time to move on and devote time and energy on other prospects instead. Make the needed adjustments and plan the final steps, being certain no prospects have fallen through the cracks.

Process evaluation. Finally, it's time to evaluate your interpretation of the moves management strategy as implemented. What aspects of the plan were the most successful, which the least? Did it have the desired effect in bringing potential donors to either a firm denial, a gift, or a pledge? Did it cultivate any major donors for ongoing stewardship giving? Should moves management techniques be used with most new prospects? Do you have the staff to do it successfully?

This is just a nutshell view of moves management. Modify it to meet the fundraising aspirations of your own organization or institution. Use an Internet search engine to find more detailed information on moves management strategy or software products.

All along, the researcher, who attends all strategy planning sessions, should be attentive to names in the moves management system. Knowing those names, the researcher can keep alert for any news about prospects, perhaps using push technology, services available at several Internet sites that will forward news about a person or company to those who have requested it.

Proactive research

Regardless of what formalized plan is in process, proactive researchers are constantly on the lookout for new names to put into the prospect hopper. Some researchers devote one-third to one-half of their time to this activity. Others set a goal of a certain number of new names per week or month to suggest as potential donors.

Researchers who read the local newspapers and other appropriate magazines, keep on the alert for news of current prospects, and scout for new potential prospects are doing the job they were hired to do. Even if these activities are your lunch hour reading or, better yet, your breakfast reading, they must be done. Allow yourself a smug feeling when you can point out a lengthy article on a donor that no one else spotted.

Consider writing a memo with just a few facts to whet the appetite of a development officer. Something like this: "I saw an article in the *Wall Street Journal* saying that Swen Johnson just retired as CEO of XYZ Corporation with a golden parachute. His wife graduated from our college and the article said the Johnsons will be moving back to this city in retirement. As I remember, his wife and our board member Susan Johnson were college roommates." Don't hesitate to ask, after an appropriate amount of time, if an initial contact was made.

Bring in your own programs and playbills from local theatre and musical performances and ask others to do the same so you can scrutinize the donors' lists for potential donors. Look at lists of benefit event attendees, check the business sections of the daily newspapers and the business journals for mergers and sales, and try to get membership rolls of country and golf clubs by asking your board to bring in lists for clubs where they belong. Do the same for names of women who belong to the Junior League, exclusive garden clubs, or similar organizations. Look for donor names in annual reports for local nonprofit organizations. Banks always seem to be merging with other banks. Might that be a good time to contact their officers? Has your organization lost track of former board members who should be brought up-to-date on activities and needs?

Use DataQuick or a similar real estate service to find neighbors of your major gift donors. Any linkage to those donors or your board members is worth investigating. Hint, through the director of development, that your organization's chief executive take some community leaders to lunch every now and then to mine for prospect names to be researched. She or he may already be going to lunch with them, but may be missing that opportunity for advancement.

Don't be timid. The hierarchy, culture, and personality of your office will determine how you present new names. You may be able to present new prospects in a formal manner at a meeting so everyone knows of your proactive ventures. Or you may have to work new names into conversation with a development officer or your superior. If you feel the prospect has great potential, make him or her sound exciting, although I'm not suggesting you do full research just yet.

Let other staff members notice your proactive activity for finding new prospects. Proactive research activity may make your position more interesting than just waiting for names to appear. As a proactive researcher, you can get instant satisfaction in knowing you are an important member of the development team.

There's nothing wrong with claiming *ownership* of those prospects you have found and initially researched. After the name has been turned over to a development officer for further cultivation, you have the right to ask how things are going. You're not being pushy, just curious. Your interest may prompt more active cultivation and if a major gift is received, you can hope your input will be acknowledged. Some organizations require progress reports on new prospects at regular staff meetings with officers and researchers.

As part of your proactive stance, you might suggest an electronic screening from your database or a peer review screening with a few donors. The electronic screening may turn up names already known to your organization but with new-found potential. The peer review sessions may find colleagues and local community leaders with current connections to other donors.

Assuming you have been successful in finding and tracking prospects, don't be afraid to blow your own horn. With all humility, of course, you can casually remind staff members of your part in obtaining that major gift.

⇒•⇐

7

Using Search Engines
on the Internet

"Ah, so they've got the Internet on computers now."
—Homer Simpson

The World Wide Web has been described many ways. It is a phone book with half the pages ripped out. It is a library with the books strewn across the floor. Using it is like looking for a needle in a haystack. It's not surprising that organizing the Web with its estimated billion pages, loosely tied together by 7 billion hyperlinks, is daunting. Each day more than a million pages are added to the Web. Even the best search engines do not cover a large number of those pages, but they cover *enough*.

Contrary to popular belief, every bit of knowledge in the world is not on the Internet. Still, it is astonishing how much is. With some patience and a lot of time, if the information you seek is there, you may be able to find it using one or more search engines.

First, determine which search engines work best, then learn how to use them. Learn the difference between regular search engines, directories, library sites, and metasearch engines, and know when to use each. This chapter will give some clues about which engines have proven most useful for nonprofit research, but only by trial and error can you determine which works for you.

For a quick tutorial to search engines, take "Bare Bones 101: A Basic Tutorial on Searching the Web." Compiled by Ellen Chamberlain, head librarian at the University of South Carolina at Beaufort, it is based on her campus workshop on improving searching techniques. Some of the tips and suggestions used here are from that tutorial.

http://www.sc.edu/beaufort/library/bones.html

For descriptions of particular search engines with ongoing news about searching, subscribe to Danny Sullivan's *Search Engine Watch*. A real search guru, Danny will let you know when the ultimate search engine comes along. Until then, he will explain what is good and bad about the current ones.

http://www.searcheginewatch.com

Several distinctly different types of search services are available on the Web and it is important to know the difference to pick the one most suited for your research.

Full-text indexes

Full-text indexes of Web pages use software robots called spiders to go looking at millions of pages each day to put keywords into the index. No humans are involved as the search engine tries to match keywords with those in the index. The primary advantage of this type of engine is size. It leads to millions and millions of Web pages, but you may be lead astray by a lot of irrelevant sites. The goal of a search engine is to return the most relevant sites to the top of the list. To do that, they look for locations and frequency of keywords and phrases. Ironically, the larger the Internet gets, the more difficult it is to find a simple, accurate answer to a question.
Examples of full-text indexes are these:

Google: http://www.google.com Google is the search engine of choice for many who are amazed by its uncanny ability to rank the most useful and relevant sites first. *Google* is my favorite!

AltaVista: http://www.altavista.com This search engine lets you search for free, but charges a small fee for full-text articles.

HotBot: http://hotbot.com Give this general search engine from *Lycos* a try.

Northern Light: http://www.northernlight.com Most searches are free, but *Northern Light* provides links to newspaper and periodical articles for which there is a charge.

InfoSeek: http://www.infoseek.com Many researchers recommend *InfoSeek*.

Fast Search: http://www.alltheweb.com This search engine originated in Norway and was launched in May 1999. It is one of the newest, largest, and fastest of the search engines with a stated goal to index all Web sites that are publicly available.

What Google found

While searching an estimated 1,346,966,000 Web sites, Google found this number of references to words or names. Perhaps the most astonishing detail is that each search was done in less than half a minute. How *can* even a computer count that fast?

Donor	1,120,000	Advancement	
Contribution	4,470,000	research	872
Nonprofit	1,440,000	Bill Gates	625,000
Non profit	1,930,000	William Gates	7,350
Philanthropy	259,000	Bill and Melinda	
Fund raising	810,000	Gates Foundation	35,000
Fundraising	1,030,000	William and	
Prospect		Melinda Gates	
research	5,460	Foundation	29
Development		John Doe	88,900
research	149,000	Helen Bergan (sigh!)	55

Directories

Directories are collections of links to Web sites compiled by people, not those software robots. Directories are similar to telephone yellow pages. They organize data by category or topic and often include more information than found by the other type of search engines. Examples of directory type engines that annotate their links with descriptions or comments are these:

> *About.com:* http://www.about.com
> *LookSmart:* http://www.looksmart.com
> *Yahoo!:* http://www.yahoo.com

Links provided by directories are more likely to be of higher quality, but with smaller returns, than full-text search engines so sometimes miss what you are looking for. This type of search engine is useful when you want a quick overview of a topic.

Metasearch engines

Metasearch engines look through several search engines or directories and organize the results so you can see at a glance the best Web sites found on a subject. Because no two search engines index exactly the same set of Web pages, metasearch tools give a wider scope of results, but more is not necessarily equal to better. Examples of metasearch engines are these:

Dogpile: http://www.dogpile.com It's got a strange name, but it works.

MetaCrawler: http://www.metacrawler.com This searches other search engines in a piggyback fashion and allows searching by phrases as well as single words.

ProFusion: http://www.profusion.com *Profusion* promises to find "Invisible Sites" overlooked by other search engines.

Taking the metasearch description a bit further, subject search engines and subject directories let you refine your search to Web sites determined to be best for your type of search. For example, *Yahoo's FindLaw* provides legal information. *The Chocolate Lover's Page* directs you to more than 700 Web sites for chocolate. You may not need that for prospect research, but it is nice to know it's there.

Library sites

Library sites are another category of search engine. These are portals to Web site information on specific topics that are often compiled by librarians or researchers. As such they have been analyzed and declared useful. Many link to library collections or sites developed by colleges and universities. *The New York Times* maintains a super Web site leading almost everywhere. It includes a good business glossary.

http://www.nytimes.com/info/contents/siteindex.html

One example of a library site of interest to nonprofit researchers is *Gary Price's List of Lists.*

http://www.gwis2.circ.gwu.edu/~gprice/direct.htm

Others have been established especially for prospect researchers:

APRA Home Page:
http://www.APRAhome.org
David Lamb Research Page:
http://www.lambresearch.com/
Princeton University Development Research Links:
http://www.princeton.edu/One/research/netlinks.html

University of Vermont:
http://www.uvm.edu/~prospect/research.html

(See the chapter on Best Web Sites for Prospect Research for more examples of prospect research sites.)

Understanding URLs

When using any Web site, determining its validity is crucial. Check who put the information on the Web. You can often tell by its address or URL. Using the Web address for the Bare Bones Tutorial shown above as an example, here's what its Web site URL means.

http://www.sc.edu/beaufort/library/bones.html

- "http" is the protocol
- "www" is the host computer name
- "sc" is the second-level domain name
- "edu" is the top-level domain name
- "beaufort" is the directory name
- "library" is the sub-directory name
- "bones" is the file name
- "html" stands for hypertext mark-up language (that's what the computer reads)

Only a few top-level domains are currently recognized, but more are coming. Here is a list of the domains generally accepted by all:

- edu — educational site
- com — commercial business site
- gov — U.S. governmental/non-military site
- mil — U.S. military site and agency
- net — network, Internet service provider, organization
- org — U.S. nonprofit organization and others

Knowing only that basic information, you can make some judgements on the validity of data found on a Web site.

Tips for searching with search engines

More than likely you have bookmarked some Web sites that have proven useful. The fastest way to an answer may be to go where you think the answer might be, using one of your own bookmarks to sites you've found useful in the past.

When you use a search engine, take a few minutes to read the help screens for shortcuts and easily overlooked, but helpful, tools. If you are looking for something really obscure, use a metasearch engine for a wide sweep of Web sites. Researchers who learned techniques doing fee-based online searching on *Dialog* may benefit by writing a search statement to use with search engines.

- Think about words you'd expect to find in the site and use them as keywords.

- Use very specific nouns and objects. Put most important terms first in your keyword list, then combine them into phrases. Spell correctly.

- Use the plus sign (+) before terms to indicate that term *must* appear and a minus sign (-) to exclude the term in searches. (NO space between the sign and the keyword.)

- Use double quotation marks (" ") around phrases to ensure they are searched exactly as is, with the words side by side in the same order. (Do NOT put quotation marks around a single word.)

- Type keywords and phrases in lower case to find both lower and upper case versions. Typing capital letters will usually return only an exact match.
  EXAMPLE: *president* retrieves both *president* and *President*

- Use truncation and wildcards (e.g., ★) to look for variations in spelling and word form. It's useful when you are unsure how to spell a name.
  EXAMPLE: librar★ returns library, libraries, librarian, etc. Lars★n can be either Larson or Larsen.

- Know the default settings the search engine uses (OR or AND). This will have an effect on how you configure your search statement because, if you don't use any signs (+, -, " "), the engine will default to its own settings.

Quick tips for Boolean logic searches

The mere mention of the word "Boolean" sends many searchers into a tailspin. Named after a 19th century British mathematician, George Boole,

Boolean operators are words like AND, OR, and NOT used in electronic research to narrow or refine a search.

- OR allows the search engine to find either one term or the other. EXAMPLE: ireland OR eire

- Using AND means that all search terms must be present on the Web pages listed. EXAMPLE: bush AND gore

- NOT excludes certain listed terms. EXAMPLE: gore NOT clinton

- NEAR indicates each term must be close to the other. Search engines, using their own default, differ about how close the words must be to each other. Or you can set the limit yourself by adding NEAR/ 10. ADJ searches for items that contain words right next to each other, in any order.

- In Boolean searches, always enclose OR statements in parentheses. AND operators should not be used inside parentheses. EXAMPLE: (college OR university) AND "financial aid"

- Always use CAPS when typing Boolean operators in your search statements. Most engines require that the operators (AND, OR, AND NOT/NOT) be in caps. The engines that don't will accept either CAPS or lower case, so you're on safe ground if you stick to CAPS. EXAMPLE: "eating disorder" AND (bulimia OR anorexia)

- A good tutorial on Boolean searching is from SUNY Albany.

http://library.albany.edu/internet/boolean.html

Stop words

Know whether the search engine you are using maintains a stop word list. Stop words are small or common words normally not considered in your search. Examples are: a, an, and, as, at, be, if, into, it, of, or, with. To be safe, don't use known stop words in your search statement.

However, on some search engines, stop words can function as a way to find a name that may be listed with a middle name or initial or as a couple. By adding a stop word, "of" for example, the engine will find the name with one word between the first and last name. Used twice, it will allow two words between. Putting it in quotes eliminates hits with only one of the names. "John of Doe" allows for a middle name; "John of of Doe" allows for John and Suzie Doe.

Conclusion

After some searching, most nonprofit researchers decide which two or three search engines, including at least one metasearch engine, they like the best and continue to use them. They discover the best search techniques by experimenting. Just for the fun of it, search for your own name and see what appears. You might be surprised by what you find—and what others can find about you. Have fun searching the Web. Just think, it was just a few short years ago when there was no World Wide Web. How did we live without it?

⇒ 8 ⇐

Best Web Sites for
Advancement Research

*When Mae West found out she wasn't in the
big red* Who's Who in America *book, she cooed
coolly, "Well, the old boy who publishes that
isn't in my little black book either."*

Although recommended Web sites are scattered throughout this book, this chapter will list and describe some of the most useful sites for prospect and donor research—most free for the using. This may serve as a training lesson for new researchers or as a short course in Internet searching for others in the nonprofit office. Many sites were highly recommended as most used by subscribers to PRSPCT-L, the listserv for nonprofit researchers. Colleagues recommended others, and I discovered some while searching the Internet.

Most researchers, after some months on the job, determine the best sites for their type of research. They bookmark those sites into their computer browser. Few things are as frustrating as finding a super Web site once, then never finding it again—or having to plow through dozens of "hits" to locate it.

Don't risk losing your bookmarks when you upgrade browser software or when a hard drive crashes. That can ruin your week! To prevent that calamity, every now and then print your bookmark list, or better yet, copy your bookmark list to a floppy disk and squirrel it away in a safe place. If it is needed, you simply reload the floppy disk bookmark list back into your browser.

Another solution to the lost-bookmark problem is to place your bookmark list on a Web site offering a private, password-protected area where your links appear on personal Web pages that you can easily edit and rearrange. With your bookmark list secured, you can access your bookmarks online from any computer. That's a useful tool at an APRA conference, for example, when you want to recommend a useful site to a colleague.

Pick your favorite from the Web sites listed below. All seem to offer similar services.

http://www.blink.com/
http://bookmarks.yahoo.com
http://www.favoritesanywhere.com

Prospect research composite sites

Several university researchers allow access to their favorite online resources with links from the APRA homepage, but use is not restricted to members. Each mega-list contains a unique set of links found most useful for identifying and qualifying prospective donors. To see the list of Web Resources for Advancement Research, click on Links.

http://www.APRAhome.org

Web collections with links compiled by experienced prospect researchers include these:

University of Vermont:
  http://www.uvm.edu/~prospect/research.html
David Lamb's Prospect Research Page:
  http://www.lambresearch.com/
Princeton University Development Research Links:
  http://www.princeton.edu/one/research/netlinks.html
University of Southern California Development Research Department:
  http://www.usc.edu/dept/source
University of Virginia Prospect Research Page:
  http://www.people.Virginia.EDU/~dev-pros/
Northwestern University Research Bookmarks:
  http://pubweb.nwu.edu/~cap440/bookmark.html
Veritas Information Service
  http://www.veritasinfo.com/training.htm
Bucknell University Research:
  http://www.departments.bucknell.edu/univ_relations/ais/research
Rowan University's Wealth of Internet Resources:
  http://users.rowan.edu/~au

Gary Price, a reference librarian at the Virginia Campus of George Washington University, has assembled a super list of links to over 1,000 searchable/interactive tools for research. His *List of Lists* is at:

http://gwis2.circ.gwu.edu/~gprice/listof.htm

The *Internet Prospector* Home Page includes the current newsletter, archives of monthly postings for one year, and a Reference Desk.

http://www.internet-prospector.org/

To find recent topics discussed on PRSPCT-L, go to its Archives at

http://groups.yahoo.com

then click PRSPCT-L and the Search Archives box.

Company research sites—public and private

CEO Express searches for company executives in many resources, including newspapers and magazines. As a one-stop resource and gateway to many Hoover databases, it includes IPO Central and Business Boneyard, a listing of defunct businesses.

http://www.ceoexpress.com

MarketGuide.com provides very good company snapshots with lists of insiders, stock histories, and a concise glossary of financial terms.

http://marketguide.com

Business.com offers somewhat the same information on companies. Pick the one you like best.

http://www.business.com/companies

Dun & Bradstreet's CompaniesOnline gives basic corporate data on over 500,000 companies. It includes a yellow page lookup for addresses and telephone numbers. (This site shut down in 2001 with a promise to re-launch soon. Check it out.)

http://www.companiesonline.com

EDGAR includes all kinds of Securities and Exchange Commission filings (including IPO and insider trading) and makes them available to the public free of charge. It's searchable by individual name, company, industry, SIC code, and area code.

http://www.secinfo.com

To search the SEC by individual name, use

http://people.edgar-online.com/people/

SEDAR (*System for Electronic Document Analysis and Retrieval*) is the Canadian database that compares to *EDGAR* in the United States. *SEDAR* links to Canadian stock exchanges.

http://www.SEDAR.com

Hoovers allows free searching for capsule profiles, but a subscription is required for full company profiles with company history, financial information, officers and their compensations.

http://www.hoovers.com

Insiders, officers, directors, and major stockholders are listed at the *InsiderTrader* Web site with information on buys and sells of stock.

http://www.insidertrader.com

IPO Central brings information on recent and future Initial Public Offerings.

http://www.IPOhome.com

10KWizard gives access to full text searches on SEC documents, allowing searches by company or individual.

http://www.10kwizard.com

Refdesk.com—a gateway to knowledge

Ever since Colin Powell was quoted in *The New York Times* saying that Refdesk.com was his favorite Web site, visits there have touched a million a day. Speaking of the passion he has for his Web site, Bob Drudge (not seeking the publicity his son Matt of the *Drudge Report* gets) says he gets real satisfaction from helping people. "I'm the quiet reference desk librarian, sitting in the back of the library." Well, he's not a librarian, but his mother was. Close enough. (*The Washington Post,* March 26, 2001)

Big Charts can display a prospect's stock portfolio in a graph going back to 1988, showing how fortunes can rise and fall. Use this Web site to find the highs and lows on a specific date when accepting gifts of stock.

http://bigcharts.com

International Business

Type in a country name, then find lots of information on that country, including business listings.

http://www.corporateinformation.com

Demographics

The *U.S. Bureau of the Census* site includes population data about the people and economy of the United States. You'll be surprised at some of the statistics. Use the second site for income data.

http://www.census.gov
http://www.census.gov/hhes/www.income.html

Foundations

The *Foundation Center* Web site includes general information about foundations and how to apply for grants, but for data on individual foundations, you will need one of many products from the Foundation Center. This site links to the *Philanthropy News Digest* archives where grants are recorded.

http://fdncenter.org/

Use *GuideStar* to find the Form 990 that must be filed with the IRS each year by nonprofit organizations, including foundations. Type in a name to check if there is a family or independent foundation. If so, the 990 gives crucial financial information.

http://www.guidestar.org/index.html

Genealogy

Family Search is the colossal Web site from the Church of the Latter Day Saints. Take a look at the array of court and legal records, land and property data, and family genealogy possibilities. Try searching for your family name.

http://www.familysearch.org/

General Reference

RefDesk is a portal that links almost everywhere on almost any topic you will ever need. Bookmark it. It may become your first stop for any kind of research.

http://www.refdesk.com

Geographic and location research

The zip code lookup site from the *United States Postal Service* tells in which county a city is located and supplies zip codes and other postal information from the National Customer Support Center.

http://www.usps.gov/ncsc/lookups/lookups.htm

Government Grants

Federal Commons is a portal serving those seeking federal government grants from the General Services Administration's *Catalog of Federal Domestic Assistance (CFDA)*.

http://www.cfda.gov/federalcommons/

Individuals

Chris Sherman from *about.com* offers a good article about finding people on the Internet. He explains what is available and how to find it.

http://websearch.about.com/cs/peoplesearch1/index.htm

People Tracker is a service from *Forbes* magazine for researching corporate executives and the *Forbes* Rich and Celebrity lists. It's updated as events happen and includes job title, compensation, stock options, and news. You can sign up for e-mail alerts for breaking news on your prospects. Free, but you need to register.

http://www.forbes.com/pt

Person Finder links to several sites for name, address, and telephone number and searches for them at one time. If you search for a deceased person, it links to the *Social Security Death Index*.

http://person.langenberg.com

Newspaper and magazine searches

Northern Light indexes thousands of periodicals and newspapers. Searching is free, but a small fee via credit card is required for downloading the complete article.

http://www.northernlight.com

NewsLibrary site lets you search archives of many newspapers. Searching is free; most retrieved articles are $1.

http://www.newslibrary.com

The regional *American City Business Journals* include good articles on businesspersons and private companies. This site is an index to all journals.

http://www.amcity.com/

For international research, try the *Financial Times* with millions of free business articles in its Global Archive.

http://www.FT.com

Political contributions

The *Federal Election Commission* database tells who gave how much to political candidates. Check for presidential election contributions or state campaigns.

http://www.tray.com/fecinfo/

Somewhat the same, *OpenSecrets* gives political contributions and analyzes which industries influence what issues.

http://www.opensecrets.org

Mother Jones magazine lists the top 400 political donors of soft money and gives a donor profile at this site.

http://www.motherjones.com/web_exclusives/special_reports/
mojo_400/

Public record research

The *Pacific Information Resources* lists more than 2000 free searchable public records databases, nicely arranged by state and locality. The site links to State Attorney General offices where business applications and Doing Business As records are filed.

http://www.pac-info.com/

Real estate research

Use the *Yahoo! Real Estate* database as a free method to find recent sales prices for an exact address or other houses in the neighborhood. It also lists houses for sale.

http://realestate.yahoo.com/realestate/homevalues

Domania gives similar information on house values for the areas it covers. Check the list by state, then enter an address and get a list of nearby houses sold during the last 10 years.

http://www.domania.com

University of Virginia's Web site, compiled by their development research office, tells where to find property value appraisals nationwide.

http://www.people.Virginia.EDU/~dev-pros/Realestate.html

Looking for a guide to real estate multipliers to determine the market value from the assessed value? *Northwestern University* Development Office can help.

http://pubweb.nwu.edu/~cap440/bookmark.html

Look at the guide to wealthy zip codes at this site from the University of Southern California.

http://www.usc.edu/dept/source/zipcode/index.htm

Salary information

The *Executive Compensation* database gives salary, bonuses, and stock options back several years. Check by company ticker symbol for a list of executives and their total annual compensation.

http://www.ecomp-online.com

Look at the *Federal Bureau of Labor Statistics* Web site for salary surveys nationwide with job descriptions and number of those jobs available in the United States.

http://www.bls.gov

The *Salary.com* site offers brief but thorough job descriptions with regional salary information and comparisons of salaries in several U.S. cities.

http://www.salary.com

Telephone and address directories

A compendium Web site from *AT&T* gives links to a large collection of sites for telephone numbers and addresses. At the home page, click on Directories for a variety of choices.

http://att.com

Many directories give much the same information, but some are somewhat out-of-date. If you have moved within the past two years, check for your name and see what address is given. Some include only telephone white pages, others include both white and yellow. Pick your favorite. Reverse directories connect a phone number to an address.

Switchboard: http://www.switchboard.com
AnyWho: http://www.anywho.com

555-1212.com searches several directories and is useful as a reverse directory. It allows 30 free searches a month, then requires a fee.

http://www.555-1212.com

The *Ultimates* searches many telephone and address directories at one time. Most searches are free; others require a $12 per year subscription.

http://www.ultimates.com

Many researchers consider *Bigfoot* the most up-to-date Internet directory. It reports the date when an address was updated.

http://www.bigfoot.com

Verizon's entry as a Web site phone book is *SuperPages*. It includes an "include nearby area" option, the date when the data was updated, reverse-directory lookups, and a map to the address.

http://superpages.com

That's it—a quick and easy guide to useful Web sites for advancement research.

❖ 9 ❖

Using Fee-Based Services

*"Content needs to be paid for on the Web just as in any other medium.
And it probably has to be paid for the same way most
other things are paid for: by the people who use it."*
—Michael Kinsley
Slate magazine

Wouldn't it be wonderful if everything needed for nonprofit advancement research were available on the Internet for free? Dream on. It just isn't so. Sometimes you will have to pay for information. Using fee-based services you will pay with either an annual or a monthly subscription fee and, quite often, with additional charges to print reports, articles, or gain access to a specific database. If you are willing to pay for data, often you may save time and get exactly what is needed.

I think it is an accurate assumption that we are living in the golden age of free information on the Internet. Several companies put amazing amounts of information there and made it available to anyone who clicked on. They hoped advertising revenue from banner ads scattered throughout the Web site would pay the way. Now, a few years into the Internet era, it seems that just isn't happening. Already some sites are changing from free to fee. It's unfortunate, but watch for this to happen quite frequently in the future.

This chapter will give information on the most popular fee-based services used in nonprofit advancement research offices.

Whatever happened to *Dialog*?

In those days of yore, before there was the Internet, there were CD-ROMs, and before that, there was *Dialog*. Most researchers and librarians trained within the last 20 years started their careers using *Dialog* and thought it would last forever. It offered researchers a method of research beyond the printed book. With it, more than 300 databases could be accessed online. *Dialog* had something for everyone. No matter how obscure the topic, *Dialog* probably had a database on the subject.

In 1963, Lockheed founded *Dialog* and it became the pioneer of the data industry as a way to manage voluminous amounts of data. *Dialog* went on a binge of database licensing and began getting commercial clients in 1972. It practically invented electronic indexing and Boolean search technology. As library users began demanding more detailed information, academic, business, and public librarians saw *Dialog* as a means to that end. With *Dialog*, researchers gained access to databases never before known, and *Dialog* thrived. Prospect researchers saw *Dialog* as a way to get biographical, foundation, and business information and went for *Dialog* training or taught themselves the intricacies of the system.

Prospect researchers used *Dialog* for its *Master Biography Index, Marquis Who's Who, Disclosure* for SEC reports, *The Foundation Directory*, the *Grants Index, Standard and Poor's Corporate Descriptions, Dun's Market Identifiers* and *Million Dollar Directory*, and many newspaper archives.

Dialog could be accessed with a subscription password after an annual fee was paid. Add to that monthly access fees, connect time fees, access charges for each database used, and download fees for anything copied.

Dialog was not very user friendly, but because it had the needed information, researchers learned searching techniques. Because the meter was running on each search, researchers were advised to work out their search strategy before logging on. They learned the joys of Boolean (AND/NOT/OR) searching. In my three previous books for prospect researchers, *Dialog* was described as the "granddaddy of data retrieval services" and it was highly recommended. So what happened?

Although Knight-Ridder purchased *Dialog* from Lockheed in 1988, the name did not change until 1995 when it became *Knight-Ridder Information*. Soon afterwards, things began to go downhill and *Dialog* seemed to be missing the boat. According to a former Knight-Ridder executive, "*Dialog* had a chance at the inception of the Web to index it, in essence to be a Yahoo. But we passed on it because we couldn't see how we could make money on it."

In 1997, *Dialog* was again sold and the Internet was creeping up on it. Pricing with the infamous DialUnits irritated most clients, bills were impossible to understand, flat rates were inconsistent, and good customer service was lacking. In an attempt to regain client confidence, *Dialog* established Web access. At some point, the company decided to overhaul the pricing structure, to charge more for searching than for the downloading of documents. Before that, researchers were routinely using *Dialog's* powerful search engines (*DialIndex* File 411) for $1 a pop to find citations, then they went to the Internet to download the documents for free. *Dialog* lost money whenever that happened.

Although some old-time researchers are still loyal to *Dialog*, most nonprofit researchers have bailed out. Much *Dialog* information became available on the Internet with direct access to the companies producing it or through other fee-based online services. On the Net, there were no nasty online connect charges—by the unit, the minute, or anything else. Granted, there were still charges for some of the information, but *Dialog* was no longer the only game in town. *Dialog* is still available with information and sign-up details at its Web site. *Dialog One* provides searches for information on people, companies, and foundations.

http://www.dialog1.com/fundraising/index.html

Other fee-based services

Before subscribing to what can be an expensive fee-based service, take a trip to a local academic or public library. If your development office is connected to a college or university, ask the librarian if your office could be added to their subscription to *Lexis-Nexis, Dow Jones Interactive*, or similar resources. If the library has negotiated a flat-rate pricing structure with the service, you may be able to get articles and reports at no additional charge. Even if you pay for downloads and printing, it will cost less than a separate subscription. Besides, you will benefit by letting the library staff deal with administrative matters. Because institutions must have credit data about their vendors, some purchasing offices have access to *Dun & Bradstreet* and may be willing to share access with the development office.

Ask which electronic services are provided at your library. Some services are available off-site, using a public library card number for password Internet access. Most libraries have very good newspaper and periodical indexes with ready access to the full-text article. Many libraries subscribe to useful financial services. Pick a nice sunny day and spend half a day, at least, visiting the library of your choice. During that time you will probably find many ways to save money for your office and new ways to get the needed information. You might even be able to get a cup of cappuccino if the library is joining that bookstore trend.

Before deciding on a fee-based service, you need to determine what information is needed. Will you be looking for private company, corporate, or individual biographical information? Are you better off turning your research needs over to one company, or should you find services with a low entrance fee and pay-as-you go pricing?

Following, in no particular order, is a list of fee-based services with their main features. It is not a complete list, but it should be enough to give an idea of what services are available. Other services that charge fees are included elsewhere in this book. Inclusion here is not necessarily a recommendation. Some of these companies do electronic database screening as well as providing online research.

Because subscription and online research fees are subject to change, prices given in this chapter were correct in early 2001. Please check with the individual service by telephone, e-mail, or online for more complete information and the current price schedule. Whenever possible, take the service's offer of a trial subscription. Pick some names from your prospect list and see how successful you are finding information about them.

Dow Jones Interactive

Dow Jones has been publishing information by and about businesses for more than a century. Most of that time, of course, they put words on paper. With the electronic information era, they are still leaders. As described on its Web site, "*Dow Jones Interactive (DJI)* is a customizable, enterprise-wide business news and research solution. It integrates content from top national newspapers, Dow Jones & Reuters newswires, business journals, market research reports, analyst reports, and Web sites." Many nonprofit researchers consider *DJI* the best service for the money.

Pricing is fairly straightforward. The two options are for corporate or single users. Corporate rates can be negotiated with a sales rep and may be a flat rate of something like $500 a month for an office with multiple users, with no additional article charges. After the first six months, the price may be reevaluated, depending on use. The single-user annual password rate is $69. There is no additional fee for searching, browsing, or viewing headlines and lead sentences. You pay $2.95 for most articles you view and there is no additional charge for printing or saving articles. A nice feature is Keywords in Context, highlighting the name or company searched for in the text. It adds $.75 per article.

Because *DJI* accesses thousands of global sources in its Publications Library, its CustomClips feature is a popular feature. For $9.95 per folder per month, enter a personal name, an institution, an event, or a company and get an alert when that appears in the news. See what your top prospects are doing. News headlines are sent by e-mail. Then, by clicking within the message, you can retrieve the full text of the article ($2.95) or SEC report ($3.95 - $5.95 per filing.) Remember time is money. Though you can get free SEC reports with EDGAR, this may be an easier method. An Executive Report, available after a Company Quick Search, is just $9.95—a lot of information for not much money. For a full list of what company and industry reports are available through *DJI*, with their charges, check this Web site.

http://askdj.dowjones.com/aboutdji/pricing/standard.htm

Dow Jones Web Center is available to most customers as part of the $69 annual fee. It works like a search engine and hunts for search terms, but many researchers have their favorite free Internet search engines and use that instead.

DJI's Business Newsstand feature provides day-of-publication access to *The New York Times, The Washington Post, The Wall Street Journal,* and *The Los Angeles Times.* Some *Dun & Bradstreet* records are included.

Since *Dialog* fell by the wayside, many nonprofit researchers use *Dow Jones Interactive* as their main fee-based research service. Although putting

Less is often more

Long ago, E. John Rosenwald Jr., one of New York's premier philanthropist who has raised almost $3 billion, realized he was good at asking others to give away their money. He contributes his success to being a good salesman, believing philanthropy and salesmanship share the same dynamic.

Acknowledging the value of research leading to "the ask," he stated the process begins with copious research. "I want to know everything about a potential big donor, including which hand she used to brush her teeth. I plan these things like the invasion of Normandy." (*The New York Times* Special Section on Giving, November 20, 2000)

Forget that bit about the toothbrush, say most prospect researchers, it is obviously an exaggeration. A lot of information is useful; but too much information may just muddy the water.

charges on a credit card is the easiest way to pay, *DJI* can set up monthly billing if that is not possible in some offices.

Lexis-Nexis

Lexis-Nexis is a favored fee-based service for advancement researchers. If you have an adequate research budget, you will be happy with *Lexis-Nexis* and, because it is "one stop shopping," you may be able to drop other services. In a one-person research shop, having *L-N* will enable you to do research otherwise available only with more staff and a larger budget. In fact, some researchers have admitted they will not accept a research position unless they will have access to *Lexis-Nexis.*

Lexis began in 1973 and provided online legal information that helped legal professionals research law more efficiently than with books. At that time, few offices had their own computers, so *Lexis* provided a custom terminal and printer to its subscribers to gain access to major archives of federal and state case law. In 1979 *Nexis* joined with *Lexis* to become a full-text news and business information service.

Now *Lexis-Nexis* offers databases from over 23,000 news, legal, business, and government sources. It is very strong with regional newspapers and business journals and excels with biographical and assets information. But beware, there are different *L-N* Universes and not all databases are available in each.

The *L-N* fee schedule is somewhat more complicated than *DJI* and not spelled out on its Web site. Potential subscribers are asked to contact the company to negotiate a plan. Each plan is customized according to what type of databases will be used and for how long. *Lexis-Nexis* has subscription contracts with many, perhaps most, colleges and universities so their students and faculty can access the *Lexis-Nexis* Academic Universe. If you are on a campus, check with the librarian to determine if your office can be attached to that flat-rate subscription or add elements to it.

The *L-N* components that development researchers most often use are People, News, Company, Public Records, and Assets Libraries. Assuming you know only a prospect's name, *L-N* may get you an address without searching each state individually. Using that name, one can find spouse's name, positions as executive on corporate and nonprofit boards, and a list of property owned and their values. If seeking the owners of property in a particular zip code with a value over one million, for example, *L-N* can retrieve that. Some states post voter registration records available on *L-N* that include date of birth, a fact that is hard to get elsewhere. Many college researchers use and highly recommend *Lexis-Nexis* Finder to track lost alumni.

In 1999, realizing that many prospect researchers were using the service, *L-N* developed a web-accessed Universe for Development Professionals. Due to what is described as "licensing restrictions," some favored databases may not be on that service. Check this Web site to see what is currently included, then ask for a trial subscription.

http://www.lexis-nexis.com/cispubs/brochures/
development_professionals/

For occasional use only, individuals can register for *Lexis-Nexis* research using a credit card and be charged for individual searches or for a weekly subscription. That may be a good way to test the service to determine how useful it will be. For details, check the Web site or call 1-800-227-9597.

http://www.lexis-nexis.com

Prospect Research Online – iWave

Prospect Research Online (PRO) was designed specifically for the nonprofit industry. When nonprofit researchers use most fee-based services, they are using products developed for other industries or for general research. With them, researchers must pick and choose what items of information will be useful for the fundraising process. They pick corporate information from a wide variety of business databases, foundation information from online or CD-ROM directories, and information on individuals from other sources.

Realizing this was true, Rainforest Publications Inc., a Canadian publisher of books for nonprofits, developed its online database to provide corporate, foundation, and individual profiles to organizations for development purposes. They asked prospect researchers and fundraisers what they wanted, then tried to create it. The American version of *PRO* was launched in 1997 and the company went public as iWave in late 1998. As a new service, it does not have the depth of either *Lexis-Nexis* or *Dow Jones Interactive* but the company strives to catch up.

PRO is an online service that combines information from five main areas into one searchable system: Corporate Research, Foundation Research, Major Gift Announcements, Executive Biographies, and Donor/Board Lists. Information is gathered from other online sources, compiled by iWave staff, and presented in an easy-to-use format.

Because *PRO* began with a limited number of records in its database of corporations and foundations, each day the *PRO* team is adding new information, about 4,000 new pages each month, it claims. Each week *PRO* sends a What's New Report to subscribers telling of new Corporate Snapshots, IPOs, and Major Gift Announcements. Customers can ask for Alumni and Hot Prospects Alerts and for custom research on potential donors.

Because the service is designed for nonprofit fundraising, *PRO* staff members gather details on the philanthropy interests and giving record of individuals, corporations, and foundations. Individual names are gathered from donor and board lists, major gift announcements, and new executive promotions. Many subscriber clients supplied their own board and donor lists to be added to the keyword-searchable *PRO* philanthropic database.

A subscription to *Prospect Research Online* is a flat rate for 12 months. Rates are available for single work groups, as well as multiple locations, starting at U.S. $1,995 per year. Call for pricing details and use the trial subscription to test the service with names from your own list.

Some of the early criticism of *PRO* involved clients not getting many "hits" for the names they sought. If the company or individual was found, most were happy with the presentation of information and felt they saved a lot of time not searching several databases themselves. Because of *PRO's* custom research option, and the continual additions to databases, it may improve with age. iWave is a Canadian company so information on companies there may be more complete than for U.S. companies. While a donor-focused service such as *PRO* won't replace a major service like *Dow Jones Interactive* or *Lexis-Nexis,* it can give philanthropic information on donors that is difficult to fine elsewhere.

Call 1–800–655–7729 or visit the Web site for more information and for a free trial password.

http://www.rpbooks.com or http://www.iwave.com

PRO Lite

Acknowledging that not all nonprofits are the same in size, budget, and resource needs, iWave established *PRO Lite,* an online service for the small shop fundraising professional. It provides philanthropic information on the top 200 corporations, the top 100 foundations, and state and federal grants available in the United States. With that limited database of information readily available elsewhere, researchers would be better served using Internet search engines for company and foundation free information.

Unlimited Internet access to *PRO Lite* is $495 for 12 months. Call 1–800–655–7729 for details or visit the Web site.

http://prolite.iwave.com

Dun & Bradstreet

If searching for information on private companies, *Dun & Bradstreet* is a good choice. It's history goes back more than 150 years. *D&B* databases are available as print directories, on CD-ROM, and via the Internet to access information on more than 11 million private and public companies. With the Internet, finding free data on public corporations is fairly easy, but small private companies are more elusive. For credit and identification purposes most companies apply for a nine-digit DUNS number and are entered into the *D&B Business Locator* service. With *D&B* you can search by executive or company name and get a short report that includes corporate family tree identification from the *D&B Who Owns Whom Directory*.

D&B is the publisher of the *D&B Million Dollar Directory* and the *D&B Minority-Owned and Women-Owned Business Directories*.

Using a credit card or some other pricing agreement, you can get short company snapshots, called GlobalSeek reports, for about $5 each, with longer reports about $24. Click on Contact Us at the D&B Web site for pricing details.

http://www.dnb.com

KnowX

KnowX is an Internet source for public records. Millions of records are from a variety of sources, including official federal, state, and country records compiled by public offices and agencies. Examples of public records include real estate records, lien filings, incorporation records, lawsuit information and court dockets, court decisions, and death records. Researchers sometimes find birth dates in voter and driver license records although a law that went into effect on June 1, 1999, restricts companies from selling data from driver licenses. States are supposed to ask drivers if they want their data released.

This service gives a clear statement that the databases come from only published sources, including telephone directories; nonpublic information is not available. There is no charge to open an account. Searches are free or $1.00 depending on time of day, with various charges for the actual record. It is charged to the credit card number given when you registered.

Prospect researchers use *KnowX* as an inexpensive way to make a quick identification of a potential prospect. Its Ultimate People Finder can find addresses and phone numbers from public records and published telephone directories—unless the person has chosen to be unlisted. In order to keep information current, *KnowX* does not store telephone directory information. Instead it gateways to providers who update their data frequently. (In late 1999 an alarming fact was revealed to persons with unlisted numbers. It seems whenever persons with an unlisted number make a toll-free call, that number is attached to their name and address and it became just another phone number sold to telephone marketers.)

The Ultimate Business Finder searches five databases simultaneously. An Owners and Officers search looks for executive names in business databases. With Incorporation Records and Doing Business As filings, you may find your prospect has connections to private companies you have not found elsewhere. Charges for company reports vary.

Checking real estate records, a researcher may get a quick idea of a person's assets. Public bankruptcy records give an opposite view. To search, simply type in an individual's or business name and the state. When the results are displayed, you click on a match to purchase the full details. You are presented with a price tag and the option to purchase or cancel. Individual records are $6.95 each or $15 for all records. An obvious problem is getting data on the wrong person with the same name, or intermingled information on several persons with the same name. *KnowX* users report that customer service understands such problems and will refund the charge.

http://www.knowx.com

AutoTrackXP

In the online magazine *Slate,* a private investigator wonders if her profession is obsolete. Instead of working as a savvy gumshoe to track down deadbeats who bought cars on falsified loan applications, she now sits at her computer, types in a name and gets most of what she needs. Pretending that then Governor George W. Bush was her client, she found out the former occupant of his residence was ex-Governor Ann Richards. No surprise there. Then she checked his voter registration and discovered George W. registered to vote in Dallas on Nov. 12, 1988—the same week that his father was elected president. The PI was using *AutoTrackXP,* an online service used by many nonprofit researchers. (*Slate,* May 10, 2000)

Using as little information as just a name, *AutoTrackXP* cross-references an enormous amount of public records—addresses, driver licenses, property deed transfers, and corporate information. Nonprofit researchers use these services to locate lost alumni or to make quick identification of prospects. In 1998 the company announced that non-law enforcement subscribers would not have access to Social Security numbers in records. That made identification less exact, but I don't think any of us want our own SS number floating around the Internet.

On its home page, *AutoTrackXP* calls itself the Premier Online Investigative Tool and states that access is restricted to information professionals who must qualify for the service. The subscriber base includes legal, professional, and insurance industry investigators and 1,400 federal, state, and local law enforcement agencies.

The online application states that businesses must meet at least two of the following criteria: 1) in business two years or more, 2) minimum of three employees, and 3) a Dun & Bradstreet account. As the company has exhibited at or attended APRA conferences, they seem willing to accept nonprofit organizations and institutions as clients. Apply online or call 1-800-279-7710 to request an application.

Interestingly, following a merger in 2000, both *KnowX* and *AutoTrackXP* are now part of ChoicePoint Inc. and share the same databases with over 6 billion current and historical records on individuals and businesses. Following the November 2000 presidential election, ChoicePoint received bad publicity after it was revealed that the state of Florida used this private company "with close ties to the Republican Party to help cleanse the state's voter registration." Potentially erroneous information was supplied on 173,000 names it targeted as ineligible because they were deceased, registered more than once, or had been convicted of a felony. Unable to certify the accuracy of all those names, many people, including many African Americans, were incorrectly taken off the voter rolls. Such incidents show the potential for misinformation from companies that rely on little more than a name to identify persons. (*The New York Times,* December 7, 2000)

Following acceptance of the Subscriber Agreement, there is no minimum usage contract. You are charged a monthly service fee of $25, which is waived if you spend more than $100 that month. *AutoTrackXP* is a "transaction-based service with no hidden fees—you pay only for what you order, with prices for each transaction clearly denoted online."

http://www.autotrackxp.com

Dataland

Let's face it. Prospect and/or nonprofit researchers are not private investigators, nor should they be. Your task is not to dig up irrelevant personal details on a prospect or donor's life. The purpose of your research is to help develop partnerships with friends of your organization with whom there is usually already a bond or connection. Searching for a prospect's evidence of wealth, professional and business affiliations, executive compensation, and philanthropic inclination is not a mandate for researchers to delve into personal financial dealings. By doing so, you risk the very relationship you are seeking to develop. (See Ethics and Privacy Issues chapter).

Dataland does public record searches about individuals. Information that once was available only to law enforcement agencies, banks, insurance companies, and attorneys is now there for anyone willing to pay a price to get it. It is a bit spooky to consider. At least I think so. Some of the services offered are rather routine people locator searches for addresses, phone numbers, and real property owned. Business searches are for professional licenses and fictitious business filings. There is a $25 setup fee plus ongoing charges of $10 per month with rather large charges for searches and records obtained.

Beyond finding the above information, I'm not willing to suggest anything further. But if you are curious, you can check the *Dataland* Web site for a listing of other types of searches they offer with their search costs. The service claims to get bank accounts, cash value of life insurance, criminal history, driving history, divorce records (apparently for Canadian searches only), and more. Look at the list in relation to the APRA Code of Ethics to see if there is any prospect research relevance or appropriateness in finding what those searches might turn up. I doubt it and even if you can rationalize any reason to get that information, are you willing to risk the possibility of your donor finding out that you have hired a private investigator firm to, in essence, treat him or her like a common criminal?

KnowX and *AutoTrackXP* state clearly they use only public records; *Dataland* does not. Instead, it is rather vague about where it finds its information.

http://www.dataland.com

WealthEngine

Another player in the online prospect research competition is *WealthEngine.* This is the new reincarnation of Prospects of Wealth & Resources (POW&R), a service for nonprofit clients dating back to 1991. It claims to offer a way to cut through information overload and provide just what prospect researchers need. Gathering information from standard commercial databases such as *Dun & Bradstreet, Market Guide,* and *Marquis Who's Who*, it provides online searches for basic information, including some records of gift giving. It is unclear where the philanthropic data comes from.

When *WealthEngine* identifies additional information, these reports and profiles are offered on a pay-per-view basis. For example, an entry from *Marquis Who's Who* sent by e-mail or on screen display is $2.00. The company offers "in-depth, individually researched profiles" of biographical and financial information on prospects. Prices begin at $300 per report for up to 49 profiles, with the price receding to $200 each for over 200 profiles.

The monthly subscription rate is $49.95 or $495 per year. Screening and list rental are other services provided by *WealthEngine.* Call 1-301-215-5980 or check the Web site for more details.

http://www.wealthengine.com

Rolodex

David Rockefeller estimated in 1991 that he had 35,000 names in his Rolodex, including leaders of most of the world's countries and major corporations. By 2000, when he appeared on the PBS Charlie Rose Show, he said he had 100,000 names. With that number, he had to hire a full-time staff member to organize the Rolodex and keep it up to date. I wonder—does Rockefeller send 100,000 Christmas cards?

P!N – Profile Builder

Is *P!N* a screening service or a research service? Actually, it's both. I've listed it here in the fee-based research category to summarize the types of research databases used to create and update a typical prospect or donor profile. *Prospect Information Network (P!N)* was founded by David Lawson. To trace Lawson's career from the late 1970s when he edited a reference volume on foundations for The Taft Group to his founding of P!N in 1997 is to trace the evolution of prospect research from the use of print directories to this electronic product. In the 1980s Lawson founded the Information Prospector, a company with 30 researchers that produced profiles of major prospects, using mostly public library resources and some early databases on *Dialog.*

As David Lawson's career advanced, he used his knowledge of what information prospect researchers needed for the fundraising process to develop electronic stock and wealth matching products at CDA/Investnet. Joining David at *P!N* as vice president is Charles Headley, a friend and colleague from The Information Prospector and CDA/Investnet. No other electronic screening/research company can claim more staff with prospect research backgrounds than P!N. Watch for speakers from this company at APRA, NSFRE, and other fundraising conferences.

P!N's Profile Builder 2.5 will screen your top prospects against an Asset File, a Business File, and a Personal File. The Asset File matches names against databases of stock ownership, private company valuation, real estate ownership, and corporate insiders. The Business File utilizes Dun & Bradstreet databases and a directory of high tech companies. The Personal File accesses who's who type directories.

Information gleaned from those databases that matches your top prospects is packaged into a profile and stored in a fully searchable database, returned to your office by a P!N staff member to ensure that client researchers learn to use the program.

Click the Request More Info button at the company's Web site or call 1-888-557-1326 for pricing and other details.

http://prospectinfo.com

Target America

Target America was created for nonprofit staff members who are seeking donors and major gifts. Using market research, it provides information on the wealthiest 5 percent of the population from many of the same standard resources mentioned elsewhere in this book.

Nonprofit clients can send their entire donor or prospect list to *Target America* to be screened to identify persons of wealth. Hits will be executives of public companies, private company owners, foundation executives, people with known assets and investments, corporate insiders, and those with individual wealth. As with any screening, there is always the potential for false hits. Some users of this service feel some parts of the database may be outdated.

Target America On-Line also allows subscriber clients to screen their best prospects on demand via the Internet. Once online, researchers can check their names against the company's databases. Some institutions use *TA* for a quick check whenever they get a new list of names. For example, hospital development officers could check daily admissions for potential "grateful patient" possibilities. (Assuming privacy regulations allow it, according to new health care privacy regulations.)

In keeping with requests from prospect researchers who lament it is difficult to find the philanthropic history and interest of individuals, this company has established a Philanthropists File of persons who have provided major funding to foundations nationwide. That's a useful beginning, but it covers mostly wealthy individuals who have established a foundation.

An annual subscription fee of $500 allows for unlimited searching against the *TA* databases. Contact the company for screening rates by calling 1-703-383-6905.

http://www.tgtam.com

Hoover's Online

Hoover's offers a lot of free business information, and for more company details, you can get an annual membership for unlimited use or pay for company reports requested.

http://www.hoovers.com

Thomson Financial Wealth Identification

Formerly known as *CDA/Investnet,* now called *Wealth ID* and owned by the massive Thomson conglomerate, this product has been tracking wealthy individuals for nonprofit organizations since 1983. The company does screening to identify corporate insiders, officers, and directors with details of their stock holdings. As an ongoing service, it provides an electronic updating service called Pinpoint.

CDA/Investnet was established before stock information was available for free with EDGAR. If you spend a lot of time rummaging around EDGAR and have many wealthy stockholders on your donor list, you may benefit from *Wealth ID.* Ask for a free trial and pricing details by calling 1-800-933-4446.

http://www.wealthid.com

DataQuick

DataQuick is a real estate information company providing clients with ownership and address data, household-level demographics, historical information about a property, sales and loan details, and property characteristics. It tracks changes in ownership from county assessor and recorder

"You'll just have to wait. Our registrar is checking your credentials on the Internet."

offices. Claiming to cover 47 states, it delivers the data over the Internet, with dial-up contracts, or on CD-ROM.

As real property ownership is one of the elements used to identify persons of wealth, a service such as *DataQuick* is used in many nonprofit research offices. It is a lot faster than calling around to assessor offices for property values and you can search nationwide on any searchable parameter, including name.

Depending on the type of service requested, search fees vary. Usually there is a start-up fee and a monthly fee of $75, deductible as you do searches. With DataQuick you can get labels segmented by elements, such as assessed value and location. Call for details at 1-800-355-2203 or 1-888-604-3282

http://www.dataquick.com

Northern Light

Researchers who were looking for information on any subject more than 10 years ago must be astonished by some of the resources now available free or for little cost on the Internet. I fit into that category—and I am astonished almost every time I click into the Internet, especially if I am using *Northern Light*. The company started in September 1995 with the lofty goal of taming the Internet to make the information available to "everyone in the world."

Northern Light is one of the largest Web search engines and a fee-based service with its Special Collection of over 7100 full-text publications. Once you identify the article or document you need from the abstract, you can purchase it quickly and conveniently for immediate view onscreen with a secure online credit card transaction. The fee is between $1 and $4 with a few documents more expensive. Do a business search from a variety of reference sources, look for stock quotes, check for individuals, and almost everything else on *Northern Light*.

Member accounts are for individuals. Enterprise accounts are for companies or organizations and allow an unlimited number of users per account and customized search folders with monthly usage reports. Sign up for an Enterprise account; you have nothing to lose. Experiment with *Northern Light* for awhile and see what you can find for just a few dollars. There is even an honor-based money back guarantee if the document you order doesn't meet your needs.

For more details, call 1-617-621-5200 or check the Web site.

http://www.northernlight.com

IQuest

IQuest can serve as a fee-based reference tool if you are a subscriber to CompuServe (owned by America Online) as your Internet Service Provider. *IQuest* is a premium service that generates fees each step along the way to an answer. *IQuest* offers these categories: Biographical Research; Business Research; Company Research; Copyright, Patents, and Trademarks; Education, Government, and Social Sciences; Medicine, Science, and Technology; and General Reference.

Each section includes many of the standard resources used by prospect researchers including the *Marquis Who's Who* database, *Standard & Poor's* directories, and the bibliographic record from *Books in Print*.

Getting the full Marquis biographical record costs $5, but there is no charge if no record is found. In most cases *IQuest* warns users what the charges will be.

➤ **10** ◄

Finding Indications of Wealth

"Bill Gates has a net worth roughly equaling the
combined net worth of the least wealthy forty
percent of American households."
—Robert B. Reich

That statement about Bill Gates may be correct. Then again, it may be wrong. It may have been true at one moment in time, but may be completely off base after Gates reportedly lost $58 billion— over half of his fortune—as Microsoft stock price shrank in 2000. (*Forbes,* January 22, 2001)

Another interesting statistic about net worth that may, or may not, be true is that 5 percent of the wealthiest households in the United States hold 68 percent of the nation's net worth. Or, as Dinesh D'Souza said, in the *Forbes 400* issue for 2000, the top 1 percent of the population owns more than one-third of the wealth in the United States; the top 10 percent has two-thirds. (*Forbes,* October 9, 2000)

Are any of those figures right? Maybe it depends on when each statistic was calculated. Economists can throw out contradictory figures like that, and who are we to refute them? The same can be said about trying to determine an individual's net worth at any one time. At best, it's just an educated guess. At worst, it's just a guess.

The net worth controversy

If there is one controversy in nonprofit advancement research, it relates to net worth—that nebulous figure telling the total assets of a prospect or donor. Development officers think—perhaps it is wishful thinking—that the researcher should be able to look at a few Web sites on the Internet, tally up some figures on a calculator, and come up with a good estimation of a prospect's total resources or net worth.

Researchers, despite their noble efforts, know it just isn't so. Researchers often feel it is their duty to educate development officers to understand that net worth is assets minus liabilities and there is no way to research the latter part of the equation. Getting everything about a prospect's financial situation would be a breach of privacy laws, to say nothing about research ethics.

What is possible is finding a prospect's indications of wealth and thus declaring the person a potential donor. Researching anything beyond what is available in public records would, and probably will, be a put-off to prospects if they realized the extent to which nonprofits were trying to determine their net worth.

Realizing that the voices of those who know it is impossible to find net worth are getting louder, perhaps officers and researchers can change the terminology to something both can understand. The best way is to discuss the issue at a staff meeting. Researchers will get a chance to tell what they can, and what they can't, find. Development officers can say why they feel an estimate of net worth is crucial to the fundraising solicitation process. With it, they feel they can more accurately assign a gift potential to the prospect and solicit accordingly. The discussion may help narrow the communication gap existing between development officers and researchers, and, for sure, it will be a lively discussion.

Instead of the term "net worth," perhaps terms such as "known assets" or "known wealth" or "indications of wealth" are better. Those terms still identify a person as a potential donor (given that everything else fits) and probably give enough information to satisfy most development officers.

Wealth multiplier techniques have been used in development offices to determine wealth during the last couple of decades. The one that always turns up in conversation on the subject is the one developed at Boston University and written about in *Case Currents* in 1995. Development Director Robert G. Millar suggested using a formula based on statistical averages of assets analyzed by the IRS, using tax returns in 1989 for deceased persons with a net worth over $600,000. The formula was devised by the IRS to help field agents determine if estate taxes were accurately reported, based on the "average person" example.

To read the complete article with tables showing assets at time of death, go to the CASE Web site and find "How Much Is That Donor in

Your Records?" (September 1999) for step-by-step advice for figuring net worth and giving ability. Click on Freebies.

http://www.case.org/currents

If fundraisers could determine one factor, for example, real estate or stock holdings, they would figure net worth based on the tables in that article. Increasingly, many persons working in development question the validity of using such percentages. For example, as the Dow Jones Index has increased so greatly since 1989, those with large stock holdings may no longer fit the statistical averages. With the IRS's *Statistics of Income (SOI) Bulletin* figures, still based on assets over $600,000 at time of death, many fundraisers think the figures are no longer reliable because the more wealth a person has, the more it is now diversified.

The IRS analyses of assets at death are broken down by age, net worth size, and sex. They give the average percentages of assets in personal residence, other real estate, stock holdings, government and corporate bonds, mutual funds, cash, farm assets, limited partnerships, and interest in non-corporate businesses. Recent "Personal Wealth" articles from the IRS can be ordered for $18 by calling 1-202-874-0410 or downloaded from their Web site. The personal wealth file is called "95perwel.exe."

http://www.irs.ustreas.gov/prod/

Some advancement offices have developed their own techniques, based partly on the average wealth of their own donors and what they consider a major gift. An example is at the Web site of the Office of University Development at the University of Virginia. It's called "Determining Net Worth: One Organization's Search for Truth."

http://www.people.virginia.edu/~dev-pros

Another site was developed at the University of Vermont. Look for the sections on "Assessing a Prospect's Financial Capacity" and "Calculating Net Worth."

http://www.uvm.edu/~prospect/research.html

Most researchers realize that upper-level donors are more sophisticated about protecting their assets. Thus, getting a complete picture of wealth is next to impossible. Knowing variables such as age of donor and liquidity of assets are more important than having a net worth figure. Most important is the person's inclination to make a large contribution to a specific institution.

Tricks of the trade

After two New York City bird-watchers were abducted by rebels near Bogota in Colombia, the Associated Press quoted the leader of the rebel group as saying they did abduct the Americans but could not decide on how much ransom to demand until they had investigated the foreigners' net worth. *(The New York Times,* April 3, 1998)

A few days later it was reported that one of the hostages had escaped by walking for six hours through rugged terrain, but the report did not tell me what I wanted to know. I wanted to know: What reference resources or online services did the rebels use to investigate the net worth of the birders.

A new way to figure giving capacity

Just when researchers thought they were getting their net worth message across, along came Claude Rosenberg, Jr., a San Francisco money manager and philanthropist, to complicate the issue. He thinks philanthropists should base their charitable giving not on annual income, as seems to be the norm, but on their net worth. He's trying to convince givers to dip into capital, saying the wealthy can and should do just that and would feel no financial pinch at all.

If wealthy Americans followed Rosenberg's advice, giving would rise by at least $100 billion annually. What an idea! His proposed formula suggests that a person with $1.8 million average income would have an average of $16 million in total assets. Using annual income as a basis, wealthy persons give, on average, 4.8 percent. Using net worth, that is just 0.5 percent of the person's average wealth. Rosenberg thinks the rich could and should give much more.

Claude Rosenberg spells out his philanthropy theory in his book, *Wealthy and Wise: How You and America Can Get the Most Out of Your Giving.* It's no surprise that some organizations were purchasing the book in quantity and giving copies to their wealthy trustees and board members. (*The Chronicle of Philanthropy,* January 25, 1996)

Following the popularity of his book, in September 2000 Rosenberg launched an interactive Web-based calculator to help people determine their optimum giving level. His New Tithing Group (online at http://

www.newtithing.org) developed an online philanthropic budgeting tool called the NewTitheCalc. It is designed for wealthy individuals who can enter a range of financial data and then explore affordable giving levels appropriate to their circumstances. Give it a try. Enter some figures and see how much donors at various financial levels may be able to give. Assuming, of course, they have the inclination.

Regardless of whether researchers and the development officers call it net worth or evidence of wealth, the figures gathered do have meaning in the philanthropy process. The indications of wealth most often gathered by researchers are real estate ownership, stock holdings and options, and annual salary.

Real estate values

It's fairly easy to research real estate values, but usually the percentage of a person's net worth in real estate goes down as income goes up. Even if you get a good handle on the value of a person's real property, it probably won't add up to a realistic net worth figure. According to a research report from Harvard University's Joint Center for Housing Studies, 70 percent of those in the lower income ranges (up to $49,000 annually) have more equity in their homes than they have in stocks. For those with over $100,000 annual income (hardly a fortune nowadays), only 40 percent have bigger home real estate equities than stock portfolios. The study implies that the gap widened considerably as annual income rose. (*The Washington Post,* July 1, 2000)

Advancement researchers for nonprofit organizations are often asked to get the value of real estate as part of a prospect-donor profile. Does it matter what a prospect's house is worth? Maybe not, except in a general kind of way. If the person is living in a $1million house, that says something, but it does not tell how big the mortgage is or how much the house may have appreciated since it was purchased. Still, the value of the principle home is one part of a total picture.

The significance of real estate values has varied through the years, as prices go up, usually, and down, occasionally. At the end of 1998, 301 families bought $1 million (or more) houses in nearby Westchester County that year. (*The New York Times,* December 31, 1998) The article concluded that you don't get much for a million these days. "If you want a mansion you're looking $2.5 million." Any analysis of a person's wealth will vary greatly depending on where the home is located—and when the house was purchased.

If the researched home is a co-op apartment in New York overlooking Central Park, it tells a lot about the purchaser. When a 14-room apartment sold in 1998 for the dizzying price of $2000 per square foot, *The New York Times* asked Barbara Corcoran, founder of the Corcoran Group specializing in luxury properties, who is in the market for such an ultra-expensive apartment. Corcoran said the typical $10 million unit would be purchased "as a third or fourth home, paid for by a lot of new money posing as old, and bought by a real somebody—with a capital S—to make the statement that they have clearly arrived." (*The New York Times,* February 14,1998) Is that a good prospect for a large donation? Your guess.

Assessment vs. market value

Prospect researchers are sometimes confused about the difference between assessed and market value. Assessed value is what the county or city's assessor office states as the property value. It is assigned locally and is the figure used to calculate the annual tax bill. If you're lucky, you can find the ratio used to calculate the difference between assessed value and market value. Ask the assessor's office staff for the multiplier formula used to get the market value from the assessed value. It's helpful to know when the assessment valuation was determined. It may have been years ago and may have been affected by rollback tax schemes. The market value is what the property would probably bring in today's market.

Real estate Web sites

Both the Northwestern University and the University of Virginia research offices have put up Web sites for Tax Assessment Resources with a state-by-state listing of assessor offices. They include phone numbers with links to those that are online and a table of multipliers by state.

http://pubweb.acns.nwu.edu/~cap440
http://www.people.virginia.edu/~dev-pros/Realestate.html

Prospects with multiple residences (perhaps a beach home in Malibu, a ski condo in Aspen, or a vacation place in the Hamptons or on Cape Cod) make good prospects and your ability to identify these assets is helpful. The *Social Register* gives second residences, either for summer or winter, for those listed.

Consider this scenario. A traditionally good prospect is the widow, without children, who lives in a paid-for house in an area that has greatly appreciated in recent years. By doing an Internet real estate search for comparable area houses, called comps, you can get a feel for the value of her property. Still, knowing that won't say much about other assets she has. It may, however, bump her into a major gift or planned giving category.

http://www.realestate.yahoo.com/realestate/homevalues/
http://www.domania.com
http://www.homeagain.com

The *Wealth Investment Network* includes a real estate dictionary to help decipher those puzzling real estate terms. Click on Dictionary in the right column.

http://www.wealthnetwork.com

Commercial real estate

While the value of a person's house gives some information about the owner, real money lies in owning commercial or income-producing investment property. If you have any doubt about that, check the annual *Forbes* 400 list to see how many gave that as the primarily source of their fortune.

Finding ownership and value of investment property is tricky because of the possibility of ownership in different corporate names. Partnerships, limited partnerships, and DBAs (Doing Business As) fictitious business names, perhaps all registered with different names, confuse the issue. *Lexis-Nexis* Assets Library may show corporate connections. If not, you may need to visit the county office that deals with corporate filings for more detailed searching. If you are lucky, the owners of commercial property you are researching make it easy to tell who the owners are. The owner's name may be on the building or in advertising copy about the property.

With the Internet, all real estate research became easier than it was just a short time ago. New real estate sites are surfacing all the time. Doing real estate research, the age-old question arises: What is more important, your time or your money? You may need to spend money for fee-based services if you strike out searching free real estate sites. It won't take long for you to realize that there is no consistent format for these sites, and you will spend time, if not money. (See chapter on Fee-Based Services.)

Gifts of real estate

Besides estimating a person's net worth, other reasons exist for knowing how to find real estate values. Don't be surprised if a director of development asks to find the value of a property offered as a donation. Sometimes a donation of property can cause problems to the recipient, but many charities are interested in such gifts because of high property values. In fact, it has been estimated that the worth of real estate in private hands in the United States is over $20 trillion! Based on that, members of the World War II generation may be searching for tax-savvy ways to bequeath property.

Because there are so many tax implications of donated property, the *Internal Revenue Service* provides a free publication that includes real estate evaluation, "Determining the Value of Donated Property." Call 1-800-829-3676 or look at the IRS Web site for full-text version of the publication numbered 0200 Pub 561.

http://www.irs.ustreas.gov

Stock holdings

If you are lucky enough to research a top officer, director, or major shareholder of a publicly held corporation, the search is quite simple. If you are looking for someone who "owns a lot of stock," but is not an officer or insider of a company, it is not simple. In fact, it's not even possible. There is no way you can find what stocks or how many a person owns. That denies the ability to determine an accurate net worth figure for many or most prospects. Even if you could, the figure put on paper one day might change the next.

Consider these stock values for five Washington area executives, as reported in *The Washington Post* just after most high-tech stock values plummeted.

	At Peak	April 27, 2000
Steve Case, America Online	$1.7 billion	$1.08 billion
Michael Saylor, MicroStrategy	$13.6 billion	$1.07 billion
Raul Fernandez, Proxicom	$898.4 million	$445.9 million
Phillip Merrick, WebMethods	$1.1 billion	$318.5 million
William L. Schrader	$691.7 million	$209.3 million

Stop! Don't cross those high-tech leaders off your prospective donor list, some stock values for their companies have since gone back up—at least a little.

Although it is difficult to be precise in determining a person's wealth based on stock ownership, stock ownership is still a good indication of known assets or known wealth. After several years of rapidly rising stock prices, American households have more of their assets invested in the stock market than at any time in the last 50 years. (*The New York Times,* February 11, 1998) For more information on researching stocks owned, see the chapter on Corporate Executives.

Annual salary

The third main determinant of wealth is annual salary. Even if you can't determine the exact annual compensation for the person you are researching, many ways exist to find approximate salary information. Use the *American Almanac of Jobs and Salaries,* an inexpensive handy reference book, as a quick way to check for salary when you know a person's

occupation or job title. The Internet is filled with salary surveys for almost every industry and if you find one from this list that seems to work, bookmark it and use it when needed.

http://www.salary.com
http://www.ecomp-online.com

Using annual income as a beginning, Stanley and Denko in *The Millionaire Next Door* have devised a simple rule of thumb to estimate net worth of the rich. They multiply the age of a person by his/her total annual income from all sources other than inheritance, then divide by 10. Fundraisers who use that formula then suggest a contribution of 5 percent of the total. It's a basic tool that doesn't take into consideration such personality traits as thriftiness or extravagance. If you think it would work for your prospects, give it a try, but don't label the results a completely accurate net worth total.

Other known assets

Adding to the mix of assets used to determine the gift giving potential of a person or family, add up the value of "big ticket" items such as airplanes, boats, classic or luxury cars, and art collections. Start with an Internet search on your favorite search engine for Web sites that give values for those items.

❖ 11 ❖

Researching Public and Private Companies

"We've been called everything—Amazon.con, Amazon.toast, Amazon.bomb,—and my favorite, Amazon.org, because clearly we are a non-for-profit corporation."
—Jeff Bezos
Amazon.com CEO

According to *Giving USA*, corporations gave 5.3 percent of the $203.5 billion given to charitable causes in 2000, up 8.4 percent from what they gave the year before. That may sound like a small amount, but not when you consider that some gifts from individuals include corporate executives. Or, consider that the 12 percent from foundations includes foundations set up by corporations. No matter how you cut the pie to show which category gave how much to charity each year, researching corporations and their executives is a worthy pursuit for a development researcher.

Corporate giving may come from company-sponsored foundations or from corporate direct-giving programs. A corporate foundation must follow appropriate regulations governing private foundations, including filing an annual Form 990-PF. Direct-giving programs are less formal. The corporation can deduct up to 10 percent of its pre-tax income for such gifts. Unfortunately, the average giving percentage is slightly more than 1 percent and includes in-kind gifts.

Evidence that corporate giving can have a dramatic effect was shown in Detroit. While federal government funding for the arts was fading, the Michigan Opera Theatre in Detroit was growing because of lavish support from the local big three corporations: General Motors, the Ford Motor Company, and Daimler-Chrysler. Despite two difficult decades in which profits lagged along with support for the arts, now that profits are soaring, so is support for the arts.

Ford Motor Company gave the opera $2.5 million in 1999, making Ford one of the biggest corporate supporters of opera in the United States. One reason is Jennifer Nasser, wife of Jacques A. Nasser, Ford's chief executive and president. An opera lover and enthusiastic fundraiser, Mrs. Nasser helped persuade Ford to bankroll opera events and her galas to raise money for opera. Her involvement with the Michigan Opera Theatre demonstrates the importance of getting influential persons involved according to their interests.

What was in it for the car companies? David G. Ropes, Ford's advertising and marketing director, said the company tries to support civic causes in cities where it has extensive operations, particularly in its hometown. It also backs its executives' involvement in local institutions. Then, admitting some self-interest, he said Ford wants to improve Detroit's reputation, "to make it easier for the company to hire the best and the brightest." That was hard during the decades following the riots of 1967 and the threat of the car companies's financial collapse in the early 1980s. As Ford corporate profits improved in the 1990s, so did its corporate philanthropy. (*The New York Times*, October 28, 1999)

Traditionally, corporate support has been to higher education, health and human services, and the environment. As government funding to the arts diminished, some corporations picked up the slack. That support was much needed. Unfortunately, corporations are not static. They are affected by external elements such as economic trends and by management decisions.

Mergers and acquisitions among large companies can have a profound impact on the company's philanthropy. A study done by the Conference Board, a New York research group financed by 3,000 companies, analyzed the effects of 26 businesses involved in the biggest mergers and acquisitions in the 1990s. One encouraging result for charities concerned about losing support from companies merging and moving their headquarters and operations was the common practice of such companies to pledge millions of dollars before leaving to organizations in the region.

An example was Honeywell of Minneapolis that merged with AlliedSignal and moved to Morristown, New Jersey. It pledged to give the same amount in 2000 to charities in Minneapolis that it gave the year before it merged. (*The Chronicle of Philanthropy*, July 13, 2000)

What makes a good corporate prospect?

Before seeking corporate funding, fundraisers for all kinds of nonprofits, should find reasons why a particular corporation might give to them. Reasons for corporate generosity might be different from those of individual givers. A company's own self-interest plays a part in corporate philanthropy. There's nothing wrong with that. Indeed, it may be to your advantage. You want to promote your organization just as the business wants to promote itself. Put the two together and you may have the reason for a big splash media event beneficial to both sides—the giver and the receiver of a corporate gift.

Most companies want to do well by doing good. It has been determined that the public's opinion about a company influences its success. Other general reasons behind corporate philanthropy are these:

Proximity. Companies are most apt to support organizations in their own community or where they have a corporate presence. Companies with a local connection may benefit from the publicity following a major gift. Community interests of the executive officers very often influence company giving. If a national corporation has a local operation, it's usually a good idea to start there, before approaching someone in the national office.

Good citizenship. Many companies realize the importance of presenting a positive image to the community. Supporting groups that provide community services can enhance that image and give a tangible return to the company. A recent survey indicated that everything else being equal, customers would buy products from a company with a good civic record.

Corporate self-interest. Just as the Ford Motor Company felt their recruitment efforts would be improved as Detroit's image improved, so other companies feel their support of community charities will benefit their own employees. Ford does not make money just to give it away, but putting the company's generosity out for public view and promoting the company's image was very important. Craig Smith, in *Corporate Philanthropy Report*, summarized this new trend in corporate giving: "Old-line CEOs used donations to get on symphony boards; today's CEOs use the money as a strategic tool."

Executive interests. Personal involvement by those who make charitable decisions is often instrumental in determining which charities get contributions. Keeping other reasons in mind, decisions are made by individuals, and an executive's personal interest is bound to be a factor in decision making.

Often nonprofit researchers are asked to target the most likely corporate givers for their organizations, then determine if the companies have a history of charitable giving. Do they have a company foundation? What is their corporate giving program? Is giving controlled from a central office, or at the discretion of regional offices? How does a nonprofit apply for a contribution or grant? Are there non-cash or gifts-in-kind options?

Colleges and universities look for an interest match between company products and any research being done at the school. They look for the number of graduates employed by the company and whether the company recruits at the college. Is the company a vendor?

The company's annual report tells most of what you will want to know. Consider just calling the company to ask for its annual report. It's a good idea to keep a file of annual reports from potential corporate donors in the region. Many public libraries do the same. Ask in the business division.

These Internet sites provide annual reports online.

http://www.annualreportservice.com
http://www.prars.com
http://www.reportgallery.com/

In an annual report, charitable contributions may be listed in the section called Accounting or under Community Relations or Contributions. By researching a company's history of giving, a researcher can better determine if there are projects within the organization that might be funded by the specific company.

For example, a utility company may provide scholarship support in fields of expertise they themselves will need in the future. We hear of the lack of persons trained for high-tech positions. Doesn't it stand to reason that a company needing trained employees may be interested in technical education and willing to support it?

A newspaper may support journalism education. Because they need readers in the future, newspaper companies have long supported literacy programs. Put two and two together and look for regional companies that will benefit by supporting your organization. Finding out details of a company's giving before you send in the proposal for funding will save a lot of rejection letters. For example, the Washington Post Company gives only to groups within a 50-mile radius of Washington, the area where its newspapers are most read, but other companies owned by the Post may give elsewhere.

Corporate philanthropy directories

Old-fashioned corporate research in print reference books is not dead. It is still a good way to get started, even before you touch your computer keyboard. Large public and academic libraries have directories of corporate philanthropy. As it does for foundations, the Foundation Center's *National Directory of Corporate Giving* includes up-to-date entries on approximately 3000 corporate foundations and direct giving programs.

For more in-depth information on the 200 largest corporate foundations, *Corporate Foundation Profiles,* also from the Foundation Center, gives all necessary information for submitting a potentially winning proposal. Using either of these directories will focus the corporate foundation application and increase the likelihood of it being accepted.

A print series, *National Guides to Funding* in specific fields, from the Foundation Center narrows the search to only those funders that are most likely to be compatible with your requests.

Keep in mind that *FC Search: The Foundation Center's Database on CD-ROM* includes information on corporate givers.

For a complete catalog of Foundation Center publications on corporate giving, see the Web site at

http://www.fdncenter.org

The Taft Group publishes the *Corporate Giving Directory 2000* with data on the top 1000 corporate foundation and direct-giving programs, including biographical information on corporate and foundation officers and directors. It lists typical recipients of corporate grants.

Taft's *The Directory of Corporate & Foundation Givers 2000* puts you in touch with more than 8,000 funding sources with enough details to narrow the search for a grant.

For those interested in the possibility of tapping into the growing trend of international giving, *The Directory of International Corporate Giving in America and Abroad 2000* is divided into two independently indexed sections, covering U.S.-based and foreign-based firms.

To identify the grant administrators who actually make corporate grant decisions the *Corporate Giving Yellow Pages 2000* includes essential contact information so proposals reach the right person.

For those who prefer a more high-tech approach to grant seeking, *Grants on Disc* and *Prospector's Choice* on CD-ROM with their powerful search features, help narrow the quest from a world of grant possibilities to only those with actual potential. Both are from Taft and include data on corporate philanthropic support.

Time is important in the fundraising process and if you can't wait for the next volume of a major directory, a newsletter may be useful. This is a way to keep up with what corporate America is giving away. Beware, many newsletters are quite expensive.

Corporate Giving Watch from Taft is a monthly newsletter put together by those who scan grant information for upcoming editions of Taft directories. Each issue includes tips, new grants, breaking news, and analysis of current corporate giving.

For a complete catalog of publications from The Taft Group, check its Web site at

http://www.taftgroup.com

Which companies give the most?

A corporate giving survey of 77 corporations done by *The Chronicle of Philanthropy* and published in its July 13, 2000 issue, details both cash donations and the fair-market value of gifts of company's brand-name products. When both types of gifts are combined, three pharmaceutical companies (Merck & Company, Johnson & Johnson, and Pfizer) landed on top of the most-generous list because all three donated significant amounts of medicine—a high-cost item. Wal-Mart gave $112 million in cash, with Philip Morris Companies coming in second. A list of those surveyed companies also tells estimated giving figures for the future.

Look for the December issue of *Worth* for its annual ranking of most-generous corporations. Bank of America ranked first for giving more than any other company in 1999. Champion International, the paper- and forest-product company, gave the largest percentage of its profits to charity. The December 2000 issue was devoted not just to any giving, but to *power giving* that could change the world for the better. At *Worth's* Web site, search for Most Generous Companies.

http://www.worth.com

Corporate directories

Many researchers will go directly to the Internet for corporate—and every other kind—of information. We'll get to that, but remember that print directories still give good corporate information. Many sources, some general and others relating to specific types of corporations and businesses, are available. The main ones are listed here, but a business library will have others.

Many directories went from book format to CD-ROM or online by subscription. In doing company research you will have to decide which is more important—money or time. Actually, that is true for most research. Those resources that are the most expensive do save you time, but you can get the same information, by spending time, by using print resources

---

What about a necktie?

Northern Virginia's high-tech corridor between Dulles International Airport and Washington has been called Silicon Valley East. It is no surprise that in the 90s technology executives joined the clubs established by developers and bankers who had benefited from the real estate boom in the 80s.

Located on the top floor of the 17-story Tycon Tower, the highest point in Fairfax Country, members of the Tower Club can see Washington 8 miles to the east or a mountain range 25 miles to the west. But most members prefer, instead, to see or be seen in this atmosphere that is ready-made for networking. In a world of mergers and acquisitions, tables are spaced at tasteful distances to hinder eavesdropping.

To draw a younger membership, those under 35 get a break on membership dues, paying $750 instead of $1500. For some potential Baby Billionaires, the difference may not matter, but some see requiring a jacket in the dining room an unnecessary restriction. (*The Washington Post Business,* April 13, 1998)

Three years later, about a year following the Nasdaq stock descent, the Tower Club relaxed its requirement for wearing jackets in the dining room to a "jackets preferred" policy. Perhaps those young entrepreneurs could no longer afford one.

in a local library and photocopying what you need. Does that sound a little prehistoric?

Because corporate reference books are expensive, consider cutting back on buying print directories in the nonprofit office. Why pay for the entire corporate directory when you can get the information more cheaply with a fee-based service that allows paying for only what is needed. Better yet, look for it free on the Internet.

Dun & Bradstreet Million Dollar Directory is a multi-volume print set (also on CD-ROM and online as a fee-based tool) for financial information on companies. In the nonprofit offices that can afford this resource, it is where a researcher will look first for information on companies and their executives. A geographic index makes it easy to find companies in your region. Because it gives basic biographical data, you can check by school or university name for graduates who are successes in the corporate world. Some organizations use the DUNS number assigned to companies by Dun & Bradstreet as the unique ID number for companies in their own database.

Rather than try to explain all Dun & Bradstreet products, my best advice is to check the Web site for a complete listing with prices or call 1-800-526-0651.

http://ddnb.com
http://www.dnbmdd.com

Some D & B Business Information Reports on companies can be ordered as needed for about $20 each. With D & B Online, individuals can order company reports for that price using a credit card. Look for details at this site.

http://www.dbisna.com

Corporate information from the SEC

A wealth of free data is available on the Internet from the Securities and Exchange Commission (SEC). Few areas are as well represented on the Internet as corporations and those who run them. Early on, the desirability of finding stock market information quickly led to Web sites making that possible. Everyone benefited—those who wanted stock information for their own investments and those who are researching a corporation as a potential donor.

Without doubt, putting SEC information on the Internet in 1995 was a crucial decision in an information age. Before that happened, companies

Philanthropy as fun

Steve Kirsch, Silicon Valley philanthropist, tells his high-tech friends to stop "sitting on your assets." When asked if philanthropy is really fun, he replied, "It's not the most fun thing I do, but it's in the top five. I think of it as work, but a satisfying kind of work." (*Worth* magazine, December/January 2001)

such as *Primark* (formerly Disclosure) offered information from SEC filings online for a fee—often a rather hefty fee. That is still one way to get historical SEC filings. Check their Web sites or call 1-800-669-1154.

http://www.primark.com/pfid

Many who needed the information felt it wasn't fair that taxpayers had to pay for SEC information twice. First they paid the salaries of the government employees who collected data at the SEC, then they paid a company to retrieve the data. EDGAR to the rescue. Okay, who remembers that EDGAR is the acronym for the commission's Electronic Data Gathering, Analysis and Retrieval system?

SEC registration was established in 1934 to protect the integrity of the security system. It required periodic reports of publicly owned companies to be used by investors and others who did research, for whatever reason. Among those reports, the most useful parts of SEC filings for nonprofit research are the annual report and the proxy statement. The annual report (the 10K) gives a list of directors and executive officers, including executive compensation. It gives stock transactions of major stockholders and an analysis of how the corporation is doing.

Proxy statements (DEF 14A) sent to shareholders before annual meetings give financial and biographical information on company executives and board members. Besides career information and stock ownership in that company, they may give membership on other corporate and philanthropic boards for those listed. This gives some clue to the interests of the person you are researching.

No one reads SEC reports for the fun of it. Those dense, dry documents are not easy to decipher. "To the uninitiated," according to *The New York Times,* "EDGAR can seem an immense haystack of boilerplate, arcane and gobbledygook, in which the valuable needles of telling information can be especially hard to find." (June 21, 1998)

An EDGAR scorecard

Here is a lexicon for some of the most useful parts of SEC filings. By recognizing which forms have what information, you can cut to the chase and get what you need.

10K The official version of a company's annual report, with a comprehensive overview of the business.

10Q An abridged version of the 10K, filed quarterly for the first three quarters of a company's fiscal year.

8K If anything significant happens that should be reported before the next 10K or 10Q, the company files one of these.

12B-25 A request for a deadline extension to file a required report. When the late report is ultimately filed, the initial NT are appended to the report's name.

S1 The basic registration form for new securities, most often used for initial (IPO) or secondary public offerings. Variants with higher numbers are used for registrations connected with mergers and acquisitions (S4), employee stock plans, and real estate investment trusts (S11). Foreign companies use similar forms beginning with an F.

DEF 14A Proxy statement. Information and ballot materials for shareholder votes, including election of directors and approval of mergers and acquisitions when required. Look for biographical and financial information on directors and officers.

Forms 3, 4 and 5. Insider trading information. Directors, officers, and owners of more than 10 percent of a company's stock report their initial purchases on Form 3 and subsequent purchases or sales on Form 4; they file an annual statement of their holdings on Form 5.

EDGAR Online provides full-text search so users can get information using key words, phrases, company name, ticker symbol, names of officers and directors, and industry. Searches can be refined using the Boolean operators: AND, OR, and NOT.

http://www.edgar-online.com

Some large reports filed to the SEC (for example, mergers and acquisitions documents) may not be available on EDGAR. They, and all other SEC documents, should be available from SEC's Office of Public Reference. For more details, e-mail: publicinfo@sec.gov or call 1-800-942-8090.

Gifts of stock

Besides research on corporate giving, the nonprofit researcher may be asked for assistance when a donor offers a gift of stock to an organization. The trend toward giving stock rather than cash to a nonprofit benefits both the donor and the recipient. When the stock market is high, donors get a generous tax deduction by giving appreciated stocks.

The value of the stock gift is figured on the high and low price the day it was transferred. When writing the acknowledgement, most recipients give both figures for the day, then determine the mean or average amount, and list that for the donor for income tax reporting. Those prices can be obtained from the stockbroker who transferred the stock, or from any number of Internet sites that give historical daily stock quotes.

Through some research on the corporation, the nonprofit officers can decide to either sell the stock or keep it as part of the organization's portfolio. When a stock has gone down since its purchase, donors are advised to sell the stock first to take a tax-deductible loss, then give the cash to a nonprofit organization. Sometimes, the nonprofit researcher is asked to find the value of a stock on a particular day. For that, check *BigCharts* at this Web site.

http://www.bigcharts.com

ICQ Historical Stock Quote does about the same. To get a stock quote from years past, enter the ticker symbol and the date, then click Quote and you have it.

http://www.iqc.com/quote/history.asp

The current economic boom has caused an explosion of stock donations at many institutions. Sometimes there are strings attached. For example, an increasingly common type of gift is stock in high technology and other companies that will soon go public or have recently done so. Some of the stock donated by company officers is subject to a "lock-up" period of at least two years, during which the SEC regulations say that it cannot be sold. Charities can be offered stock options, shares in a family business, or real estate trusts—none of which can be turned immediately into cash.

Any of those scenarios can be a challenge for the nonprofit that is not prepared to handle such transactions. Traditionally, many charities unloaded donated stock right away and took the cash. Now, with the increase in stock donations, financial officers at charities are asking development officers to rethink that policy and get good advice about whether to hold or unload gift stocks. In that case, the nonprofit researcher may be asked to gather information on the company to help determine what to do. Gathering that information is similar to what any educated investor would do before making one's own stock buy or sell decisions.

Those with an interest in stocks from high technology companies can get more information on them at this site.

http://www.siliconinvestor.com

Even if the price has fluctuated between the date of the gift and the date the stock was sold, the important date is the date of the gift. That is the amount the donor can use for tax reports and pledge obligations. The thank you letter must follow the guidelines for gift acknowledgement over $250.

⋙ 12 ⋘

Researching Corporate Executives

"The goal is not to be the richest guy in the graveyard.
I don't care how much I'm worth when I'm dead.
How do I make myself feel good?
The only way I know is to make the world better.
Don't mistake that for altruism. It's egotism.
Call it enlightened egotism."
—Larry Ellison
Oracle Corporation CEO

I n 1992, America's chief executives were making about $3 million a year in salary, bonus and stock awards. In 2000, the average compensa tion had more than tripled to $11.9 million. The average corporate chieftain now makes more in a single day than the typical American worker makes in a year! Such statements used to shock people, including politi-cians, as early as during the 1996 election. No more. Compensation con-sultant Graef Crystal reports, "C.E.O. pay has been rising so quickly for several years now that it has lost its shock value."

There seems to be a changing attitude of Americans towards money or perhaps it is just that high numbers no longer astonish us. Since 1996, hundreds of recent college graduates and mid-level workers have become millionaires, thanks mostly to the Internet boom. *(The New York Times,* April 23, 2000) Only time will tell how many of them are interested in philanthropy or if their fortunes will vanish.

Those "old fashioned" ways of making money as bankers, lawyers, or real estate moguls are still with us, and it's still possible to inherit large sums of money. But in the current philanthropy gold rush, the new tech-nology fortunes are what everyone is after. Despite recent problems, a study by the U.S. Trust Corporation declared that the technology sector

But are they rich?

"Four-hundred and ninety-eight business owners were thrilled to make the *Working Woman* magazine's list of the 500 largest women-owned companies....But for Lynn Johnson, No. 25, and Gale Burkett, No. 387, the rankings caused some chagrin. Those who knew them were quick to point out that each failed one key criterion: They were decidedly male." *(The Miami Herald,* April 11, 1998)

is still one of the fastest-growing segments of the U.S. economy and the primary generator of personal wealth. Happily, those wealthy technology executives gave 6 percent of their after-tax income to charity, according to the study.

That study noted the primary concern of these new donors is to know the impact of their gifts. For them, getting a thank you note from the charity is not enough. They want to know what happened to their gift, or as a result of their gift. In fact, 66 percent said they would give more if they had better information about the effectiveness of their gifts to particular causes. (*The Chronicle of Philanthropy*, August 10, 2000) The feeling used to be, you've got to get their hearts. But the new philanthropists want to see the numbers.

If it is true—and it surely is—that fundraising is about developing a relationship with an individual, the successful young high-tech folks from the Internet world are the busiest people in town.

Michel Saylor, known around Washington and environs for flaunting his billionaire fortune from MicroStrategy, made all his money within two years. After some problems with accounting and the SEC, he has lost some and may loss a lot more within the next two. He admitted to the press he hasn't figured out how to use it, or how to share it, but one of his publicized ideas was to personally endow an online university. He hoped it would be the equivalent of Andrew Carnegie's libraries.

An overnight millionaire doesn't automatically mean an overnight philanthropist, but Saylor suggested the process: "The way it definitely starts is that you meet business executives in the region who you trust, and they invite you to these events. First you're exposed to all the different charitable organizations, then you come to your own conclusion about which are most consistent with your value system." (*The Washington Post.* April 30, 2000) Saylor was besieged with requests for time and money, but which ones get through? They are from people he knows, he said, or perhaps requests from people who shared the same table at the last fundraising gala.

Saylor didn't have to worry for long about how to spend his billions. Following revolutions that his company had filed misleading financial results to the SEC, the company stock tumbled as quickly as it had escalated. The stock had traded as high as $333; by late 2000, it closed at $10.50. That meant Saylor's personal stake in the company, once valued on paper as $14.5 billion, was down to half a billion. (That is, probably, enough to interest Washington area fundraisers.) After the SEC investigation, instead of giving millions to charity, three MicroStrategy executives paid $10 million in penalties to the SEC. (*The Washington Post,* December 15, 2000)

Best CEOs

Consider yourself lucky if one of these men (oops, some may be women) is on your donor list. *Worth* magazine rates The Best CEOs of Public Companies in its May issue. Steven Ballmer of Microsoft topped the list for 2001,

http://www.worth.com/

Forbes magazine lists Corporate America's Top Paid CEOs each year. In 2000 *Forbes* reported that only 23 percent of their compensation came from salaries and bonuses in 1999. The rest was from stock grants that vested or stock options they exercised. As recently as five years ago, 60 percent of total pay was from salaries and bonuses. Citigroup's Sanford I. Weill topped the 2001 list with his $785 million compensation. Look for other *Forbes* lists under People on the homepage.

http://www.forbes.com/ceos

Venture investors are said to be more discerning at deciding which new high-tech companies to support compared to just a few years ago. *Forbes* (February 19, 2001) provides its Midas List of the top 50 investors and the companies that have benefited from venture funds. Look at the Web site for the complete list of 100 names.

http://www.forbes.com/midas

Executive philanthropy

Information on the executives' giving is harder to come by than the numbers on their pay checks. (Plus options, of course!) Doing research on executive giving for *The New York Times*, reporters examined the pay packages of 12 executives, then tried to determine their philanthropy. "They reviewed the public records of the business leaders' personal foundations, talked to people familiar with their giving, interviewed company officials, and when they would come to the phone, spoke with the executives themselves. Those who were unwilling to answer questions may be donating more than is publicly disclosed, but it is impossible to know." (December 20, 1998)

Though reporters using *The New York Times* name could open some doors, or at least get someone to answer the telephones, most of what was discovered was from public records.

What those reporters were doing is what nonprofit executives and development research staff must do as part of their organization's fundraising process. Using the following terms, reporters arrived at the executive's total compensation.

> *Cash Compensation* – Includes salary, bonus, and other cash in an executive's pay package.
>
> *Gains from Options Exercised* – The difference between the present or strike price of the executive's stock options and the stock price on the date the options were exercised.
>
> *Additional Exercisable Options* – The gain that the executive would have realized on exercisable options accumulated over time, but not exercised, had he exercised them on the last day of the fiscal year.
>
> *Total Compensation* – The sum of the three categories above, representing the earned income that an executive could have given away, if he so chose.
>
> *Net Worth* – Estimates used for the article were from *Forbes* magazine for those executives in its latest listing of the 400 richest Americans.

As noted in *The New York Times* article, some executives were very generous. Eli Broad, chairman of SunAmerica, the insurer in Los Angeles, gave away $11.6 million in 1997. Sanford I. Weill, chairman of Citigroup, pledged $100 million over several years to the medical school at Cornell. (It's no surprise, Cornell renamed its medical school the Joan and Sanford

I. Weill Medical College and Graduate School of Medical Sciences.) But alas, the article concluded the biggest earners are not necessarily the biggest givers.

Just knowing a person's income, sex, or age won't give much insight into their charitable giving or enable you to predict it. That will take more research, especially when you realize that many of these same executives are involved in his or her companies' donations—a source of status not available to the average giver. This fact alone puts executives in high demand as board members and community leaders.

Claiming that his generosity was more than meets the eye, Dick Cheney, when he was the Republican vice-presidential candidate, insisted he should be given credit not only for direct contributions but also for corporate gifts that matched his own donations. When asked to justify why he and his wife gave only 1.01 percent to charity, he said his generosity should be measured by those corporate matching funds and by his speaking without charge to nonprofit groups, neither considered charitable contributions by federal tax laws. By his measure, his donations would still equal only 2.14 percent.

According to the Internal Revenue Service, average taxpayers give about 2 percent of their income to charity. Those with incomes over $1 million, a category in which the Cheneys fit with annual incomes over $2 million since 1992, gave an average of 4.5 percent. (*The New York Times*, September 6, 2000)

Whatever the size of their giving, the wealthiest executives are often quite ordinary when it comes to choosing recipients. Like others, they direct their giving to causes they are interested in: religion, education, and health care. The old boys' network (occasionally infiltrated by women) often gets their friends and colleagues involved, especially if they are among the highest paid executives.

Reading the listing of philanthropic donations of the 12 executives profiled by *The New York Times,* it is apparent that the connection between board membership and large gifts is very important. Colleges and universities attended by those charitable 12 have "lucked out" for they were remembered by their graduates.

As charity giving became the "ultimate status symbol among the newly wealthy," to quote *Worth* magazine in the December 2000 issue, some companies have begun offering free advice on charitable giving. It is widely thought that Cisco Systems in San Jose, California, was the first to offer a full-time counselor to help employees make philanthropic decisions. Although the company won't say how many of its employees are millionaires, it has been suggested that roughly 2,000 workers are, or were, worth at least $1 million. (*The Chronicle of Philanthropy*, December 14, 2000)

Knowing of the Cisco interest in philanthropy, one can assume executives of nonprofit organizations in the community are working hard to inform the Cisco counselor of their organization's financial needs so she can pass the information on to donors. Here the tables are turned. Instead of researchers finding information on a prospective donor, donors are researching giving opportunities in order to make appropriate gifts.

An often-quoted comment about the new high-tech dot-comers and their charitable giving is that they are able to make substantial gifts, but are demanding that charities show they can produce specific results, as expected in the business world. If the newly rich folks don't see a nonprofit they like, they form their own organization, often in direct competition to an established one.

Researchers should consider keeping a "watch list" or a "future prospects" file—call it whatever you wish. If it's a paper file, add newspaper articles on local high profile young entrepreneurs, watch the IPO (Initial Public Offering) for local companies and stuff the article into the file, read *Red Herring* magazine for its list of IPOs, and read the regional business newspapers and magazines. In short, keep your eyes open for names. Also watch for names of persons who are likely to inherit wealth. It's proactive research—and when a development office asks for information on one of the persons on the "watch list," you are two steps ahead. Using names that can be even loosely connected to your organization, you have a list of persons to invite to special events or ask to serve on committees.

Researching executives and their compensation

Researching executives involves knowing how to do a combination of individual biographical research and corporate research. The executives are, despite all, still an individual with their personal likes and dislikes. The corporation must be making money in order to give it away!

Do you ever wonder what's in those employment contracts of CEO's of large public companies. Read some in the *Corporate Library*.

http://www.thecorporatelibrary.com

The best way to find the compensation received by corporate executives is the proxy that is part of the Securities and Exchange Commission filing from the company. In most cases that document will spell out basic salary plus information on bonuses and stock options. When Graef Crystal, a leading researcher on executive salaries, does his compensation analysis, he notes that there is not always a connection between stock options and corporate performance. Some companies, he said, give out so many stock options that they represent about 10 percent of total stock. As you research an executive, be aware that stock options are a "gold mine" for a chief executive as they almost always carry no risk and can be exercised over a period of 10 years and are easy to cash out, according to Crystal. Begin research with the *EDGAR* online database for executive compensation.

http://people.edgar-online.com/

Since Crystal drew everyone's attention to those high executive salaries, several other Internet sites were set up to give details. *EComp Executive Compensation Database* is useful because you can search by state to find potential prospects. Search by company name, ticker symbol, or industry sector to get officers and their full titles.

http://www.ecomp-online.com/

As the gap between the compensation for average workers and the executive widens, it is no surprise that the *AFL-CIO* union would be interested. This site includes a pull-down menu for How to Track Down Executive Pay and lists companies in alphabetical order.

http://www.aflcio.org/cgi-bin/aflcio.pl

Researchers have expressed a word of warning about trying to equate salaries of executives of corporations with those in private companies, even if it is a similar business. Salaries of executives in private companies may appear less than for corporate executives. What is significant is how much of the private company the executive owns. It also matters how well the company is doing. And, were other businesses spun off the original company? If so, the executive may receive compensation from those as well.

If the executive is with a family-founded company, he or she may be gaining equity in the company. Although it's not cash in hand, it may pay off when the company is sold or goes public. Of course, if the private company is not doing well, what might have been salary may be plowed back into the company. Beware! There are many variables in researching both corporate and private company executives. Don't assume they are comparable; but also, don't assume one is always more than the other.

It started with salad dressing

Paul Newman tastes and accepts each Newman's Own product the same as he approves every charitable grant. Although his company was started as a lark as a for-profit enterprise, Newman promised to give away the after-tax profits. By the end of 2000, he had turned over $100 million to charity. Mr. Newman said his ability to tap publicity by using his face on the product "was tacky enough," so the brand motto became, "Shameless exploitation in pursuit of the common good." Over 1000 groups have benefited from Newman's Own charity.

First Call from Thomson Financial with its Investnet Insider Watch online gives alerts and details about past and upcoming stock transactions. Take a look and be amazed at the details. If you want more, look at an online sample issue of *Insiders' Chronicle,* a print publication detailing the stock transactions of insiders, giving their total stock holdings. Published 50 times a year, with four quarterly summaries, it is a bit pricey, but worth it if you discover an insider transaction that leads to a major gift. Since most development officers and prospect researchers can spot the names of their own top donors, passing around a copy of *Insiders' Chronicle* is cause for excitement. Call 1-800-243-2324 for subscription details or check the Web site for a download copy.

http://www.cda.com/investnet

Several Internet Web sites serve as portals to a wide variety of information about corporate executives. Consider bookmarking one of them to make your corporate and corporate executive search easier. Using just a couple clicks you can navigate to annual reports, executive compensation, and corporate financial data. This site is from the *Wall Street Executive.*

http://www.executivelibrary.com

13

Researching Foundations

*"Patty Stonesifer, the woman Bill Gates has put in charge
of distributing his money, may be as important to this world—certainly
as powerful in terms of her ability to effect change—as anyone who
has come before her, including the Buddha, Jesus Christ, Copernicus,
Freud, Marx, Einstein, Alexander Fleming, and Elvis."*
—From a profile in *Elle* magazine

Buoyed by the robust stock market and some large gifts to form new foundations, the nation's 47,000 foundations gave away a record $24.5 billion in 2000, up 15.7 percent from the year before. As the stock market soared, foundation assets grew and their donors became more generous. Overall, in 1998 foundation endowments grew by 16.7 percent, partly due to the huge foundation established by William and Melinda Gates.

Since then, endowment figures continued to climb. By March 2000, the William and Melinda Gates Foundation, with an endowment of $21.8 billion, is the world's wealthiest foundation. Other high-technology entrepreneurs have dived into philanthropy with large foundations. In 1999, Michael Dell, founder of Dell Computer Corporation, established a $114 million foundation to focus on education and children's health. Steve Case, chairman of America Online, has a foundation worth approximately $100 million.

Under IRS regulations, foundations must distribute at least 5 percent of their total worth annually. Some give more, and advocacy groups argue that Congress should set the floor at 6 percent. Whether or not that happens, as foundation endowments increase, so does the amount of the 5 percent that must be dispersed. Also, some foundations have set a time limit when their total endowment must be liquidated.

Unconventionally rich

When she died at the age of 80 in 1993, Doris Duke was reported to be the richest woman in the United States. She cared about children, animals, and the great outdoors. She worried about people with heart disease, cancer, AIDS, and sickle cell anemia. The only problem was that she didn't leave instructions in her will about how to distribute the $1.4 billion in the Doris Duke Charitable Foundation. Her will directed that money go toward "the improvement of humanity." By the time the foundation began giving grants in late 1997, Joan Spero, president of the foundation, said because of the announcement that the initial grants would be over $1 million, she was "everyone's best friend in New York."

The initial grants went to the performing arts, the environment, and medical research. Ms. Spero said, "Doris Duke was not a conventional lady. She was a free spirit, an iconoclast. And I certainly feel we have a mandate from her to not be conventional." About the future, Ms. Spero said, "We have over $1 billion that we can put to some definition of the public good, and that is awesome. It is frightening."
(*The New York Times*, November 4, 1998)

Foundations are typically created by wealthy people who use them as vehicles for giving during their lives and gaining certain tax advantages. *Forbes* magazine estimated in late 2000 that three-quarters of the very wealthiest Americans have their own private foundations. The bulk of the money in private foundations flows in at the funder's death, when bequests leave much of an estate to the foundation. So while the number of foundations grows, the greater effect will be when the funders die and their bequests are made. According to Foundation Center research, the average span between creation of a private foundation and execution of a bequest is about 18 years.

Perhaps your nonprofit organization benefited from that $24.5 billion foundation generosity. If not, you may be wondering how to go about getting foundation funding. You need to find foundations that give to your type of organization and then determine the foundation's giving history and the typical range of its grants. Once identified, you need to get and follow that foundation's guidelines for funding. New technology has made finding the answer to those questions easier.

In the golden days of yore—not very long ago—that old reliable print *Foundation Directory* from the Foundation Center was about the only way to research a foundation. Using data from the Foundation Center is still the best way. The *Foundation Directory* in print form is still with us and available in libraries around the country. The Foundation Center also provides electronic ways to get information on both long-established foundations and newly established ones.

To understand the range of Foundation Center services and publications, visit its Web site, considered a gateway to philanthropy on the Web. It links to about 1,600 grant-making foundations, includes an Electronic Reference Desk with FAQs about nonprofit resources, provides a common grant application for downloading, and gives general information about top U.S. funders. The Foundation Center's catalog of publications is online and users can order from it with a credit card. New items are constantly being added to the Web site, so check it often.

http://www.fdncenter.org

Sorry, not all the information in Foundation Center publications is free. But then, you didn't expect it would be, did you? Helpful as its Web site is, you will still need to refer to the directories (in whatever format) for extensive searching. If you are lucky enough to live in New York City, Washington, San Francisco, Cleveland, or Atlanta, you can visit Foundation Center collections or field offices to use their publications there. (See addresses on the Web site.) Check to see if your public library is a cooperating collection.

Electronic searching

Those who have used the print *Foundation Directory* will marvel at *The Foundation Directory on CD-ROM*. The searchable database of over 20,000 of the largest foundations will dramatically reduce the time spent searching for grants and researching a foundation. Best of all, it finds those grants you might have missed with a conventional search. It's a good way to find lost alumni who may have a connection with a foundation and to create customized prospect lists. The CD-ROM directory offers direct links to foundations with their own Web sites. See the Foundation Center Web site or call 1-800-424-9836 for single-user or network pricing and special offers that combine the CD-ROM and the print *Foundation Directory.*

FC Search: The Foundation Center's Database on CD-ROM includes data from several of the Center's print directories all combined in a searchable database of over 53,000 foundations, corporate givers, and grant-making public charities. With its 21 search fields, it provides access every which way you may be searching. I've always felt that doing research on a CD-ROM is more fun than playing most video games!

Foundation researchers in Washington, D.C., and surrounding areas have a new *Guide to Greater Washington D.C. Grantmakers on CD-ROM* from the Foundation Center.

For those who prefer the convenience of Internet access, *The Foundation Directory Online* made its debut in spring 2000. It offers fee-based access to the same set of over 10,000 large foundations, accessed by easy-to-use search methods. Using a credit card, you can subscribe and be online to the information in minutes, using your own user name and password. The benefits of electronic access rather than the print directory are the seven search fields you can use to refine your hunt: foundation name, fields of interest, foundation state, types of support, foundation city, geographic focus, and text search.

With a subscription of only $19.95 for a single user per month, organizations can control costs by subscribing only during times when they do the most foundation-grant searching. Special offers provide savings for online users who want the print directory also. To subscribe, visit the Web site or click on a link from the Foundation Center Web site.

http://www.fconline.fdncenter.org

Another online option from the Foundation Center is *The Foundation Directory Online Plus.* It combines the *Foundation Directory* and a searchable database of grants awarded by the top 1,000 foundations. In addition to the seven search fields listed above, several grant search fields are added: grant recipient name, recipient city, recipient state, subjects, text search, and types of support. Access to this database is $29.95 for a single-user per month. Expand your list of potential funders with *The Foundation Directory Online Premium* for an additional fee.

By joining the Associates Program, you have access to Foundation Center resources. For an annual membership fee, presently $595, members can make ten toll-free telephone reference calls per month and top-notch researchers will do the searching for you. Customized computer searches for potential foundation funders and photocopies of research materials are available for additional fees. Call 1-800-424-9836 or see the Foundation Center Web site for details. Click Marketplace for a complete list of products.

http://www.fdncenter.org

Those grant seekers who want a print guide to foundation and corporate grantmakers may want to order *The Foundation Center's Guide to Grantseeking on the Web.* The all-new 2000 edition teaches how to maximize use of the Internet for funding research. It gives general information about this new method of looking for grant funding and abstracts hundreds of grantmaker Web sites. It is also available on CD-ROM.

Each Wednesday the latest issue of *Philanthropy News Digest (PND)* is put online on the Foundation Center's Web site. It gives abstracts of major philanthropy-related news articles, including grant-seeker success stories and profiles of new foundation executives. Keyword access to archived issues is available.

http://www.fdncenter.org/phil/philmain.html

Another source of foundation grant information is *The Chronicle of Philanthropy's* Web site. It gives a summary of the current issue's articles, a list of upcoming conferences and workshops, new grants that have been awarded, upcoming deadlines for grant applications, employment opportunities, and links to other sites related to the nonprofit world. Some portions of the site are restricted to subscribers.

http://philanthropy.com

Small foundations are being formed constantly. Previously it has been difficult to get data on them, but now, at least, there is the ASF Web site for member foundations with assets from under $100,000 to over $250 million. The defining aspect of membership is the concept of few or no paid staff. Members pay an annual fee of $300 and must make grants annually to two or more entities to be included. The 2,000 small foundations listed can be searched by state.

http://www.smallfoundations.org/index.htm

The Taft Group's *Prospector's Choice* is a CD-ROM product giving financial information on foundation and corporate giving with biographical information on the people who make funding decisions so you can better design your application for the best results. The database is searchable in many ways—including by person's alma mater—and once the appropriate grant is determined, the product gives application information. *Grants on Disc* supplements *Prospector's Choice* by helping users access information on the grants themselves. Visit Taft on the Internet for further information on its products and services or call 1–800–877–TAFT.

http://www.taftgroup.com

Aspen Publishers's *GrantScape: Electronic Fundraising Database* on CD-ROM provides information on nearly 15,000 private, community, and corporate foundations. *GrantScape's* text-search system leads to qualified donors at a cost below some of the other CD-ROM search products. Call 1–800–392–7886 or visit the Web site at

http://www.aspenpublishers.com

Form 990s

Form 990 for nonprofits and 990PF for foundations are documents that must be filed annually to the IRS by tax-exempt organizations with a budget over $25,000. Thus, many small charities are not involved. The arcane document goes back to 1942 when it was established to prove exemption from taxes, but not intended to inform the public about the efficacy or efficiency of organizations and foundations. Unfortunately, there is no similar mandated document that does, so Form 990 was called into service to provide a window into the operations of a foundation. As the 990 is filed to the IRS "under penalties of perjury," it should be accurate. Now, with public scrutiny, organizations feel an obligation to make their 990s not only correct, but also informative.

When the Internet became what it is today, it seemed the logical way to make Form 990s information available. Philanthropic Research in Williamsburg, Virginia, the parent of GuideStar, offered to host the forms on its Web site.

GuideStar is a free database of over 700,000 nonprofits that the Internal Revenue Service has determined to be a 501(c)(3) organization. It can be searched by anyone who wants to determine a nonprofit's purpose and to see financial reports about the nonprofit's operations, expenses, staff, and board members.

With knowledge of a foundation's total assets, and the awareness that it must give at least 5 percent each year, you can get a clue to the amount of its grants. A foundation's Form 990 should list grants made and show the organizations it supports. As the form shows foundation officers and board members, searchers look for a potential link to the foundation.

The sunny sister

Most people know Warren Buffett for his billions, but most don't realize that his sister, Doris Buffett Bryant, is making a name for herself in philanthropy. Her Sunshine Lady Foundation is low-key and "charmingly eccentric," according to *Worth* magazine. But it has assets of $16 million. "It's a uniquely hands-on, folksy, person-to-person kind of enterprise—the un-foundation." Most grant recipients are the hard-luck cases that bigger foundations won't touch, with amounts between $58 and $280,000.

Ms. Bryant avoids what she calls the SOB's—the symphony, opera, and ballet, as well as "other high arts whose glitzy patrons too often carry 'multiple-type agendas.'" She tries to keep her philanthropy homey, "real clean, real simple." Even at that, she admits that done properly, giving money away is the "hardest thing I've ever done." (*Worth* magazine, October 1999)

Based on public disclosure law, the plan is to receive all electronically filed 990s from the IRS and post the complete document, including donor attachments, on this Web site.

http://www.guidestar.org
http://www.guidestar.org/index.html

On *GuideStar*, enter a foundation name in the search box. When the basic foundation data appears, look to the left and click on 990. Click on the latest date and the document will appear, as a Microsoft Word document. In most cases you won't want to plow through the entire 990, as you can look for just what information you need. In fact, *GuideStar* reports that each week 6,000 visitors view a 990 and click on 2.5 million individual Web pages. (*The New York Times*, November 20, 2000)

The *GuideStar* Web site includes articles that tell which foundations support what types of activities. Each article then links to a state-by-state listing. Click on your state to get appropriate funders.

http://www.guidestar.org/news/features/

Form 990s are also on file at the Department of Charities Registration (or similar department) at each state's attorney general office where they should be available for inspection by the public. The 1987 Tax Act requires that those who file 990s must make forms for the last three years available for inspection during business hours, but they are not required to make copies of the form for those who request them. That used to be the only way for potential donors and grant seekers to see the 990s for foundations and charities.

To see the information each nonprofit must file on the 990, you can download a blank form from the *IRS*. (It's also useful if you have to make notes from a 990 at a state office.) The site includes a "Frequently Asked Questions" file of special interest, including how to get a copy of an organization's 990 forms.

http://www.irs.gov

If the 990 is not available on the Internet, for whatever reason, a copy can be ordered from the regional IRS office where the foundation or nonprofit is located.

Independent foundations

Independent foundations are run by families or individuals and are also called private or family foundations. According to the Foundation Center, 41,750 such foundations existed at the beginning of the 21st century. This number showed an increase of 52 percent since 1988. Not incidentally, that period also saw the huge rise of millionaires and billionaires in this country. Some of the largest foundations, including the Bill and Melinda Gates Foundation and the David and Lucile Packard Foundation, can be called family foundations, but generally foundations set up by families are smaller.

When the economy is booming, a rule of thumb indicates that the number of private foundations rises in proportion to the number of wealthy people. So do the total assets of foundations, reaching $326.9 billion in 1998—a $100 billion gain since 1996—and assets continue to rise. *Forbes* magazine estimated that about three-quarters of the very wealthiest Americans have their own private foundations. (*Forbes*, October 30, 2000)

Those are interesting details, but irrelevant unless a nonprofit organization can determine a way to benefit from those figures. It is often a task of a nonprofit researcher to find those foundations most apt to support the work and mission of the nonprofit organization seeking funding.

The best way to find out about an independent, private, or family foundation is in its annual report. That's where a foundation tells why it exists and defines its interests. Many foundations post these reports on their Web sites. Try typing the foundation's name into a search engine and scan the results looking for a foundation's own web site or home page. Then, to find that foundation's Form 990, use the sites listed above.

Another source for finding information is *GrantSmart,* a resource with data on over 60,000 private foundations operated by Canyon Researchers, a San Diego–based private foundation. You can use this Web site to find foundations that support projects similar to yours. Search by state, zip code, or subject to find general information including contact details. The site includes a Hot Topics section and articles on public disclosure and privacy obligations.

http://www.grantsmart.org

Tips when seeking a foundation grant

- Use the resources listed in this book to carefully research foundations that give to your type of organization and note the amount of their average grants.

- A foundation must give 5 percent of its total assets each year. Knowing that figure will enable you to make a realistic request to improve your chance of success.

- Research how your proposal fits the mission of the foundation, its geographic area of support, and the strength of your linkage with them.

- Think about your proposal request very carefully. Does it thoroughly outline the problem and convincingly describe the proposed solution? Does it tell how the foundation can participate in that solution?

- Check the Internet for the foundation's Web site. Look there for a sample grant proposal and follow the directions carefully. Note the deadline. Look for other sample winning proposals at the Foundation Center site.

- Proofread your grant proposal. Then proofread it again the day before you send it.

- Hope for the best. If the proposal is rejected, learn from the experience and try again.

As an attempt to match those who have funds with those who need some, *GrantMatch* hosts information from both grant makers and grant seekers. Developed in Michigan by a tax and estate planning attorney who saw the need, his site appeals to smaller organizations who hope to attract grant makers looking for a nonprofit to support with both funds and involvement. A useful part of the site is a complete listing of the National Taxonomy of Exempt Entities (NTEE) code developed by the Urban Institute and the Foundation Center for organizations to classify themselves.

Because GrantMatch does not screen the listed nonprofits, grant makers are asked to be cautious before writing a check, advises *Bloomberg Personal Finance* (June 10, 2000).

As can be expected at a site developed by an attorney, there is a long legal disclaimer. GrantMatch's motto is "Where smart money funds nonprofits."

http://www.grantmatch.com

⇨ 14 ⇦

Board Selection

"You can bet that even as museum directors and curators
are whispering about other people's billionaires,
they are conspiring to woo one, or more, of their own."
—The New York Times

Oone of the most significant tasks a researcher can do for the organization or institution is to assist in the selection of board members or chairs of a major fundraising campaign. This research will be similar to researching major prospects, but the consequences may be even greater if the nomination of a board member is not carefully done. Board development is the process of identifying, researching, and recruiting a group of individuals whose fiduciary commitment and other talents will advance the mission of the institution or organization. One principal responsibility for board members is to see that the organization has sufficient resources to operate effectively. Read that as fundraising.

An effective board must provide leadership in financial development. According to many in the nonprofit world, trustees who approve the budget must also support it with their own personal and corporate resources. Those who take that position estimate that half of the trustees should be wealthy enough to make a leadership gift to a capital program. One-fourth should be able and willing to spend a substantial amount of time on development and fundraising, and all should be willing to support the mission of the nonprofit. As new names are added to prospect and donor lists, an astute researcher will keep an eye open for potential board members.

In *Mega Gifts: Who Gives Them, Who Gets Them,* Jerold Panas states that major donors give their largest gifts to the institutions where they serve on the board or in some official capacity. He says that not all on the board will be able to make a "sacrificial gift," but most large gifts will come from those deeply involved. In fact, Panas found that 20 out of 30 persons who gave over $1 million in one year were on the boards of the recipient institution. New technology multimillionaire Scott Oki, former Microsoft executive, serves on 27 nonprofit boards and has become an influential young philanthropist. (*Town and Country* magazine, June 2000)

When the Corcoran Gallery of Art and College of Art and Design announced the largest single donation in the museum's 132-year history and the largest to a Washington art museum from the area's suburban tech community, it noted the donor's board membership. The two American Online executives and their wives jointly pledged $30 million. Robert Pittman had been on the Corcoran board for three years; Barry M. Schuler joined the Corcoran board the year before the gift.

Irving Warner, author of *The Art of Fundraising* and long a practitioner of the profession, puts being rich on top of a list of qualities most needed for board members and campaign chairs. He writes that being rich and having clout almost always go together, an ideal combination for a board member. Clearly, Warner wrote that before the days of the high-tech baby billionaires, but he argues that the rich person will have social, business, religious, ethnic, professional, and cultural contacts. He or she may be politically connected and probably will know other community leaders—all pluses in influencing potential major donors.

The donor community's perception of an organization's leaders will be a major factor in the success or failure of a fundraising campaign. In fact, these persons influence the total operation of a nonprofit. More and more, organizations strive to put persons of wealth on their boards, expecting those members to lead the way by setting an example with their contributions. Those on the board should communicate confidence that the organization is deserving of large gifts because they will be used properly by the organization executives. It truly does matter whose names are on the organization's letterhead.

When he resigned as chairman of the board of WNET Channel 13 in New York, Henry R. Kravis was praised for his skills as a board chairman. It was not only because he helped the station raise $78 million in a capital campaign, the largest ever by a public television station, but also because of his skills as a board member.

Steven Rattner, chosen to succeed Kravis, said, "Henry has left the station in much, much better shape that ever before, not just financially but in terms of mission and spirit." Rattner praised Kravis for knowing, "how to motivate management by showing them you're involved, but not de-motivate them by meddling." William F. Baker, the station's presi-

A board from the 'hood

An example of the importance of putting people on the board who may become high-end donors is shown by the example of the Central Park Conservancy. Leaders of that group did not have to look far for donors—thousands of the country's richest persons lived in luxury buildings within a block of the park. As tradition has shown, the wealthy give to causes for which they themselves will benefit. That explains why cultural institutions are an "easier sell" than social service agencies. In this case, some potential donors had played in the park as children and had seen it become "a disaster zone."

Elizabeth Barlow Rogers, who had written a book on Frederick Law Olmsted, the principle designer of Central Park, became administrator of the park and promoted the park as a cultural institution, rather like the Metropolitan Museum of Art. It was an easy sell, mostly because of the park's neighbors. One was William S. Beinecke who had just retired as chairman and chief executive of Sperry & Hutchinson Company. He happened to have a penthouse apartment with a splendid view of the park.

Mr. Beinecke recruited members for the board and they were later urged to give to the park and to pressure their peers to do likewise—a long-standing fundraisers' technique. Now, after $233 million in donations, Central Park is a national model for restoration and right up there with the museums as a source of personal satisfaction for its donors.

dent, agreed. "He set parameters....He was all over us about education being our heritage. But he never tells you how to do it; he gives management their heads."

Every organization can hope to find board members with those skills, and it doesn't hurt if they have considerable wealth also. As a board member, Henry Kravis took his role in fundraising seriously and gave a $5 million gift to start the Kravis Multimedia Education Center to forge new ideas for the convergence of computers, CD-ROM, DVD, and the Internet with television.

In no other type of nonprofit institution are executives seeking wealthy persons more than on art museum boards. In "A Billion Reasons to Be on Board" (*The New York Times*, November 17, 1999) the author said that David A. Ross, director of the San Francisco Museum of Modern Art, "was in his glory. He was feeling very secure in the knowledge that his museum had no fewer than five billionaires on its board of trustees, among them Helen Schwab, the wife of Charles R. Schwab of the brokerage house fortune, and Donald G. Fisher, the founder of the Gap." At that time, the Whitney Museum of American Art had only one billionaire among its trustees, Leonard A. Lauder. According to the article, New York's Metropolitan Museum of Art "appeared to have five billionaire trustees."

The point was made that museum board members traditionally came from the social set whose members grew up surrounded by art, but many of today's billionaires, who are pretty much self-made, are eager to enhance their social standing by joining a prestigious board. In the search for new board members, museum directors are scanning the business pages of newspapers, thinking some of the very rich high-tech persons also may be useful for their counsel on technology.

James Kimsey, co-founder of America Online Inc., has been chairman of the Washington Opera Board, a member of the National Symphony Orchestra's executive committee, and a presidential appointee to the Kennedy Center's board of trustees. "They don't do this because of my personality," says Kimsey. "One, I can write a check." (And he did. One check, for $10 million, went to the Kennedy Center.) He continued, "Two, I'm a magnet for other people who can write checks. Three, my business skills." Landing Kimsey for the opera board was key because he became a bridge from local charities to new money. The money may be new, but the rules of the charity game are as old as time: What matters most is who you know and when you know them.

With this high-tech group, it may take a while for institutions to develop a relationship with potential donors. That approach takes time. Nevertheless, in a gold rush, the sooner one stakes a claim, the better the chance of striking it rich states "The New Philanthropists: Charity Networks Eagerly Woo the Region's High-Tech Millionaires." *(The Washington Post,* April 30, 2000)

Family and regional connections do matter. Although not (yet) a trustee of the Seattle Art Museum, the world's richest man, William H. Gates 3rd, gave $10 million to the museum, which happens to be directed by Mimi Gardner Gates, his stepmother. Michael S. Dell, the young computer magnate from Texas, gave over $7 million to the Austin Museum of Art.

Most nonprofit organizations cannot depend on even one billionaire for their board, but still there is the hope and expectation that those in a leadership capacity will also be leaders in giving. It is not unusual for the highest administration officer to meet with prospective board or trustee members to describe what is expected of board members, including an expected gift amount. This can include distributing a quite formal "statement of expectations" describing the role of a board member—almost like a job description.

At Carnegie Hall, candidates for the board are evaluated for financial capacity, as described in "Concerted Efforts: Even CEOs Sweat Out Carnegie Hall Tryouts; For the Board That Is." (*Wall Street Journal,* July 30, 1998) Nonprofit affiliations with other organizations are reviewed to determine the size of the candidate's gifts elsewhere.

A top-notch trustee on many New York organization boards, E. John Rosenwald Jr., has his own rules for board selection and fundraising. Among them: 1) Think twice before naming a trustee who can't make a substantial contribution. 2) Sell the excellence of the institution. People want to be associated with winners. 3) Never send a thousand-dollar giver to make a million-dollar *ask.* 4) Nobody is insulted by being asked for too much. (*The New York Times* Special Section on Giving, November 20, 2000)

Because board members and trustees are the public face of the organization, the chances of embarrassment are great when wrong choices are made. Remember the following incident?

Executives at American University in Washington, D.C., were embarrassed in the late 1980s when a major controversy erupted and was reported in local newspapers. Adnan Khashoggi, the Saudi financier and international arms broker, was asked to sit on the university board of trustees and then pledged $5 million towards a sports center to be named for him. (A donor got more for $5 million then than one does now! See the chapter on Naming Opportunities.)

This offer from the flamboyant Khashoggi immediately stirred debate on campus. Then, before the new technology billionaires, Khashoggi was considered the "richest man in the world." But his $5 million gift would only realize $500,000 annually for 10 years. Not much from a man who said he spent $330,000 per day for necessities. (*The Washington Post,* January 11, 1987)

When word of his offer got out, the student newspaper called the gift "blood money." It led to the resignation of a board member, the vexation of the college's Jewish donors, and questions about why the college presi-

Is *that* art?

Things do not always run smoothly even if the executives, with the help of a good researcher, have assembled a board of wealthy individuals interested in the mission of the organization. Marylou Whitney, one of about 60 members of the Whitney Museum's national committee, each of whom contribute about $5,000 to the museum annually, was so incensed over an art installation she said she would stop giving money to the museum.

That very controversial Brooklyn Museum 2000 exhibit called "Sensations" featured a portrait of the Virgin Mary with a clump of elephant dung. The piece, "Sanitation" by Hans Haacke, caused Mayor Rudolph Giuliani to attempt to stop city funding of the museum. Also, the 73-year-old heiress, whose mother-in-law was Gertrude Vanderbilt Whitney, founder of the Whitney Museum, left the national committee and said she wished they would take the Whitney name off the museum. "I had intended to make a big contribution to the Whitney in my will, but not now. This is a horrible work. I can't even call it 'art,'" she told the *New York Post*. (*The Washington Post*, March 14, 2000)

dent solicited this gift. The university did need a new sports center, but one professor suggested that the center be named the "Khashoggi Sports and Guerilla Warfare Center." As time went on, Khashoggi had his own financial woes and spent some time in jail. The university president left for unrelated reasons. Khashoggi didn't last long on the board. He attended one meeting and left after half an hour. When the president was asked why he was on the board, he admitted it was because the media was calling Khashoggi "the richest man in the world."

Undoubtedly wealth has to be considered one factor in board selection for organizations that rely on private contributions. As Panas stated, it's a basic nonprofit truth that the largest donors are actively involved with the organization. Lulu Wang, who with her husband made the largest-ever gift to a women's college in 2000, had been on Wellesley's board of trustees since 1988. Organizations should consider board selection a continuing process, not an emergency situation when money runs low. It takes a while for new board members to size up the organization before they are convinced it is worthy of a large donation.

As executives keep their eyes open for potential board members, they may wish to cast a fairly wide net for candidates. They should consider people in these categories: top professional managers of leading corporations or leaders of local successful businesses, persons who have a sizable inheritance in a family known for its generosity to charities, self-made individuals who can offer organizations a thrust to the future with technological skills, and community leaders in professions like law, real estate, banking, and accounting. In short, people in positions to identify wealthy persons.

Within each of the above groups there is an expectation that the person is affluent enough to make sizable contributions and has influence in the community. You hope they will solicit their peers to become involved with the organization. One perk an organization can offer its board members is community status and camaraderie with like-minded individuals.

Serious research on an individual being considered as a board member is crucial. It's much more difficult to take a badly chosen person off the board than to do research before the appointment. Any past financial or legal impropriety should be known at the beginning, not after it becomes an embarrassment. Traditionally, board members were chosen through the old-boy network. That is not as easy now with more competition for good board members. Many leading citizens are overwhelmed with requests to sit on boards, so smaller organizations may wish to seek out young executives or middle managers of companies instead of top officials.

When board or trustee candidates are being considered for your institution and the research office is asked to gather information on the candidates, where do you begin?

With biographical and financial research, of course. As with any research on a person, begin with a general resource such as *Who's Who in America, Who's Who of American Women,* and *Who's Who in the World.*

If not in those volumes, check the name in *Who's Who in the East, Who's Who in the Midwest, Who's Who in the South and Southwest,* and *Who's Who in the West* using the *Index to Marquis Who's Who Books.* Most biographical sources give complete name, birth date and place, education, publications, activities, marital status, family names, home and office addresses, career history, memberships, military record, religion, and political affiliations.

If you begin using basic print reference sources, you can get a handle on the person you are researching before you get into that "great reference resource in the sky"—the Internet.

Once the basic biographical information is compiled, it is necessary for the researcher to go further. As the person is being solicited not only for his or her station in life, but also because of leadership qualities, the researcher should look for in-depth newspaper or magazine articles about the candidate.

The researcher can use a general search engine to the Internet and other online resources described elsewhere in this book for newspaper and magazine articles. Use stock market and real estate databases to begin estimating the person's financial situation.

Several organizations dealing with nonprofit boards have Web sites of information about choosing board members and their function within their organizations.

The National Center for Nonprofit Boards Web site offers advice to charity trustees online. Users can ask questions on any nonprofit board-related issue such as fundraising and executive salaries and get an answer within two days. And, they can get information on NCNB training programs and publications.

http://www.ncnb.org

Look at *Trustee* magazine online for more information on board member topics. Although it is subtitled "The Magazine for Health Care Governance," the subjects relate to other types of boards.

http://www.trusteemag.com

Keep reading other chapters in this book. The same print and Internet Web sites useful for researching prospects and donors can and should be used for the ultimate prospect—the board member. Once the person has been installed as a board member, it is often a function of the research office to maintain a file on each board member, updating the files as new material is available.

❧ 15 ❧

Naming Opportunities

"Be careful whose names you put on your buildings.
Today's financial heroes could easily wind up as
tomorrow's license plate makers."
—Art Buchwald

D o you know how your institution got its name? Why is Harvard named Harvard? What about Duke? If you are at Brown University, you probably know that in 1804 the former College of Rhode Island became Brown University because of multiple Brown family benefactions. More recently, Florida Presbyterian College in St. Petersburg, Florida, became Eckerd College in the early 1970s when Jack M. Eckerd gave the school $10 million.

And why are there name plaques on many benches in Central Park? Why does each school within your university have a different name? The procedure of attaching a name to a building, a hallway, or even those park benches, is called naming. As more institutions realize the fundraising potential inherent in naming, don't be surprised if soon each cushioned seat in a concert hall, each hallway in your school, each bench on campus, and each tree in the park will have a name attached to it. The name plaque won't tell you the type of tree, but it might say the tree is dedicated to John Q. Public who gave money for its care.

Capital campaign naming

Many naming opportunities coincide with capital campaigns at academic institutions. Capital campaigns, which most colleges and universities schedule once every 10 years or so for a three-to-six year period, require an institution to step up its normal fundraising by listing long-term priorities. It requires the school to rigorously research its alumni, parents, and other friends. Then key university officials ask major donors to dig deeper than ever before to support the school. A carefully orchestrated *ask* may include opportunities to have the donor's name attached to a building or something else around campus. For a price, of course.

In 1998 Middlebury College in Middlebury, Vermont, started its capital campaign for $200 million with a detailed list of what a donor must give to have his or her name on a particular structure or item. Here's a partial list from the article "Behind Every Gift, A Careful Plot" in *The New York Times* (November 18, 1998).

Science library	$5 million
Ice rink	$4 million
Residence hall	$2 million
Endowed professorship	$1.5 million
Lecture hall	$500,000
Observatory dome	$500,000
Snow bowl ski trail	$250,000
Greenhouse	$50,000
Swimming pool lane	$25,000
Library work station	$25,000
Ice hockey locker	$10,000

Before college president John M. McCardell makes *the ask*, he needs the development office's well-researched estimate of the donor's net worth. When the president says, "I would like you to consider a gift of $1.5 million," it shouldn't come as too great a shock to the potential donor. Sometimes using reverse psychology, McCardell might say, "I know you are capable of $10 million, but can you give us $1 million?" Then, more than likely, a naming opportunity on campus will be mentioned, according to *The New York Times* article.

Colleges and universities look to each other to see who is charging how much for what. You can be sure the sky is the limit. From the West Coast, at the East Asian Library and Study Center at the University of California at Berkeley, we have these numbers for naming opportunities.

- To name the Library Building $ 15 million

- To name the Institute for East Asian Studies $10 million

- The C.V. Starr Library already has gone for $6 million

- A seminar room costs $50,000

A message for the future

After his daughter enrolled in the Maryland Institute, College of Art, Eddie C. Brown became a parent trustee of the school's board and at his second meeting decided to make a $6 million gift. The gift from Brown and his wife, Sylvia, will help finance the first new academic building on the campus in nearly 100 years.

Brown is the founder and president of Brown Capital Management Inc., one of the country's leading management firms, and a regular investment analyst on the television show "Wall Street Week With Louis Rukeyser." With the gift, Brown steps forward as a key African American philanthropist. "It is not too often that there is an opportunity for an African American family—and that was not a condition—to have their name on a world-class building. That will send a message to this generation and future generations." *(The Washington Post,* March 27, 2001)

• Naming rights for Chinese, Korean, and Japanese studies and the Department of East Asian Languages are going for between $5 to $10 million each.

The university didn't plan to start any of the above buildings until it raises the $40 million building cost, according to *The Washington Post* (December 9, 1999).

Research to the rescue

Offering to put a donor's name on a building, a professorship, or a classroom is the biggest reward a university or college can dangle. As one vice president for advancement stated, "A thank-you note works well for a $50 donation, but for a $50 million donation you're trying to find something that's more relevant to that size." These gifts are not spontaneous. They usually are the result of years of cultivation and subtle persuasion. Seldom, if ever, do people show up on campus saying they'd like their names on something. Said a vice president for institute relations, "As we say in the business, first the resources, second the interest, and third the inclination, because you need all three to make it work." It sounds like a job for some behind-the-scene research, doesn't it?

I do not mean to imply that most donors give only to have their name on a building or a classroom. But, assuming the prospect has philanthropic intent, the possibility of recognition may pique his or her interest and focus on a specific purpose for the donation.

The price goes up

When Harvard University came into being almost four centuries ago, all Massachusetts minister John Harvard did was give away his books to get his name on the new school.

In the early 1700s, a wealthy English merchant named Elihu Yale was persuaded to send several bales of cotton, goods worth 562 pounds and 12 shillings, 417 books, and a portrait of King George I to the Collegiate School in New Haven, Connecticut. It became Yale.

Now it takes a whole lot more to rename a school. For his $100 million gift, furnace company founder Henry Rowan persuaded Glassboro State University in New Jersey to change its name to Rowan College.

In today's world most donors will get their name on a new building or on a business or engineering school within a university if they give an eight-figure amount. Henry Samueli, a founder of Broadcom Corp., doubled his chance for immortality in late 1999 by giving two universities enough to have engineering schools at each named for him. He gave $30 million to the University of California at Los Angeles, his alma mater, and $20 million to the University of California at Irvine. Because government aid to higher education has been cut in recent years, state schools have adopted a more aggressive attitude toward fundraising. They are using the same tactics as private universities—including an emphasis on naming.

Further up the California coast at Stanford University, Jim Clark, the former faculty member who helped found Netscape, gave $150 million to the school for the James H. Clark Center for Biomedical Engineering and Sciences. Clark got his name on the center for that amount, but in the 19th century, railroad baron Leland Stanford was able to name the entire university to memorialize his late son for a fraction of that. Of course, dollars went further in the 1800s.

As it started its largest-ever fundraising campaign, Harvard University passed out a shopping list of naming opportunities priced between $5,000 for a class endowment account to $5 million for its Fine Arts

Library. Sorry, the Division of Engineering and Applied Science is already taken. Alum Bill Gates and his Microsoft sidekick Steve Ballmer paid $25 million to name it for their mothers!

Big spenders don't have to look to academe for an opportunity to attach their name to something. Just take a stroll in the park—Central Park, that is. Six hundred park benches have been endowed for $5,000 each for a standard bench, $25,000 for a handmade rustic one. Trees in the park go from just $1,000 for a sapling to $2,500 for a "historic tree."

If music is a donor's preference, he or she may consider a naming opportunity at the Kennedy Center for the Performing Arts in Washington, D.C., as part of a $100 million campaign. For $20 million, the Millennium Stage program would be christened for its benefactor. As part of the center's outreach programming, the Millennium Stage offers free concerts and is the only daily online performance of any arts group in the world. The center hopes high-tech millionaires will be interested.

The Kennedy Center is offering naming rights to several series of performances, including theater and ballet and the National Conducting Institute. In early 2001, Alberto Vilar, a Cuban-born billionaire and arts patron, gave the Kennedy Center $50 million to support a 10-year series of appearances by the Kirov Ballet and Opera as well as a training program for arts management.

In a capital campaign, with the hope for a large donation that ends with a naming opportunity, researching a prospect's *net worth* has some validity. It provides a watermark for the institution president or top executive who will be making *the ask*, so a possible amount can be requested. Advancement researchers debate the necessity of determining a person's net worth. Most agree it is, at best, just a rough estimate used to set a lower limit of the person's actual net worth.

The ultimate non-naming

Despite these examples of conspicuous giving, some donors still prefer to give anonymously. A 1991 survey found that only 1 percent of money contributed is given anonymously. The rate was 1.3 percent for gifts of $1 million or over. Those who want to hide behind anonymity do it for many reasons, according to a study on anonymous giving at Boston College.

Reasons stated in the study included: 1) a desire to hide the fact that one is wealthy—to shield oneself from subsequent requests, 2) to protect one's family and simply to maintain privacy, 3) to increase the effect of the gift by not making the recipient feel the donor is *hovering*, 4) ethical

Mr. Smithson's was the first

Following are excerpts from an editorial by Lawrence M. Small, secretary of the Smithsonian Institution, in *The Washington Post*, May 31, 2001, after he was criticized for accepting private funds that came with some conditions.

"As a nation, our lives are enriched by the generosity of others. . . . Today, for example, there is a simmering debate over 'naming opportunities,' the process by which a building or a room is named for a donor. Some argue that naming opportunities can warp an institution's mission. But history proves that this notion is incorrect. Simply accepting a gift does not create a conflict. Indeed, many great public institutions date their excellence to such a donation.

"The Smithsonian is one example. It takes its name from its benefactor, British scientist James Smithson. For those who object to 'conditions' placed on donations, consider the little-known fact that Smithson imposed three conditions. He specified the name (Smithsonian Institution), the location (Washington), and the purpose ('the increase and diffusion of knowledge.')

"Government funding cannot do it all. We make no apologies for seeking private support to develop programs or facilities that the public wants and benefits from. . . . Although we live in an era of great cynicism, there is ample proof today that private philanthropy is a vehicle for good work. . . . We should embrace those whose generosity enriches our lives, not reject them."

concerns that the giver becomes more important than the gift, and 5) protecting the recipient from embarrassment. (*The Washington Post*, January 11, 2000)

Conversely, benefits of going public with a gift include a chance for direct participation in a funded project and an opportunity to encourage others, by example, to be generous. More than likely, the recipient won't feel the donor is *hovering*. Instead, the donor will have a chance to ensure that the gift is well spent.

One of the prime reasons nonprofit researchers look for the interests of a prospect is to match a specific project to an interested person. Researchers working to determine the interests of Elizabeth B. Noyce had an easy time. If it involved her beloved Maine, she was interested. By the time she died in 1996 at the age of 65, Betty Noyce had given away $75 million, primarily to Maine charities. One of her most unusual projects is the Portland Public Market, modeled after the Pike Place Market in Seattle. Mrs. Noyce saw the downtown market as a way to revitalize Portland's downtown and provide help to Maine's farmers. Using millions she won in a divorce settlement from her husband, Robert N. Noyce, a co-inventor of the microchip, she also helped support the Portland Museum of Art, the Maine Maritime Museum, the University of Maine and the Maine Medical Center.

None of Mrs. Noyce's projects bears her name. She never wanted any kind of a memorial to herself, nor did she want her name on scholarships, endowments, or buildings. In the same spirit, she refused honorary degrees, saying that "just giving money was not the appropriate measure for an honorary degree." On the second floor of the market, a sculpture of an old woman pushing a cart laden with vegetables and feeding corn to a crow was originally named Henrietta and the Heckler. After Elizabeth Noyce's death, it was renamed "Betty Sharing the Bounty." The benefactress is anonymous no more. (*The New York Times,* January 1, 1999)

The naming rules

Although many institutions have their own regulations, there is no consistency about what amounts different institutions require to put a name on a building or to name an auditorium. Most realize the best thing to do, especially if the economy is good, is to put as high a price tag as possible on each naming opportunity. Officials usually have an idea about what the market will bear, depending on their own potential donors.

One fact seems true. The more prestigious the institution, the higher the amount. Like anything else, it is a question of supply and demand. The amount should be high enough but not too high, or no one will accept. Even though a naming opportunity may solicit larger contributions than ever before, officials should take a long and hard look at the history of gifts to their institution before setting a naming price.

One strategy often used is a careful analysis of the institution's potential top donors. Are they board members or trustees? (They probably should be.) What might they be able to give? The research staff can help with these decisions using basic prospect/donor research on estimated net worth.

It varies, but many institutions assume it will take a gift of at least 51 percent of the building cost to attach a donor's name to it. If it takes that amount to name the whole building, naming opportunities inside are priced accordingly. If a classroom building costs $10 million (but most cost more), the charge could be about $5 million for the name and another 1 percent for upkeep and improvements. Within the building, it may cost $500,000 each to name 8 classrooms for a total of $4 million, and $1 million for each fully equipped science lab. Some colleges and universities add up to 25 percent over the building cost for maintenance and upkeep, assuming it is easier to get money up front rather than later.

In the past, and possibly still, some buildings or parts thereof on campuses will be named for a beloved faculty member, a former president, an academic dean, or someone whose name will add luster on the campus without that person paying the full naming price.

Naming is an impure science. It's easier to determine a naming amount for a new building, than for improving an older building. Some schools determine a figure from what it would cost to replace the building at today's costs. But what if the old building was already named and the descendants presumed it would be in perpetuity? There is no concrete rule to deal with that reality; each case is different. With the assumption that naming is here to stay, institutions should begin setting guidelines about how long a name stays on a building.

Building costs are usually provided by the taxpayers at state-assisted universities, but sometimes the school is required to raise a certain percentage of the total cost or to furnish the building interior—everything inside the bare walls. Could a contribution of half the figure left, after the

Give money, get a plaque, but you better ask where

"The most creative and puzzling example of fundraising was at a school where there was a plaque to an alumnus outside the men's room," said Mr. Blake of the University of California, Irvine. "I couldn't figure out if the donor had a great sense of humor, the school was just a terrific fundraiser and raised money for everything, or if this was just for a donor who reneged on his pledge." (*The New York Times*, March 18, 1998) state chipped in its part, win a name on the building? Perhaps. Many naming decisions are made on an ad hoc basis, case-by-case.

To complicate things further, some schools are thinking about adding a *footprint charge* to the cost of the building construction. The theory is that the building will occupy space that then becomes unavailable for other uses. A department of a university, for example, would have to pay to take the land out of future use that might otherwise become another department. As you might imagine, this is rather controversial.

Many colleges and universities are putting their naming opportunities on Web sites with rules and regulations governing such gifts. Do an Internet search on a search engine such as Google for the term "naming opportunities." Putting the term in quotation marks helps you get only appropriate hits.

Other names on campus

Schools are becoming more creative at finding new naming opportunities, but for a long time colleges and universities have put a price on faculty endowments. The standard price used to be $1 million, but that

"Thank you for the check, Mr. Johnson. Are there any strings attached to your gift?"

price is going higher as faculty salaries rise. In 1998, Harvard Medical School charged $2.75 million for an endowed named chair. The U.S. Naval Academy received a $2 million donation in 2000 from Kevin Sharer, president and CEO of Amgen, the nation's largest biotechnology firm, to endow a professorial chair in aerospace engineering.

At other universities, department chairs, endowed and distinguished professorships, dean's chairs, research chairs, and teaching chairs may go for less, but are usually at or well above $1 million. Fellowships often start at $100,000 and go up from there.

During the 1990s, business schools were vigorously competing for students and rankings while a roaring economy created massive wealth. Consequently, many business schools acquired a new name. According to the American Assembly of Collegiate Schools of Business, a trade association, the total amount of money raised for renaming went from $29 million in 1994 to $87 million in 1997. Joseph Wharton started the first business school at the University of Pennsylvania with $100,000 in 1881. Nowadays, at major schools, the cost is varied: $18 million at Babson College in 1998, $34 million to Vanderbilt in 1996, and $50 million to the University of Texas at Austin. In early 1998, Columbia University was trying to interest someone in naming its business school for $60 million.

Renaming a business school does more than raise money; it can raise a school's visibility and give it new connections. (Call it networking, if you wish.) For the donor, the payoff is increased status and recognition. For the school, an association with a famous entrepreneur, a notable industrialist, or a Wall Street Wizard makes a statement about the school's image and identity.

The New York Times (March 18, 1998) chronicled the naming of the University of South Carolina's business school after Darla Moore with an article that provided a thumbnail sketch of Moore's life. She was born on a small farm in South Carolina, went to Wall Street and became the queen of capitalism, married a fellow worth $1.5 billion, and appeared on the cover of *Fortune* magazine as the "toughest babe" in bankruptcy financing. Darla Moore wrote a check for $25 million and the Darla Moore School of Business at the University of South Carolina came into existence, the first major business school to be named for a woman.

Luckily for business schools, their graduates go out and often make a lot of money. But sometimes they lose it. Karl Eller, a business entrepreneur who gave money to have the business school at the University of Arizona named for him, subsequently went bankrupt. Fortunately for him and the school, he recovered and is back in business.

Corporate naming

Across the nation, local and regional sport and performing arts facilities are following the example of professional sports, where almost every new stadium bears a corporate signature. Although many Washington Redskins fans would like the team to change from a name that is offensive to many Native Americans, the only thing that changes is the name of its stadium. Currently it's named for the delivery company, Fed Ex. Many nonprofit groups, as well as local and state governments, see that as a way to pay for big projects without dipping into their own coffers. Montgomery County, Maryland, with the nonprofit Strathmore Hall Foundation, is looking for a corporate or individual naming gift of $15 million for its concert hall and education center.

The University of Maryland at College Park announced in early 2000 that it had a $20 million deal with Comcast Corp. that will emblazon the Philadelphia-based communications company's name on the new arena for the next quarter century. It was one of the richest naming deals in collegiate sports history. Although corporate naming is now common-place and part of the growing proliferation of advertising in society, many consider it *adcreep*. In 1998 in Maryland, a bill was introduced, but not passed, that would have prohibited state colleges from putting corporate names on campus buildings. (*The Washington Post*, June 18, 2000)

Pitfalls to avoid

Sometimes a college or university is stuck with a building name it does not want after negative publicity puts the donor in a bad light. Such was the case when Ivan Boesky went to prison for insider trading violations. He had to withdraw a $1.5 million pledge to Princeton University's religious center after it was decided "it just would not look right."

Another bit of good advice is to have the check in hand before the name is chiseled on the building. Robert O. Anderson gave $500,000 to the business school at the University of New Mexico. The school was named after him with the hope that he would give more. To everyone's dismay, he did not.

Naming major donors

A different type of naming involves creating categories for major donors. The first step is to determine the amount of a major gift. Work from there to determine category amounts, then think of appropriate names for each category. What those groups are called should depend on the type of institution, using terms from the services or programs provided. For example, theatre groups may place their major donors in the Director's Circle, with other theatrical terms used for lesser gift amounts.

Here are some group names for major and not-so-major donors.

President's Circle
President's Club
President's Roundtable
Founder's Circle
Donor Society
Leadership Circle
Director's Circle
Conductor's Circle
Friends
Sponsors
Patrons
Benefactors
Fellows
Associates
Colleagues
Partners' Corner
Pacesetters
Sustainers
Conservators

That's a start. For other ideas, look at theatre and symphony orchestra programs, public radio and television publications, alumni publications, hospital foundation letterhead, and anything else that lists donors to any type of organization.

⇒ 16 ⇐

Women as Donors

"Philanthropy is the next frontier of the women's movement.
The challenge is to see where we can change—
or have some influence on—society."
—Andrea Kaminski,
Women's Philanthropy Institute

An alumna of Wellesley College in suburban Boston and her husband made the largest donation ever to a women's college in April 2000. The $25 million gift from Lulu and Anthony Wang was announced as the college began a five-year campaign to raise $400 million. That campaign had the most ambitious fundraising goal ever set by a women's college, although it is no longer unusual for coed universities to succeed in $1 billion campaigns.

According to the article in *The New York Times* announcing the gift, it has been assumed women traditionally lagged behind men in charitable giving. Therefore, women's colleges have had less success than coeducational institutions in fundraising. (April 16, 2000)

Commenting on the gift, Wellesley's president Diana Chapman Walsh said the gift from the Wangs "shattered that shibboleth." She continued, "This says women are loyal, and they care, and they care about causes that have to do with women and the institutions that help women to make a difference in the world." At the end of the college's successful campaign, Walsh said it would prove that women are just as capable of raising money as they are in any other realm.

Mrs. Lulu Wang is the founder of Tupelo Capital Management. As a member of Wellesley's board of trustees since 1988, she was the first woman to head the board's investment committee, which is in charge of investing the college's endowment valued at about $1 billion. She and her husband,

153

What? I'm rich?

Although she had given millions to many cultural, educational, and medical charities in the San Francisco area, Louise M. Davies is best known as the one who in 1980 gave the city a 3,000-seat, modern concert hall that is home for the San Francisco Symphony. Ten years later, when asked why she had financed the Davies Symphony Hall, the down-to-earth woman who was born fairly poor answered, "Because I had the money, and we certainly needed the hall." She added, "I'm just learning after all these years that I have quite a lot of money. Isn't that something?" Her husband, Ralph K. Davies, was an oil millionaire who died in 1971. (From her obituary in the *The New York Times,* June 25, 1998)

prominent collectors of American art and furniture, decided to announce the gift publicly "to raise everyone's sights."

Although it may take a while to improve the image of women as donors who have the financial ability to make large contributions, a study by the Independent Sector showed that 71 percent of women give to charity, compared to 65 percent of men. The average amount of annual contributions from women is rising steadily.

Another survey, this one supported by a grant from the W.K. Kellogg Foundation in 1999, compared people's beliefs about men's and women's finances and philanthropy. It found that more than two-thirds of men and women believe that men control more wealth than women. The summary noted that perception runs counter to federal data on consumer finances, which show that women control more than half, or 51.3 percent, of the privately held wealth in the United States.

Still, women are often stereotyped as being less secure about their finances than men and more reluctant to part with their money. Financial independence is still relatively new for women, especially single women. Marie Wilson, president of Ms. Foundation for Women, believes that executive women demand a hands-on role in philanthropy because "women have to work very hard to earn their money, so they want to do something worthwhile with it."

Women expect to outlive their husbands and sometimes fear for their future well-being. They may even suffer from "bag-lady syndrome"—a concern they will find themselves impoverished in old age. Women may be less secure than men about giving while they are still alive, so women's gifts to women's colleges tend to be in the form of bequests—an assurance that they will no longer need the funds. Hence the term "stealth wealth," which refers to previously unknown donors who leave multi-million dollar gifts in their wills to women's colleges. When this happens, development officers are shocked to hear from the woman's estate lawyer that their institution will receive such a large gift.

Development officers at women's colleges are encouraged to focus on developing strong connections with their alumna who may have the capacity to make a major donation. Doing that requires skillful prospect and donor research with an understanding of women's ability as donors.

A study was done as part of the Kellogg Foundation's effort to support women's groups that work to get women to recognize their philanthropic potential and to increase giving to programs designed to benefit women and girls. The study found that programs designed exclusively to benefit females receive less than 6 percent of all grants distributed by foundations. Conversely, two-thirds of adults below the poverty level are women, and women aged 46 to 64 are twice as likely as their male counterparts to lack health insurance. Who better to benefit from the increasing philanthropic instincts of women of wealth?

As some women amass significant wealth, they have the means to help less fortunate sisters. Bringing those two disparate groups together is the goal of the *Women's Funding Network*. It represents more than 70 funds that raise money from women and distribute the donations to causes that benefit females. Leaders of women's funds in many cities stress that women need to learn how to influence society with their gifts. Educating women to this need is the challenge for fundraisers at organizations. Private and public women's funds are listed on this site with online publications about women as donors.

http://www.wfnet.org/

Now may be the right time for the networking of women. The number of women-owned businesses nationwide, for example, grew by 103 percent between 1987 and 1999 and made up almost one-third of the nation's entrepreneurs. Today, 9.1 million companies are owned by women, and they generate annual sales of $3.6 trillion. In the 1990s, women started companies at three times the rate of men. That's good news for fundraisers because a survey done by the National Foundation of Women Business Owners found that senior-ranking female executives and business owners give to charity at a significantly higher rate than other women. Ninety-two percent of them donated to charity, and many gave at least $25,000 a year.

Still, women make up only 5 percent of the executives on *Forbes* 500 executives who head the magazine's Super 100 list of top U.S. companies. Hewlett-Packard's Carleton Fiorina is the only female CEO.

Check the Web site for the American Business Women's Association for membership directories and networking opportunities.

http://www.abwahq.org/

Realizing the need to study the subject of women as donors, the late Ann Castle, while director of development research at Hamilton College, began to compile an extensive bibliography and analysis of women in philanthropy. Later Ms. Castle helped compile the annual most philanthropic list for the online magazine, *Slate*.

After Ann Castle's death, the University of Michigan office of development took over maintenance of her *Women in Philanthropy* Web site. It includes an alphabetical list of major women donors and what they gave to whom, a bibliography of online publications and articles, and links to other sites about women as donors.

http://www.women-philanthropy.umich.edu

The *Women's Philanthropy Institute* is an organization dedicated to enhancing the role of women in major giving and volunteerism. It provides information and publishes a newsletter on the history and current status of women in fundraising and maintains a speakers bureau. One of the institute's purposes is to educate professionals about how to encourage women as major donors. It links to similar online sites.

http://www.women-philanthropy.org/

We can count on *Fortune* and *Forbes* magazines to give us valuable lists of successful and wealthy women. The "50 Most Powerful Women in American Business" article appears in an October *Fortune* issue each year and on their Web site. Put Powerful Women in the search box at the homepage, or use the second site.

http://www.fortune.com
http://www.fortune.com/fortune/mostpowerful/

Forbes list of corporate America's most powerful women is at

http://www.forbes.com/superwomen

A generous endowment

Dolly Parton's Imagination Library has given away 150,000 books to children in her native Sevier County, Tennessee. "From the day they're born until they start kindergarten, children get a book every month in the mail," stated Ms. Parton.

She said the kids get so excited about the book and she thinks this gets them off on the right foot in an area where illiteracy is too prevalent. Presented with an award from the Association of American Publishers for her efforts to promote literacy, Parton announced an additional $7 million gift to expand the Imagination Library nationwide. She asked for others to help, adding, "I have to keep a little money back, because it costs a lot to make me look so cheap." (*The Washington Post*, March 23, 2000)

Sure, we know some names of men who have made it big in Silicon Valley, but what about the women? Find them on *Silicon Salley's* Web site. Each online newsletter includes fascinating profiles and pictures of prominent women in information technology.

http://www.siliconsalley.com/

Women in Internet and information technology are featured in *Girl Geeks—The Female Side of Commuting* Web site. It includes interviews with women running multimillion dollar high-tech businesses and takes a light-hearted approach.

http://www.girlgeeks.com/

Working Woman magazine compiles its annual list of the top 500 companies headed by women. It's online with the executive's name and profile along with her company's data.

http://www.workingwoman.com/

In its September 1999 issue, *Working Woman* profiled young women under 30 who were already leaders and achievers. As a token gift to college development officers, it gave the women's alma maters. *Working Woman's* annual salary survey in October 1999 stated that Julia Roberts is the first woman to break the $20 million per film barrier. And, compared to male basketball players, women dribblers make only $50,000—but at least they now have a league of their own.

Do you ever wonder how the stocks of women-owned public companies are doing? *Bloomberg/Women.Com 30 Index* tracks stock histories of the top 30 women-owned companies. Development researchers will appreciate the profiles of those women. To get bios of the women executives, click on Meet the Execs.

http://www.womenswire.com/30index/

The organization *Resourceful Women* helps women who have inherited wealth or are newly wealthy make positive social change by educating and empowering them to consider making a major contribution. The site lists affinity groups with the same purpose for women at various ages.

http://www.rw.org/

DistinguishedWomen.com includes short bios of women, with hundreds of links to other sites about women in many professional categories. Search by name or subject and also look for links to prominent African American women.

http://www.distinguishedwomen.com

Foundations for women and girls

Many staff members at organizations serving women and girls feel their requests for grants are most successful when sent to foundations whose main purpose is the funding of such organizations. Using *FC Search* from the Foundation Center, you can search keywords relating to women or girls to find foundations that support programs for women. (See also chapter on Researching Foundations.)

One Web site that lists foundations that give to programs for women and girls is from The Feminist Majority Foundation. The second site is the Foundation's List of Notable Women of the 20th Century.

http://www.feminist.org
http://www.feminist.org/other/wh_20thcent.html

Members of the Association of Professional Researchers for Advancement can refer to *APRA Connections*, Spring 2001, for a special issue on Women and Philanthropy with Internet search techniques.

❧ 17 ❧

Genealogy and Family History

*"I was born into it and there was nothing I could do
about it. It was there, like air or food or any other
element....The only question with wealth is what to do with it."*
—John D. Rockefeller, Jr.

Philanthropy is often a family undertaking. In the San Francisco area, for example, the names Stern, Goldman, and Haas are well known as donors to programs to promote education, good government, the environment, and culture. Their names are not as well known as that of their common ancestor, Levi Strauss, the founder of the multibillion-dollar clothing empire that started with a pair of denim pants.

Private foundations set up by Strauss' heirs have more than $1 billion in assets, and the family itself is one of the world's wealthiest, estimated to be worth $12.3 billion. As each generation of the family leaves its assets to the next, it is likely that many millions will be used to benefit those in the San Francisco area. Each of the Strauss family funds has an independent interest, but several family members serve on the boards of more than one foundation. (*The Chronicle of Philanthropy*, May 21, 1998)

Prospect research is very much about finding family ties and links within a donor family. You may want to answer the question of whether Jim Smith on your prospect list is related to the John Smith who last year made a major contribution. Just knowing Jim is John's brother won't prove that he will give, but it helps to know that both are sons of Peter Smith who died recently, leaving a large estate to both sons.

Many of the persons who have money today got it through inheritance. Finding biographical information about the person's family, or about the ancestor who made the family fortune, is useful. Clues to the family's interests and charities may be helpful in understanding the present generation. When researching an individual, you may wish to research the family from whom he or she inherited wealth.

Although the Internet has drastically changed the way we research living individuals, many historical reference books in libraries make it easier to find information on the deceased than on the living. After all, the lives of most persons, even the most reclusive, are revealed in their obituaries. Obits often give family details about relationships that will be useful for the fundraiser who is soliciting a major gift from a person with inherited wealth.

Deceased Americans

Doing research on your prospect's family history is a good excuse for you to visit a large public or academic library. It will also remind you of how research was done in those prehistoric days before the Internet.

Begin your search with the one-volume *Historical Biographies Master Index*. Because this indexes the very important *Dictionary of American Biography* (known as the *DAB*), the *National Cyclopedia of American Biography* (*NCAB*), and *Who Was Who in America* (*WWWA*), you will find the names of many deceased persons for whom you are searching. If you don't find the exact individual, you may be able to get your questions answered by reading the entries for other members with the same family name, especially if it is not a common name.

Who Was Who in America, published by Marquis, is the most extensive listing for deceased notable Americans. It includes an historical volume covering persons who died between 1607 and 1896. Since then, several volumes have been published for the 20th century. An index to the set was published in 2000.

All of these books, the historical and the continuing volumes, contain basically the same information as the typical who's who type entry in *Who's Who in America*. The later *WWWA* volumes usually just add a death date to the last entry in the *WWA* that appeared during the person's life. A person is entered on confirmation of death, or when a person is assumed to be dead because the birth date was over 100 years ago. Some living persons, however, end up as "has beens" in *WWWA*. One man appeared at my reference desk at a public library and proudly showed me his *WWWA* entry. He didn't meet stated criteria to be listed; he wasn't dead, nor was he 100. Happily, he did not find his own death date listed. If no death date is given, look further if you want to be sure your subject is deceased.

Persons who were the most noteworthy in their field are profiled in the *Dictionary of American Biography (DAB),* the prestigious and scholarly American biographical dictionary. This reference work, available in most public and academic libraries, includes Americans who have been dead about 20 years, ensuring that the biographies are as definitive as possible. This lapse of years is necessary for the scholars to attempt to write a just and considered appraisal of the person's contributions to national history. The *DAB* also throws light on the careers of individuals who, by the caprice of fortune, have been lost from view, but who, in their times, were an important part of the fabric of American culture. These signed biographies by specialists document persons from over 700 fields of endeavor and include bibliographies. A tidbit of information, such as where the person's papers are deposited, may give insight to the interests of the deceased and thus of the descendants.

The original set, done in 1928, forms the nucleus of the multi-volume set. Each few years another supplement is added, bringing the *DAB* up to date. The first comprehensive index to *DAB* was published in 1990.

This index, much more extensive than previous indexes, makes information accessible in many new ways. All biographies are indexed alphabetically, by topic or profession, by birth date, and by school or college attended. Not until this index was it as easy to find, in one place, which

"I think you're a very good cause,
but I gave at the office."

notable Americans went to what schools. If you work at an academic institution, see if your school is listed as the alma mater for persons in the *DAB*. That person may have descendants interested in your current programs and they may become prospects.

Only the most noteworthy get into the *DAB,* so you are more apt to find the names you seek in the *National Cyclopedia of American Biography* (*NCAB*). This venerable set, begun in 1898, survived unto the late 1980s. Sixty-three volumes of the main set were published. Thirteen volumes of the current series include persons living at the time the volume was published. Family members, not scholars, wrote most of the entries, thus giving a different slant on the individual. The entries often mention the generous gifts of the deceased, with quite a bit of information about the person's family and ancestors. Like the *DAB*, the *NCAB* is written in narrative form and it may include a picture of the subject.

The NCAB set has some quirks. Volumes are not arranged alphabetically, or in any other order, as far as I can tell. Use the *National Cyclopedia of American Biography Index*, published in 1984, to find what you need. This index also picks up names other than the main entry, and includes businesses and other institutions with which the deceased was involved.

You can use the readily available *Historical Biographies Master Index* to find names you need if you do not have access to *NCAB*'s own index. A very expensive set, the *NCAB* probably won't be in many academic or public libraries. It will, however, be somewhere in most states and photocopies of individual entries can be requested through the inter-library loan system at your public library. There may be a small photocopy and postage fee.

Women and minorities are often missing, in the numbers that should represent their importance, from both of the previously mentioned historical sets. Now separate sets somewhat correct this omission.

Notable American Women, 1607-1950, A Biographical Dictionary covers women who died before the end of 1950. *Notable American Women: The Modern Period* covers those who died between 1951 and 1975.

In some cases, the woman documented in this set is the one who made the fortune or was famous. In other cases, she is the relative of those who did. To note the difference, you can use the classified vocational index. Look for the heading Philanthropists. Those entries are fascinating and surely of interest to anyone active in development work. Each entry for the philanthropists tells the woman's giving history, something that is often hard to find elsewhere. Hopefully the living descendants of those women carry on the family's philanthropic traditions.

What the above set does to include women in the biographical record of this country, the *Dictionary of American Negro Biography* does for African Americans who died before 1970. Included are well-known African Americans, as well as many generally unheard of until their lives were documented here. Some accumulated a great deal of wealth in their times, and many were generous with it. Articles in this resource are well-researched and well-written by scholars. The volume was originally published without an index, but later printings include a good index.

Sometimes all you need about a deceased person is a quick identification. For that, use *Notable Americans: What They Did, From 1620 to the Present.* That 1986 edition updates an earlier *Notable Names in American History.* Both books are useful if you think the ancestor was a high government official, the president of a university or college, a governor or mayor, or held some other high position. The names are listed by position in chronological order from whenever the position was created.

Another good source for deceased Americans is an old timer, *Appleton's Cyclopedia of American Biography*, published around the turn of the last century. This sometimes includes names not found elsewhere in historical research. It is indexed in *Historical Biographies Master Index.* Although it is old, this classic reference set is still found in many libraries.

Have you ever wondered if someone is dead or alive? This Web site may help answer your question. *Who's Alive and Who's Dead* lists only the most well-known individuals. For those listed, it shows whether the person is alive, over 80 years old, then gives date of birth and date of death. Search by category or alphabetically.

http://www.whosaliveandwhosdead.com/

Obituaries in *The New York Times* and elsewhere

The resources listed above include only the most distinguished deceased Americans. Many others who are not included may have had considerable wealth, and may have had obituaries in *The New York Times,* and can be researched in *The New York Times Obituaries Index* volumes. Even if you do not have access to microfilm files of *The New York Times* itself, the above index gives the date of death. You may then find an obit for a person, using that date, in a less-well-indexed newspaper on microfilm.

In early 2001, *The New York Times* announced it would bring the newspaper's backfile dating to 1851 to the World Wide Web. Digitizing the nation's newspaper of record—some 3,500,000 pages in total—means it will be available through *ProQuest,* an online information service at libraries and educational institutions. With monthly releases covering 10 years each, beginning in March 2001 and continuing for 15 months, the entire backfile will offer index searching and will display articles with full-page images.

Obituaries on File includes names in obits from *The New York Times* and other newspapers. It covers deaths between 1940 and 1978 with a very brief sketch about the person and the date and place of death. That's helpful when identifying persons with the same name. The resource includes about 25,000 names and may serve as the first step in finding more information about someone's family history.

Once you start reading obits with an eye towards determining a person's philanthropic interests, you will be hooked and may start reading them for fun. Most newspapers don't give much space to obits, but *The New York Times* still treats a well-written obituary as an art form and has published *The Last Word*, a collection of its best obits. As you read the obits in your local newspaper, watch for requests for memorial donations "in lieu of flowers." This may give a clue about the favorite charities of the surviving family members. Often bequests are designated to the health services facility where the deceased was treated or to the organizations working to eliminate the disease that caused the death.

Newspaper research

For any kind of research, *The New York Times Index* is a paramount resource. It began in 1913 and continues with semimonthly issues cumulated annually. That index was used to compile the multivolume *Personal Name Index to The New York Times Index,* covering from 1851 to 1974 and continuing. Because it picks up references for New York business executives and East Coast socialites, as well as thousands of others, it is useful for prospect research purposes. Remember that it refers you to the index, so you must go there for the exact newspaper citation. Most libraries that have the name index will also have the complete index.

The *The New York Times Biographical Edition* includes biographical articles, on both living and deceased persons, that have appeared in that newspaper. The loose-leaf monthly compilation reprints the actual articles from daily and Sunday editions of the *Times*. It includes some, but not all, obits plus articles on prominent living persons.

Your local and regional newspapers are the best sources of information on local prospects and most are now online and available through the Internet. Before computers (yes, life—and research—did exist before computers), how well newspapers were indexed determines how useful

"You have reached our 800 number. If you plan to give $100, please dial one. If you are giving $1,000, please dial two. If you are giving $1,000,000, please hold on and a human will speak to you."

they are now. Most large city newspapers did a fairly good job of index-ing and those indexes are at the local public library. Even if no index exists, public libraries and libraries at historical societies often kept clip-ping files on prominent persons and families. Don't neglect those re-sources.

Historical biographies by profession

Historical volumes exist for almost every profession: educators, business people, economists, librarians, actors and movie stars, musicians, labor lead-ers, and even comedians.

Perhaps the most useful for fundraisers is *Biographical Dictionary of American Business Leaders.* This four-volume set gives comprehensive cov-erage of business leaders from colonial times to the present. Although most persons included are deceased, a few leaders are still alive. If not, their sons and daughters may be involved in the same business and enjoy-ing the fortune left by the business leaders. The set has a good index, including listings of women, African Americans, and business leaders by geographical location. If several members of one family were involved in the same business, check the family name as well as individual listings to sort out those confusing relationship questions.

Another multivolume set, *International Directory of Company Histories,* tells how companies began. Names you are now researching may be the descendants of business leaders documented in these sets, and that may explain the origin of the family wealth.

Noted scientists are well documented in the *World Who's Who in Science.*

For American politicians of the past, see the *Biographical Dictionary of the American Congress.* It's online at

http://bioguide.congress.gov/biosearch/biosearch.asp

See also the print *Biographical Directory of the Governors of the United States 1790-1978* and the *Biographical Dictionary of American Mayors, 1820-1980.*

For show business names, *Who Was Who on Screen* and *Variety Obits* are useful. The latter refers to full-length obits that appeared in *Variety* magazine. Although it lists mostly living celebrities, *Celebrity Sources* include some deceased persons in popular film, television, music, and sports.

Try these directories of deceased persons if the individual you are researching is from "old money" or is a member of a distinguished family. Having information on former generations may help you deal with the current prospect or donor who may be flattered by your knowledge of the ancestor.

When researching a foundation begun many years ago, find as much as possible about the founder. The current foundation officers probably reflect the intentions and philosophy of the individual who established it. Look through biographical directories published during the lifetime of the foundation donor. Also check for periodical and newspaper articles. When the deceased person is well documented, your focus can next turn to current members of the family. Many current family members may be in the news, even if not listed in biographical directories. Use periodical and newspaper indexes on the Internet or at libraries for current research.

The more you do historical biographical research, the better you will become at it. Clues picked up along the way will help you and the librarian who is helping you proceed. Even if you meet an occasional dead end, you will probably gather some useful research techniques for the next family history or biographical search you do.

Wills and trusts

When wills are probated, they become public documents and are available in the probate court office of the country courthouse. But not all wills are probated. A will can be probated in any county where the deceased owned property, including second seasonal residences. Wills may include an inventory of valuables, art objects, real estate, and other items of significance. Knowing if your prospect inherited such items will be useful in determining suggestions of net worth. If you are gathering data for an art museum, this information is especially crucial. Wills are often probated 30 to 90 days after a death, but it sometimes takes much longer. The complete probate process is usually finished within two years, but some cases seem to drag on forever.

Some court records in computer databases go back only a limited number of years, so ask if other records are available beyond that. At the county recorder's office, ask also if there are other files that may give information on the deceased.

Be discreet when seeking family history from will probate records. Prospects may be upset, and perhaps rightly so, if they discover your interest in these family documents.

Instead of a will, some people transfer their assets into a family trust. This is becoming more popular as more individuals have more to leave behind. Unfortunately, these documents are private and not available to the public. If the trust is a charitable trust, it is treated like a foundation and information will be available, but if the trust benefits individual family members only, it is not available.

The *Social Security Death Index*

If you wish to determine if a donor or prospect or a family member of a prospect is living or dead, the *Social Security Death Index* is the first place to check. It is available online at several sites, including this one at *Ancestry.com*

http://www.ancestry.com/search/rectype/vital/ssdi/main.htm

Because it includes only those U.S. deaths for which a death benefit was filed or claimed, not all deceased persons are listed, although the death index is extensive, with over 63 million names. The index includes those who have made claims for railroad benefits. It gives social security number, date of birth, and place of last residence. Obviously, if you have only a name, you will have better luck identifying deceased persons with unique names. At the above site, read the Frequently Asked Questions.

An index to obituaries at the *Obituary Daily Times,* gathered from local newspapers, is on the *RootsWeb.com* Web site. The actual obit is not given, only the citation to it. The site includes Obituaries on the Web in New England and Obituaries on the Web in Canada with links to newspapers in those areas.

http://www.rootsweb.com/~obituary

Genealogy

Genealogical records are often overlooked as sources of historical information on a prospect's family. Most public libraries have a genealogy or local history section with published, and even not-published, family histories for families who lived in their region.

A good list of such family histories is *Genealogies in the Library of Congress*. It will show if a family history has been written and deposited there. If there are several histories listed with the same family name, you may be able to identify the family you are researching by the place of publication of the genealogy. If you find the family history listed at the Library of Congress, investigate getting a copy of parts of the publication (or the whole thing, if it is not too long) through the photocopy service at the Library of Congress. Or you may find a copy in a library in the state of publication.

Ask at your library for other bibliographies dealing with family histories, including listings arranged by state where family and local histories are deposited. As you might suspect, there is a *Directory of Historical Societies and Agencies in the United States and Canada*. Check for a location near the residence of the family you are researching.

Waltman Associates has compiled a *Book of American Family Trees* for prominent families. It has a comprehensive index by names showing family linkage. *Book of Minnesota Family Trees* does the same for that state. For ordering information, see this Web site.

http://www.waltmanassociates.com

On the Internet

Genealogy sites on the Internet have accelerated the possibilities for family research almost beyond belief. The need to visit physical sites with microfilm holdings of records has diminished as the computer brings the information to you. Doing a basic family chart for a prospect or his or her family history won't be quite as much fun as doing your own, but it may be more beneficial for your institution.

Family Tree Maker from Broderbunds Software is the genealogy software most used in development offices, including those who use Macs. It is considered easy to use, available at most software stores, and inexpensive. (Call 1-800-474-8696) With it, you can compile family charts on your prospects/donors for several generations, adding other family members as you locate information and establish relationships for them. Tracking generations on a chart is especially helpful when dealing with school or college alumni, or it can be used for linking those on corporate boards of directors.

The regular version of *Family Tree Maker* (8-CDs for $45) may be all you need if you only wish to make family charts for information you already have. The deluxe version ($80 for the 15-CD package) can't be overlooked if you are at all interesting in pursuing a family history—for a prospect (or yourself). It includes a compilation of 1.5 billion names including the digitized *Social Security Death Index* and an *International Marriage Records Index*, plus discs containing American military records. This amounts to 900 years of birth records for Europe and the United States, and 15,000 existing family trees. Wow!

Several Web sites give genealogical help with tips for the beginner and tools to tap into online indexes and records, including the *Social Security Death Index*.

http://www.genealogy.com
http://www.familytreemaker.com

Genealogy research often depends on determining the county location for a piece of family property. Lots of location information is given at this Web site.

http://www.familytreemaker.com/countlst.html

Ancestry World Tree is billed as the largest, mostly free online database of family files available. It consists of millions of records submitted by thousands of genealogy enthusiasts throughout the world. It has connections to 1,700 archives that offer all sorts of vital information, including the very useful *Social Security Death Index* database with over 63 million names, marriage and death certificates, newspaper obituaries with names of surviving relatives, and much more. Most information is free, but some databases require a subscription fee of $59 for one year.

http://ancestry.com

No personal advice intended

On Monday, Microsoft announced that Melinda French Gates, wife of Bill, had given birth to the couple's second child. On Tuesday, Johns Hopkins University announced that the couple had donated $20 million for family planning in the developing world.

An advisor to the Gates family foundation said that the timing of the family planning announcement, so close to the birth announcement, was accidental. Approval of the grant to train foreign health workers at Johns Hopkins had been made some time before.

Bill Gates held company stock worth about $80 billion at that time. He has said that his children will get only a small part of his wealth and that most of it will be given away. (*The New York Times*, May 30, 1999)

The Church of Jesus Christ of Latter-Day Saints' Family History Center runs the largest genealogical library in the U.S. It's a mega-biographical resource. The much-anticipated huge online genealogy database from the Latter-Day Saints debuted in spring 1999. Coverage includes more than 35 million names in the *Ancestral File* and 285 million in the *International Genealogy Index* with name, gender, birth date and location, and parents' names.

http://www.familysearch.org/

You can order microfilm of census and other records from them at 1-800-346-6044. Their introductory Web site gives helpful information on genealogy research and a locator for local Family History Centers. From that site you can use a drop down dialog box to move around the site.

http://www.lds.org/

To find where to get birth, marriage, and death certificates, take a look at the Web site for the government *Consumer Information Center*. You can order the booklet, "Where to Write for Vital Records" or get the directions for ordering records from each state.

http://www.pueblo.gsa.gov

⇾ 18 ⇽

Rating and Screening Prospects

"Shake and shake the ketchup bottle.
None'll come out and then a lot'll."
—Anonymous

R ating prospects is done every day in nonprofit advancement offices in an informal way. Every time a name is mentioned there is
some thought or question, whether consciously or subconsciously,
about the person's giving potential. Each time an Internet search engine
is consulted, each time a real estate database is checked, each time a name
is run through an online or CD-ROM directory, the researcher is rating
a prospect. The goal of research and prospect rating is to focus the development staff on people with the highest giving potential.

Philanthropic guru Harold J. Seymour wrote that potential prospects
fall into five distinct categories:

- Those who see a need and respond without being asked
- Those who respond when told to do so
- Those who will respond when persuaded
- Those who may or may not respond, even when heavily encouraged
- Those in the inert fifth—nothing could ever get them to give

Further divided, a good prospect must have an interest in the mission
of the organization, the capability to make a major gift, and a relationship
with the organization. Finding someone with those qualities is the function of advancement research. But that is not the end of the task; once
identified, the prospect should be rated according to giving level.

What is considered a major gift varies greatly between types of institutions or organizations. In most cases the researcher won't have to give

the final answer to the question: "How much can this person give?" The development officers normally have that responsibility. Still, the financial and biographical data gathered by researchers may lead to an answer when combined with other factors such as age, affiliation with the institution, and philanthropic philosophy.

The wide variety of techniques used to rate giving potential was apparent when PRSPCT-L listserv members were asked how their institutions rated potential donors. Here are some answers.

> "An old formula that I was once taught is to take annual salary times ten to establish net worth. Then use 3-5% of that figure to come up with a rough giving ability figure."

> "We use a formula that figures 5% of the gross salary is a total gift potential. Unless the salary is very large, a prospect who is dependent solely on a salary is not really a major gift prospect, unless we figure in stock, real estate, company ownership, plus motivation and inclination."

> "We rely fairly strongly on this formula. Ten per cent of a prospect's annual compensation is equal to the amount they can give over five years' time, i.e., if a prospect makes $100,000 a year, they should be capable to giving $10,000 over five years or $2,000 per year."

> "When estimating long-term giving such as pledging with so much each year, salary is used. We use net worth for deriving an ask amount for a one-time major gift."

> "We always use 10 per cent of salary equals giving over five years, so a person making $250,000 per year would be able to make a gift of $25,000 over five years, or $5,000 per year."

These formulas using salary and net worth were established before the days of high technology with the recent escalation of salary and stock holdings, but they are a part of the history of prospect and donor research. No longer can one assume a person's net worth is 10 times the annual salary.

Consider this: In 1999, Jeffrey P. Bezos of Amazon.com got only $81,840 in "total direct compensation" (read that as salary), but the total value of his equity holdings was $8,946,424,825. That's right. It was $8.94 billion (subject to change, of course.) A *New York Times* listing to compare executives in the "New Economy" to those in the "Old Economy" (April 2, 2000) shows the disparate ratio of salary to equity holdings. The oldsters get more salary; the young executives have more stock equity.

How one determines a person's inclination to give along with his or her ability to give, then estimate how much they might give is a tricky and largely speculative concern. For a thorough examination of the procedure, look at Claire Verrette's article, "Get the Picture," in *Currents,* September 1999. It's available at this site.

http://www.case.org/currents/sept99/verrette.htm

Peer screening

Whether it is called "silent screening," "external screening," "outside screening," or "peer screening," it is basically the same thing. To distinguish it from electronic screening (to be described later), I'll call it "peer screening." The purpose of the screening is to fish major donors from a large pool of possible donors.

The volunteers chosen to do the screening are not just a group of people picked up off the street. They are members of the board of directors, trustees, alumni boards, major donors, parents who are active in school activities, development officers, academic deans or professors, and community leaders, depending on the type of nonprofit organization doing the peer screening. In short, they should be people who are actively involved with the organization and sympathetic with its need to raise funds to function successfully.

The purpose of peer screening is to take a long list and make it shorter. It focuses the work of the development office so the best prospects receive immediate attention and those with less potential as donors are given less priority. It may establish who knows whom. When it is time for a personal solicitation, that detail is significant, as friends often give to friends and support each other's charities. Many feel peer screening works better than other research because someone who knows a prospect will usually tell everything needed to begin a conversation with a prospect.

A peer-screening session can go something like this. Appropriate volunteers are personally invited to a meeting that can be a combination social and working event. Serving food is always a good idea!

Following the socializing, the host or facilitator should explain the reason for the meeting: to share the screeners' information about people who have the capability and interest in giving. The leader stresses that confidentiality is crucial to the process and that no screener will be expected to know each person discussed. He or she will say whether or not the ratings will be anonymous. (Experts report best results when ratings do not tell who made them.) Raters may be asked to categorize their relationship with the prospect. Are they personal friends, business associates, or known by reputation only? Would the screener be willing to ask the prospect for a gift?

A list of names with a short identification is distributed and screeners are asked to add relevant details about names they identify. Comments should include indications of wealth. These can include businesses and real property owned by the listed person, access to inherited wealth, and family foundations or trusts. Screeners are encouraged to add comments, but the session shouldn't degenerate into a gossip or rumor event.

Two techniques are most often used. Some group leaders go down the list, name by name, asking those who recognize a name to make verbal comments. One or two note takers should be on hand to record what has been stated—even picking up mentioned names that may not be on the list. Other groups distribute lists and ask that screeners silently add notes to the list, giving relevant details. Following the meeting, all lists should be returned and the information on them considered confidential.

Colleges and universities have successfully used peer screening when their alumni and donors are scattered around the country. Using their

organization's software tracking system, development staff can get computer printouts of those living in a specific area or city. If several people are living in an area, screening sessions are planned as a social event. An appropriate host is chosen and invited to participate. A key to the session's success is choosing the right person as host. A known and highly visible person who is committed to the cause makes a good choice. Sometimes that person may even underwrite the event. The college president, vice president for advancement, or a prominent graduate may attend. He or she will explain the rationale and procedure for the meeting that is intended to reacquaint alumni with their school and its continuing need for funding. That person can state how those attending can help their alma mater by identifying persons able to provide financial support.

It's old-fashioned prospect research—talking to people about other people. You learn information about prospects from people who know them—not cold facts from a biographical reference source.

Another type of a screening session is to convene a focus group or committee screening. At those, a small number of engaged volunteers review names and determine ratings. At these sessions, only a small number of names are reviewed as compared to a long list. The purpose, however, is the same—to obtain more details about potential donors.

Perhaps the most important aspect of peer screening is what happens after the sessions are over. Thank you letters should go out promptly to all who participated. You may also wish to send a statistical summary of the session's results so participants feel they were part of an important endeavor. The sooner the new data is entered into the main database, the quicker development officers can be assigned new prospects and benefit from the momentum created by peer screening.

Staff screening

If you have the right electronic tools, enough staff, and available time you can do some screening yourself. If you have entered relevant information into your internal data management system, many options are available. You can bring up reports on persons who have contributed a certain amount annually, live on streets known to contain houses worth $1 million (or whatever amount you choose), and/or have executive titles like CEO, CFO, or President. Data mining records should be an ongoing process in most advancement research offices to ensure no potential good prospect falls through the system cracks. Once identified, these names may be further researched and given to officers for cultivation.

What you are doing as you look for prospects in your own system is, in effect, screening. You are taking the name of one person and researching it and determining if he or she is a major gift candidate. You may chose to take some names and individually zap them against a CD-ROM or an Internet database, for example, of corporate executives. The *Dun & Bradstreet Million Dollar Directory* gives information on 1.3 million public and private companies. With it, you can determine which corporate executives are graduates of your institution, live in your city or state, and work for large corporations. Other companies provide databases online for a monthly subscription or per-use fee. With those, researchers can run a check on new prospects as their names become known. (See the chapter on Using Fee-Based Services.)

Off-site electronic screening

Is there a magic technique that will churn out the names of wealthy prospects as fast as development officers can contact them and convince them to become major donors? Nope. Sorry. Using off-site electronic screening toward that end is a topic that every development staff (and thus, every nonprofit researcher) will eventually consider. Either they will embrace the concept, spend a sizable amount of dollars on the procedure, then live with the results, or they will ignore the whole concept.

As some organizations know nothing about their donors except name, address and giving history, a screening can fill in the blanks. The hoped-for result should determine which persons have the financial capacity to make a sizable contribution.

Since its origin as a fundraising tool in about the mid-1980s, electronic screening has grown in sophistication. Now many databases of wealthy persons can be matched against a prospect list. Some screening companies even attempt to determine a prospect's propensity to give while showing the ability to give. At best, electronic screening is a quick way for a nonprofit to find wealthy persons among its database of names and to discover connections between those who serve together on corporate boards

Most development staff members agree that screening is still an imperfect science, but one certainly worth considering. It has been used successfully by both large and small organizations, yet it still has detractors who feel the results do not merit the cost. Whether the screening was successful may depend on the organization's ability to use the screening results.

For further reading on the subject, see "Finding the Needle in the Haystack: Computer Screening" by Steve Barth, *CASE Currents*, June 1998.

Those who hire a company to do a screening will always wonder if they hired the right company, if it was worth what it cost, and if the information was completely accurate. Those who don't hire a screening company will always wonder if they should have.

The screening process

In the screening process, the names on a prospect or donor list are sent to a screening company where they are filtered through databases of persons with stock holdings, real estate, businesses, executive positions, corporate insider status, corporate board connections, and other indicators of wealth. Names are matched for demographic characteristics by zip code or other jurisdiction and to biographical directories of persons of achievement. For prospects that are "matches," a profile compiled from the screened databases is sent back to the nonprofit organization. Staffs in the development or advancement office use the returned information to target those donors most apt to respond.

Determining the need

The following questions might be considered to determine if your organization should do a computer-assisted screening of your prospect and donor list. When that decision is made in the affirmative, you will want to ask lots and lots of questions to representatives of companies that do such screening. When the screening is completed, you will need to ask other questions about how to use the new data.

This list of questions are to be considered—and answered—by the entire development staff.

- What do you hope to accomplish by a screening?

- Are you hoping to identify previously unknown prospects or seeking further information on your current prospects?

- Is your database "clean" enough for a successful screening or is it filled with incorrect addresses and incomplete names?

- Should you send your list to an address verification company before doing a further screening?

- Are you realistic in your expectations about a screening? Are you aware that not all financial assets can be identified?

- Does your office have sufficient staff to get your lists ready to be screened and to incorporate the new data into your fundraising software database to make the best use of data received?

- Should you screen your entire database or only portions of it?

- Is the complete development staff enthusiastic about doing a screening and willing to work together for its successful completion?

- Can you afford to do an extensive electronic screening? Should you consider a partial screening—only for stock holdings, for example?

Because some screening companies use an address to distinguish between persons with the same name, it is essential that the submitted list be as accurate as possible. It's counterproductive, and a waste of funds, to submit outdated or incorrect addresses. It has been estimated that the U.S. Postal Service records over 750,000 address changes a month—nearly 9 million annually. Many direct mail marketing companies will take your list and run it through a program that updates addresses using postal service change of address information.

It's no secret that a person's name and address is known by companies doing direct mailing who gather the data for that purpose from almost everywhere. Where *do* all those return address labels come from anyway? The same technology that churns them out can be used to update your prospect or membership list.

If you have Social Security numbers as part of your database, you can hire a company to either update addresses or search for lost alumni. Although some are credit history companies, you will get only address, not credit information. You cannot get SS numbers from those companies, as this is considered private information. (See the chapter on Ethics for more information on using Social Security numbers.)

Choosing a company

An electronic screening will take a sizable chunk from your budget. Make sure it is well spent. The best way to do that is to research several screening companies. Find out which companies provide what types of screening and get pricing details. If possible, ask for a presentation from two or three companies. Ask a lot of questions. A well-informed representative should be able to answer your questions confidently and may even suggest ways to cut costs. Someone within your development or research office should be the designated contact person with the screening company. Don't expect the company to field the same question asked by several staff members.

Consider the company rep your best friend—or, at least, a respected colleague. Personality does count. You will need to get along with—or at least communicate well with—the rep. Contacts with the company before you sign the contract should give you clues as to how their staff will communicate with you before, during, and after the screening. If they have trouble answering your questions, or give inconsistent answers, or don't return your calls or e-mails promptly before the contract is signed, you may wonder how they will be after they have your signed contract. Don't expect miracles, but expect good service.

Here are examples of the types of questions to ask screening companies before making a decision.

- How will the company assure that the information on your list will not be sold or shared with anyone else for any purpose?

- What is the required minimum number of prospects screened?

- Will the company run a sample test, using some of your names? Can you pick which names you want tested?

- Will the company give you a list of their nonprofit clients for whom they have done screenings so you can get opinions of the company's reputation?

- What databases are matched? Do they own or rent the databases? Are the databases current? How far back do the databases go?

- Can separate services be purchased individually?

- What stock wealth is revealed? Does it include options and vesting schedules?

- How is real estate evaluated? Does it include multiple properties and investment property or just the main residence?

- Can the company find private company executives?

- If Social Security numbers are included for some names, will they be used for definite matches?

- Is there an analysis of inclination to give, or just ability to give?

- How are persons with the same names distinguished from each other?

- Does the company screen using middle names or initials, if available?

- What demographic factors are used?

- Will you be assigned a representative who will come to your office for a consultation either before or after the screening? Will that person make recommendations on how to use the data following the screening?

- Will screening results be delivered on a printed list, a software database, or a CD-ROM? Will the results be searchable?

- Will results be delivered in a format that is compatible with your prospect tracking software?

- Can the company databases be purchased on CD-ROMs or online so research staff can screen prospects themselves?

- Are matches returned in separate tables for sure matches and possible matches?

- What will the screening cost? How is the cost determined?

- What is the turn around time?

- Ask the sales rep what questions you should ask that you forgot!

(See the appendix of this book for companies that do electronic screening.)

Names to screen

Based on the answers to the above questions and much discussion in the development office, other things must be decided before the final choice of a screening company. For example, how much of your list do you want to screen? Because most screening companies charge a basic fee, then charge by the number of names analyzed, you may want to screen all names with the hope that they may reveal some surprises. Consider these questions.

- If you are at a college or university, do you want to screen all alumni or just those who graduated more than 10 years ago?

- Do you want to screen only donors who have given above a certain amount?

- Do you want to screen only new names added to the donor list during the last five years, for example?

Father knows best

As father of the world's wealthiest, Bill Gates Sr. is co-chair of the Bill and Melinda Gates Foundation. In that role, he told *Town and Country* magazine, he doesn't expect to see overnight results. He feels the foundation's long-term results will improve the lot of millions of people around the world. "I see the numbers and I'm really awed by what the potential is," he said.

The "numbers" he spoke of indicated he understood the implications of the federal requirement that foundations must spend 5 percent of its previous year's assets. That means the Gates' foundation must give away $2.3 million *a day*!

While the 2001 Congressional debate on the estate tax was going on, Bill Gates Sr. became co-founder of Responsible Wealth's Call to Preserve the Estate Tax. He felt repealing the estate tax would have a tragic effect on charitable giving and the nonprofit civic sector. One hundred years ago, wealthy people took a stand in favor of inheritance taxes, he said. In fact, Andrew Carnegie testified before Congress in favor of the tax. This time, according to Gates, more than a thousand prominent investors and business leaders have called for estate tax reform, not repeal.

Gates acknowledges that society has played an important role in the creation of wealth. He suggests, "Take anyone of the *Forbes* 400 and drop them into rural Africa and see how much wealth they would amass." He concludes, "What's wrong with the most successful people putting one-quarter of their wealth back into the place that made their wealth and success possible? Many people repay their universities this way. Why not their country?" (*The Washington Post,* June 1, 2001)

- Do you want to remove names of those you already have a continuing relationship with: board members, trustees, and major donors?

- Have you weeded out names that should not be screened—dead people, duplicate names, international addresses, corporate, and foundation names?

- Have you run your names through an address update service such as the NCOA (National Change of Address) service?

After screening

When you look back on the entire screening process and analyze whether it was beneficial, much will depend on how your organization used the results. It has been estimated that up to one-third of off-site screenings fail because of poor planning about the use of the results. Before you start, plan how you will finish.

The happy results may be that the screening process unearthed hundreds—or thousands—of persons capable of making a large contribution. The reality is that your office will need to add those names to your own database system and do further research on each one. You might want to spot check some returns for accuracy, especially those you will be asking for a very large donation. A successful screening will allow development officers to prioritize their donor solicitation to the very best prospects.

If the screening turns up even a few very good prospects that become major donors, most nonprofit organizations consider the electronic screening money well spent.

❧◈❧

⇒ 19 ⇐

Finding Lost Alumni

"To conceive of fund-raising as making a pitch is missing the point.
Money's only one part of what you need to ask for.
I ask for their vision of the university, I ask for their political support,
I ask for their membership on committees, I ask for their children."
—Dr. John Casteen, President
University of Virginia

Whenever the topic of lost alumni comes up at meetings of advancement researchers in educational institutions, some one will mention the cartoon showing two men shipwrecked on a tropical island. One says to the other, "Don't worry, my college alumni office will find us."

Whether his optimism is warranted may depend on several factors. Has he ever filled out an alumni survey? Does he own or is he an executive or insider in a business or corporation? Does he live in a wealthy zip code? Best of all, has he made annual gifts to his alma mater and been identified as a potential donor of a major gift? Only then are his chances of rescue realistic.

Perhaps the biggest challenge to staff in the development office of an educational institution is tracking down lost alumni. Once found, many of those elusive former students tend to be generous, even years later. Although someone as well-known as Philanthropist Walter H. Annenberg was not literally lost, his major gift came 66 years after he graduated from Peddie School in Hightstown, New Jersey. Then Annenberg gave the school a $100 million gift, the largest ever to a preparatory school. Since that 1993 gift, Annenberg has provided the school with $50 million more. Surely he is an alum worth keeping track of. Other private schools are using what they call "teenage nostalgia" to solicit gifts.

"It's very exciting," said Brian Davidson, associate director of development at the Peddie School, "because it makes you realize the impact the school had on one individual and how important that education was to him." Happily for those in educational development, many feel as Annenberg does and attribute their success and prosperity in life to their education.

Dr. John Casteen, president of the University of Virginia, understands the importance of staying in close touch with alumni who are capable of making a major contribution. According to a profile in *The New York Times Magazine,* "The enduring image of President Casteen on campus may well be a man schmoozing up alumni at the president's residence; last year he opened Carr's Hill, the president's home, for more than 150 fundraising events....At one meeting of Dr. Casteen's cabinet, nobody blinked when he explained what he would be doing in the next months. 'I plan to get pretty deeply into people's pockets,' he said." *(The New York Times Magazine,* August 1, 1999)

According to the Council for Advancement and Support of Education (CASE) standards, "Alumni are defined as former students—full or part-time, undergraduate or graduate—who have earned some credit toward one of the degrees, certificates, or diplomas offered by the reporting institution." Although most major gifts come from graduates, sometimes loyalty to a school is more important than a degree. That's the reason nongraduates Philip and Ruth Clark Holton left stock worth $128 million to DePauw University in Indiana to be used for scholarships. Lucky DePauw. While waiting the two years for the estate to be settled, the value of the Time-Warner stock climbed, doubling the estate's value.

Try not to lose them

The simplistic answer to the question on how to find lost alumni is to never lose them in the first place. Easier said than done. Techniques used at some schools begin long before the student graduates. They start with the college application form and depend on a good working relationship and a policy of sharing that information between the admissions and development offices.

Before going further, it must be stated that many schools have established restrictions on who has access to student applications and financial aid forms from the admissions office. The registrar's office may limit who can see records of courses taken, credits earned, or if the student graduated. As useful as these records are in confirming identity of alumni or their parents as potential donors, they may be inaccessible. Some schools have a database of general identification on students that can be accessed by authorized personnel. Others allow staff from the development office to get limited information from the admissions or registrar's office.

FERPA

How student records are regulated depends on the institution's interpretation of the federal Family Educational Rights and Privacy Act (FERPA). Because the act states that employees at an institution cannot view student records without the permission of the student, there are "gray areas" open to interpretation. Does that include those in the development office? Depends on how the school understands the act. For details, read "The Ethics of Using Student Records for Prospect Research" by Cyrus Mulready (*APRA Connections,* Fall 1999) and read these Web sites.

http://www.ed.gov/offices/OM/append.html
http://www.ncjrs.org/txtfiles/163705.txt

If the school's code allows it, the admissions office can copy and send to the alumni or development office the first page of the admission form for all entering freshmen. There a staff member can go through the pages looking for indications of wealth, such as parents' job titles, mother's maiden

On the job training

When the American Council on Education (ACE) conducted its National Presidents' Study in 1998, it found that with the demand for student financial aid on the rise and the proportion of revenues for state funding of higher education on the decline, college leaders must pay more attention to marketing. Other highlights:

- Presidents at private colleges and universities said they spend most of their time fundraising—82 percent of it.

- Presidents at public institutions said they spend 45 percent of their time fundraising.

- More than 50 percent of presidents wished they'd had more training or experience in fundraising.

name, high school attended, or home address. Most development offices in educational institutions do not use a student's grade point average or whether a student applied for financial aid (or was denied such aid) as significant information.

Once some information is known about the parents of incoming students, all of the skills of the nonprofit researcher go into play to establish potential donors. That may involve using electronic screening tools mentioned throughout this book and other old-fashioned research techniques.

Parents selected from that sampling may be asked to form a parents committee or become involved in school activities or the annual fund drive. A letter or card sent to the parents may include a question about their own alma maters and the names and alma maters of the student's grandparents. (Might the parents or grandparents be lost alumni themselves?) It's been said that the most generous person is the doting grandfather of his college freshman granddaughter.

Having selected parents involved in school activities remains the best way to build school loyalty that may lead to a major contribution even years later. While the student is in college, many parents feel they are making a contribution just paying the tuition and school fees. Identifying a student's family of wealth does not answer any questions about the family's expenses. Are there other children in college or in high school—getting ready for an expensive college? Are grandparents in a nursing home? Did the family lose a lot of wealth in the spring 2000 high-tech stock disaster? Such questions have significance in the development process.

Any further information about a student's family is useful and should be coded to the student's name and entered into the development tracking software as the first step in keeping track of alumni after graduation. Alumni who have been identified as likely to one day inherit a large fortune can be coded to indicate that.

Since new graduates move around quite often in the 10 years following graduation, the home address may be the best way to keep in touch. Most parents will forward their child's mail—even if they know it may include a request for a contribution to the alma mater.

How you enter new graduates into the alumni database may determine how well you can stay in touch with them later. Software tracking systems should allow adequate fields for information, including parents' addresses, maiden names, married names, and connections. Some alumni offices file all women by their maiden name with cross references from the married name.

Just as the development office was in contact with the admissions office for information on incoming students, the career development office, by whatever name, may provide updated addresses and professional information on recent graduates. Many graduates will have submitted requests for college transcripts when applying for new positions. Most college public relations offices subscribe to clipping services to receive news items that mention the college and its alumni. Throughout this book are mentions of Internet sites offering similar tracking services. Called "push technology," some are free and others quite inexpensive. What used to be a real chore is now made easy with the new technologies.

Graduates who were college athletes often keep in touch with coaches and others in the sports information office. Others keep in touch with department faculty members and senior dissertation advisors. Theatre majors may send play announcements to those who directed them while in college. Membership records for fraternities and sororities may be checked. Many schools designate class agents who attempt to keep contact with their classmates. Others hope alumni who have not been in touch with their college will discover the college Web site and fill in an online form to update their current address and occupation achievements. This may alert the development office to new prospects.

By doing two or more mailings to alumni each year, there is a good chance they will be forwarded. The U.S. Postal Service honors forwarding instructions for only one year. Get to know the person who services your postal meter or handles return corrections at your local post office. Ask about return correction requests available on first class mailings as a way to catch some new addresses and other available options. Even after the forwarding time has expired, you may get the returned piece with a label giving the new address.

Using e-mail to keep in touch

Increasingly, colleges and universities are offering lifelong personal e-mail accounts for its graduates and home pages for each graduating class as a way for graduates to keep in touch with each other—and for college fundraisers to find them. The e-mail addresses allow e-mail to be forwarded to alumni, even if they change their Internet service providers. Using those e-mail addresses to publicize reunions has increased attendance, according to an assistant director at the Association of Yale Alumni. It also has fund-raising implications. "It keeps people connected to the university, and that's what fundraising is all about—keeping people connected who want to contribute," said a fundraiser at Washington State University in Pullman.

Speaking of Wake Forest University's "seamless" communication service which extends from the time a new student pays an application deposit until they become alumni, a fundraiser at the university said, "Nothing we've ever done has been able to bring people closer to the university than this technology. It has personalized and extended our communication…. If they feel fulfilled in that way, then the money follows." (*The New York Times*, March 26, 1998)

That doesn't mean all graduates keep their alumni office up-to-date with every address change or job promotion. It often depends on the ingenuity of college staff members to find those who may become major donors.

Find alumni e-mail addresses the same way you seek to discover mail addresses. Put a space for e-mail address on every form alumni may complete. If you do an alumni directory, with Harris or other firms, make sure their questionnaire includes a space for e-mail addresses. Once e-mail addresses are collected, make sure there is some good reason to have them. Some colleges do a weekly or monthly e-mail newsletter telling of campus activities, alumni events, sports events, and college/university press releases. Don't make an e-mail message just another plea for contributions.

Using class notes

Most colleges and universities alumni newsletters and magazines have a class notes section by graduate year. Use a student assistant or volunteer to index those and add pertinent facts into the database. Those publications sometime announce children born to alumni, job changes and promotions, and deaths—all facts for the database. A posting on PRSPCT-L mentioned the Harvard University Archives as an example of the type of information one university keeps on its alumni. The biographical sketches on file were gathered for special anniversary reports—10, 25, or 50 years after graduation. Call (617) 495-2461 or e-mail to *archives-ref@hulmail. harvard.edu* to request information on a Harvard graduate.

Whether the alumni office and the development office are the same or separate, there should be a close working relation between the two. Keeping track of alumni is a science onto itself and staff members with that responsibility in both offices can learn from each other. Many of the best articles on college development and alumni services are in CASE's monthly publication, *Currents*. Call the membership office at (202) 328-

5996 for details about membership in the association or how to subscribe to the publication. Some articles are available as "freebies" at the CASE Web site.

http://www.case.org

Staff members involved in alumni relations can get together on the alumni listserv, ALUMNI-L. Send an e-mail message to listserv@brownvm. brown.edu. It should read: subscribe ALUMNI-L <insert your name>

Many college and university researchers are active participants on PRSPCT-L. To access PRSPCT-L archives and files of useful documents go to this site and follow directions after signing in as a list member.

http://groups.yahoo.com/group/PRSPCT-L

The Alumni Records Clearing House (ARCH), a project from Snow & Associates is a non-profit resource designed to help educational, fraternal, and professional institutions relocate lost alumni. It provides a way for qualified institutions to share location information on alumni on the premise that many colleges and universities have overlapping populations whose names will be gathered into a central database. For details, see the ARCH Project Web site.

http://www.arch.org

Finding lost alumni

Just a few short years ago it used to be almost impossible to track down lost alumni with only a person's name. With the Internet, it is not quite as difficult, but still not a walk in the park.

As the first step in renewing contact with alumni, find their current address and telephone number. If you have a limited number of names and a good student or volunteer, you can start with these directory Web sites. Pray that everyone on your list has an unusual name!

http://www.555-1212.com
http://www.AnyWho.com
http://www.bigfoot.com
http://www.teldir.com

Here's a useful portal that links to a number of search Web sites for addresses, e-mail addresses, and telephone numbers. If you want to confirm a death, link to the *Social Security Death Index*.

http://person.langenberg.com

A fundraiser for the military

There won't be a bake sale, but the U.S. Naval Academy announced it is launching a $175 million capital campaign, the first time it will seek support from donors. Even though the military institution will rely on the Pentagon to fund its basic needs, it needs extra funds to enhance the campus and lure top faculty.

The Naval Academy faces some challenges in raising private dollars. The superintendent is prohibited from soliciting gifts, as are all the military officers and students. That means there will be no phone banks when students ask alumni for funds.

Naval cadets have an obligation to stay in military service for five years following graduation in exchange for free tuition and the academy hopes its alumni will support the campaign. Perhaps the main incentive will be the traditional Army vs. Navy rivalry. The U.S. Military Academy at West Point set a $150 million goal in 1999, but now expects to surpass $200 million when the campaign ends in 2002. (*The Washington Post,* June 9, 2001)

Names of lost alumni can be printed in alumni publications with a request for a recent address from someone who knows the person. Phonathon callers can call parents or the last-known phone number for the lost person to get a phone number change. Some schools send out a postcard to parents of lost young alumni asking for their child's address or phone number.

Getting addresses from companies

Several companies, including those listed below, can help by running names through databases of, for example, 90,000,000 credit card holders. If you have Social Security numbers in your database, the percentage of matches is around 80 percent. If you have only a name and last address, the results may be more like 50 percent. Prices per name vary greatly.

Although many records in nonprofit files include Social Security numbers, for ethical reasons, the current trend is to avoid collecting them. Most people are protective of their SS numbers, and rightly so, because identity theft using those numbers is prevalent. Before you release any lists containing SS numbers, check with your attorney about confidentiality laws.

By law, credit companies that provide address and phone number services will not provide more than that. When negotiating with a company to screen your lost alumni lists, ask for a trial run of a few hundred names to see the results, then negotiate the price based on the accuracy rate of the sample. Also ask what records are used to compile their databases and whether the company strives to protect a person's privacy.

In April 2001, a federal appeals court told Trans Union Corp., one of the nation's largest credit bureaus, that it must stop selling lists from loan information in credit reports. Based on the Fair Credit Reporting Act (FCRA), the two other major credit bureaus, Equifax and Experian, had long ago agreed to stop selling information gleaned from credit records. Trans Union argued that it should be allowed to sell targeted lists unless a customer "opts out." The court thought otherwise. Whether this ruling based on privacy legislation will affect companies that offer name and address services remains to be seen. As long as database information does not come from credit reports, it should continue to be available.

Companies doing alumni searches

Including companies in this list is not an endorsement of that company by the author, nor is exclusion meant to be the opposite.

Anchor Computer, Inc., 1900 New Highway, Farmingdale, NY 11735. 1-800-728-6262

Anchor is a licensee of the U.S. Postal Services databases, including the NCOA (National Change of Address), with more than 108 million changes reported to the USPS in three years.

http://www.anchor-computer.com/

Business Credit Information (BCI), 251 Rhode Island, Suite 207, San Francisco, CA 94103. 1-800-382-1735 or 1-415-861-4224

BCI offers information from various sources, including NCOA address changes, with its address retrieval service.

http://www.alumnilocators.com

Can she find them?

"It was a job seeker's nightmare," writes Peg Mancuso of Hicksville, NY, as four high-ranking officials of a university were taking turns questioning her about how she would handle the role of alumni relations director for the institution.

"The university had lost track of many of the alumni and needed to regain contact," said the applicant. "I had some ideas and answered all the questions with the confidence that I could do the job for my alma mater."

But then one of the vice presidents asked, "So, do you think you could find all of the lost alumni?" Mrs. Mancuso hesitated. The tension built.

"I felt that if I answered 'yes,' I would be showing overconfidence and a lack of knowledge about the challenges of the job," she recalled. "But to answer 'no' would be to admit to the possibility of failure."

Mrs. Marcuso repeated the question and with a smile, gave her reply: "No, I don't think that I'll find all the alumni, at least not those in the Witness Protection Program."

She got the job. *(The New York Times, April 25, 1999)*

Boyd's City Dispatch, 185 Millerton Road, Millerton, NY 12546. 1-860-435-0861

Boyd's offers alumni search service and has databases of business owners and affluent individuals.

http://www.boydscity.com/

CDB Infotek (subsidiary of Equifax), 6 Hutton Centre, Santa Ana, CA 92707 1-800-427-3747

This is one of the three largest credit card reporting agencies with access to 3 billion records, including public records and Dun & Bradstreet business records.

http://www.cdb.com
http://www.cdb.com/public/services/locate.shtml

DataQuick Products. 1-800-355-2203

DataQuick is a real-estate company with records from county recorder and assessor records throughout the U.S., searchable by name and address and including phone numbers.

http://www.dataquick.com

Dun & Bradstreet, 3 Sylvan Way, Parsippany, NJ 07054 1-800-526-0651

D & B will do a custom search of their entire database, looking for executive biographies to match your alumni list.

http://www.dnb.com

Equifax, 1-888-202-4025

This company offers consumer information, including that from the R.L.Polk Co. Equifax is one of the three largest credit information companies.

http://equifax.com

Executive Marketing Services, Inc., 184 Sherman Blvd., Ste. 300, Naperville, IL 60563 1-800-367-7311

Using known Social Security numbers from your alumni list, EMS will run the list through various sources to find recent addresses and telephone numbers from a database of 90 million households.

http://www.emsphone.com

Experian Information Solutions (formerly TRW), 701 Experian Parkway, Allen, TX 75013. 1-888-397-3742

This major credit reporting service also includes databases of public records including state motor vehicle records, USPS National Change of Address database, and others.

http://www.experian.com

Harris Publishing Co., 3 Barker Ave., White Plains, NY 10601. 1-800-326-6600

While doing a directory of alumni, this company will try to locate lost alumni and give address changes, if found. The company does not do separate lost alumni searches.

http://www.bcharrispub.com

Lexis–Nexis Finder

As one of the many services from Lexis–Nexis, Finder is most useful for finding lost alumni. At a cost of about $200 a month (with a two month minimum subscription), subscribers get unlimited access to the service and can search by name and get current address, past addresses with date changed, and sometimes birth dates and spouse's name.

http://lexis-nexis.com/

Marts & Lundy, 1200 Wall Street West, Lyndhurst, NJ 07071. 1–800–526–9005

M & L provides several levels of screening for your alumni, with giving levels. It can include a changed address option with a NCOA database as part of a screening, but not as a separate service.

http://www.martsandlundy.com

Trans Union Corp., P.O. Box, Chester, PA 19022. 1–800–397–2131 or 1–800–888–4213

Trans Union is another large credit card information and service company that can search for alumni addresses.

http://www.transunion.com

≫ 20 ≪

Ethics and Privacy Issues

"The iron rule of organizational ethics is this:
If you gain people's trust, you may gain their money,
but if you lose people's trust, you absolutely will lost their money."
—Michael O'Neill
Institute of Nonprofit Management

Sometimes a simple answer to a complicated question says the most. That may be true when considering ethical questions in your nonprofit research office. Can everything you do pass the "light of day" test? Would you be embarrassed to read about your work in the morning newspaper? The answer to the first question should be yes; the second answer should be no.

Fundraising is the building of relationships between those who give the gift and the institution that receives it. It is a partnership. If, or when, a prospect discovers that research is being done, you have no reason to be embarrassed unless you have been less than candid and ethical in your research and documentation. Every aspect of prospect research must be aboveboard.

Few wealthy prospects and donors are surprised to learn that information about them, including indications of their wealth, is being collected by nonprofit organizations that hope to receive a gift. They must be aware that this information, sometimes quite detailed, is out there and available in public sources through electronic databases. Putting this information together and making assumptions about that prospect and his/her relationship to an institution is prospect research. Most donors understand that.

Public records vs. the right to privacy

The right to privacy is a treasured hallmark of the American way of life. In fact, it was acknowledged by our Founding Fathers in the Fourth and Fifth Amendments to the U.S. Constitution. Alas, that was long before the era of advanced computer technology when most details of our lives are in a database somewhere. It was before the days when aggressive direct marketers collected information on us to sell to mail or telephone solicitors. One can only wonder how those Constitution authors would write the amendments today.

The American public has indicated that privacy is among the things that matter most. One recent poll found that nine out of ten Americans are concerned about threats to privacy. Articles in journals as dissimilar as the professional *Chronicle of Philanthropy* (March 23, 2000) and the popular *Town and Country* (May 2000) have included ominous warning to development staffs about donors' concern that information is being gathered on them.

Both articles should be required reading by nonprofit prospect researchers who must do their required and necessary work in the light of prospects' and donors' right to privacy. Research should be based on ethical principles with the assumption that staff members will do right and avoid doing wrong. Still, as with the Golden Rule, there is room for interpretation.

You, as researchers in the world of electronics, are more aware of what is electronically available than the average citizen, but public awareness is growing. Public records that used to be available only in courthouses, in halls of records, or state offices are now available on your computer screen. Remember that using those public records is not unethical! The fact that so many records are public is a barrier against corruption. For example, having real estate assessment records online is a way an owner, by making comparison, can know if property is being taxed fairly. The advancement researcher can use the same real estate records to establish evidence of wealth.

Ethics is not law. Some things may be very legal, but very unethical.

Sometimes, though, law and ethics collide in court. In Washington, D.C., *Regardie's* magazine did its own "100 Richest List" some years ago. The research was similar to what is done by *Forbes* to compile its 400 richest list and similar to what prospect researchers do in nonprofit offices every day. The difference was that *Regardie's* planned to publish the results. A real estate investor did not want to be on the list. He went to court, saying the magazine was guilty of "ferreting out facts about his financial affairs in a cynical, snooping, conspiratorial, privacy-invading and gossip-mongering manner." He filed suit against the magazine for invasion of privacy, intrusion upon seclusion, and the publicity given to his private life. He demanded $120 million in compensatory and punitive damages.

The judge threw out the case, saying, "Such intrusion, from a legal point of view, is obviously not upon his own private 'personal space,' to borrow a pseudo-psychological term...[and] that is all the law protects." He added that the "matters publicized about the plaintiff were not private, that they would not, as a matter of law, be highly offensive to a reasonable person." (*The Washington Post*, May 4, 1987)

This type of financial research seldom becomes a court case, but it is comforting to know the law protects your right to gather and use publicly available information. The trouble with increased access to information is that we think we are entitled to it and a person's privacy may be threatened. We should ask ourselves, is it possible to collect so much public information that it becomes an invasion of privacy?

Each year at meetings of the Association of Professional Researchers for Advancement (APRA) any discussion of ethical questions in the research office is guaranteed to result in spirited debate. When APRA was a new organization without a code of ethics, several ethical dilemmas were discussed: Does a researcher have to identify him or herself when seeking information? Can a researcher take information gained with one organization along when moving to a new position? Do prospects and donors have the right to see their own files?

The first two questions were resolved when APRA's Statement of Ethics was adopted. The ethics statement simply said researchers "shall be truthful with regard to their identity and purpose." To answer the second concern, "Constituent information is the property of the institution for which it was collected," and "Constituent information for one institution shall not be taken to another institution." Those issues were settled once and for all.

The question about a donor's right to his or her researched report is still in debate in many offices. It's not a hypothetical question. In many public institutions "sunshine" or open-records laws require that files be available if requested. Experienced researchers often advise new researchers to put nothing into a file that they would not want the prospect to read. That means anything that would cause embarrassment or anger. Just because no one has requested his or her file in your organization doesn't mean it won't happen.

It is worth noting that research files may be subpoenaed in a lawsuit that involves a contribution to your organization. For example, if a donor's will is challenged by disinherited heirs, the file may become part of the "discovery" legal process. That's another good reason to be careful about what comments go into the file. What's not there won't become a problem later.

Sensitive information

Issues that require sensitivity include divorce and alimony settlements, lawsuit decisions, employment terminations, dysfunctional family issues, alcoholism or drug addiction, suicide, mental or physical conditions of family members, inappropriate sexual behavior, drunk driving, criminal charges, incarcerations—to name just a few possible skeletons in a donor's closet.

Your organization should discuss the issue of using sensitive information before it becomes an issue. The Privacy Act of 1974 passed by Congress provided certain safeguards for an individual against invasion of privacy. It stated that the individual has the right to know about government records pertaining to them, and must be told who else sees them and how the information is used.

Nonprofit organizations can get *header* data from the large credit card reporting companies, Trans Union, Experian (formerly TRW), and Equifax, to verify addresses (using a person's previous addresses) and phone numbers. Those companies, by law, cannot sell financial information or get data from credit records. To access someone's credit record requires that person's authorization or a compelling legal reason. You can get your own credit record, but no one else's.

In your office, protecting a donor's privacy may be as uncomplicated as deciding if you will use any court records in your research. Beware! Based on the Privacy Act, courthouse regulations require that the name and address of persons who photocopy documents be recorded. Do you want your prospect to know you were digging that deeply into his or her private life? It may abort that priceless relationship you hoped to develop.

Researchers are often in conflict between a development officer who wants to know *everything* about a prospect and the researcher's own feeling of what is appropriate—and available. Thus, part of a researcher's task is educating officers. On occasion a donor may ask the development officer what information the organization gathers about donors. The officer should be able to say, in all truthfulness, that what is gathered is only from public records, newspaper and magazine articles, real estate data, and in-house information. That may include giving patterns, areas of interest, and information the donor has offered during visits.

Speaking of call reports, the development officer who made the visit may lack tact and may use offensive language in the written report. You don't want that to become part of a permanent record. Someone in the office should look at each report before it becomes part of a profile. The same information can be recorded in many different ways. Use words that aren't derogatory or pejorative. Stating that the donor is divorced may say enough. There is no need to label it a "messy divorce," even if it was. It may be necessary to mention an alimony judgment, if it was found in some publicly available record or mentioned by the donor. That fact may be relevant to the fundraising process, but some details should stay in the development officer's head—not in the file.

Considering how much useful information is available through legitimate sources, there should be no need to go beyond that. After all, no development officer who is building a relationship with a potential donor needs to know *every personal detail* about that person. Nevertheless, some controversial items that may surface, assuming they can be verified and are not just gossip, innuendo or personal opinion, can be relevant to the fundraising process.

When damaging information is uncovered that might embarrass the institution or change the potential of the person becoming a donor, it is relevant. When that happens and the researcher thinks the officer really needs to know about it, the information can be shared with him/her. But before it is put into the file, it must conform to the relevancy principle. Relevance means the information is appropriate to the fundraising efforts of the institution. Sometimes that's a matter of professional judgement.

Here's an example: The researcher turns up bankruptcy records and other disturbing financial information about a donor who is considering making a multimillion dollar gift over 10 years. Your organization will be dependent on that money coming in to fulfill your mission. That's relevant information. Research can reveal both good and bad things about a potential donor.

Many recent articles in the national press have given the impression that everything—bank records, credit card balances, unlisted phone numbers, long distance telephone records, and criminal records—is easily available to everyone. But it's not true. Because a lot of information is online, though supposedly restricted to those who need it (such as law enforcement officers and private investigators), some data may be revealed. Credit companies restrict what information they sell to the general public, but their information is still available to the estimated 60,000 licensed private eyes operating in the United States, many of them without licenses. Regulations dealing with privacy have not kept pace with the speed that personal information becomes available online. Too often it may be retrieved by unethical persons. As the editor of *Privacy Times*, stated, "A lot of things most Americans assume are illegal or wrong are not prohibited by law."

Use of Social Security numbers

When Congress passed the Social Security Act of 1935, it stated that an individual's number was not to be used as an identifier for other than Social Security purposes. That fact got lost along the way and the number became required information on applications for almost everything, including a driver's license in many states.

Social Security numbers present an ethical dilemma for many nonprofit researchers. Many records in their databases include numbers, put there before those numbers became the most sought detail by those involved in identity and credit theft. Many alumni records include those numbers, recorded when students used that as their ID number. In the past, some SS numbers were copied from gift checks when numbers were routinely printed on checks. Whether or not to use those numbers to gather precise information on those donors is a much-discussed topic by researchers. If Social Security numbers are stored in nonprofit databases, development staffs must be very vigilant to keep them secure.

There are reasons for using Social Security numbers in a research office, but better reasons for not collecting and using them. Using those numbers improves the possibility of getting exact hits when seeking address verifications from credit report companies. It improves the chance of identifying the correct person with a common name. Having that number verifies a death when using the *Social Security Death Index*. Because part of the number indicates where it was issued, that fact gives researchers a hint to a person's residence at that time.

However, in considering the potential for damage if someone misuses the numbers against the minor research benefits of storing and keeping the number as part of database records, many organizations are deleting that information. I doubt if any nonprofit office now asks for the Social Security number on surveys or other forms seeking information on a prospect.

The APRA Statement of Ethics reads, "Prospect researchers shall seek and record only information that is relevant and appropriate to the fundraising effort of the institutions that employ them." Further, "Constituent information...shall be stored securely to prevent access by unauthorized persons." If an organization, in light of recent thinking on the subject, decides to remove the numbers from records, they must be "irreversibly disposed of when no longer needed."

Writing your code of ethics

Because different types of nonprofit organizations have situations unique to themselves, it is desirable that each development office write an internal code of ethics and confidentiality. The exercise of writing these statements brings the reality of operating ethically into everyday discussion. A statement dealing with prospect research can be a part of your development office's code of ethics and can begin by stating that your office will adhere to the APRA Statement of Ethics.

Check within your organization to see what other policies are in effect. You will need to know about policies in the admissions and registrar's offices, if you are an educational institution. If there are local or state laws that affect research (perhaps dealing with privacy or access to information), your statement must acknowledge that.

In your code, define why you are collecting information, what type you will gather or avoid gathering, and how you will store and use it. You should say who is authorized to enter information into the database, who can see the information, and how the confidentiality of the profiles will be protected in both paper and electronic files. The code may state that disposal of documents must be done by mechanical shredding. If you use volunteers, what restrictions apply to them? Who will have the ultimate authority to enforce procedures?

It's a good idea to have your ethics document screened by your organization's counsel before it is adopted. Once finished, it should be widely circulated to all staff members and volunteers, and reviewed periodically.

Confidentiality of records

Assume that *all* information about a prospect or donor in your files or databases is confidential and treat it as such. To meet the APRA Statement of Ethics standards, you must deal with information about your donors with confidentiality, accuracy, relevance, accountability, and honesty.

Because of the sensitivity of information within profiles, some research offices stamp each file as confidential or put a confidentiality statement on the cover. Such a statement should detail ownership of the file and say it is provided under the guidelines of the institution's development office. It should emphasize that reproduction, copying, and distribution or sharing of information within the file without prior authorization is prohibited. It may ask that the file be returned promptly to the research office after use.

When real or potential ethical dilemmas arise in a nonprofit research office, the staff member involved should talk with the head of the research office. She or he may wish to make the situation a topic of discussion at a department meeting with development officers. When this happens, it emphasizes to all that issues of privacy and confidentiality are not just textbook issues, but may happen at any time.

When researchers and development officers deal with sensitive and confidential matters regarding potential or actual donors, there is always danger that established trust between the person and the organization may be harmed. When that happens, it goes without saying the purpose of the research is thwarted.

The dilemma in healthcare philanthropy

Both in the field of healthcare philanthropy and throughout the nonprofit world, the question of using a patient's hospital admission records for philanthropy prompts intense discussion. In late 1999, the U.S. Department of Health and Human Services proposed new rules to protect a patient's medical records.

For years development officers in hospitals have used admission records to prospect for potential "grateful patient" gifts. Fundraisers used those names and addresses for direct mail campaigns and to determine major gift prospects. In 1999 that procedure was questioned. Many healthcare fundraisers felt denying a list of patients for hospital development was comparable to a college having no access to its alumni.

A spokesman for the American Hospital Association said it made sense that former grateful patients were the ones most apt to respond to appeals. About 65 percent of funds raised by hospital foundations comes from former patients. For example, Philanthropist Alberto Vilar gave $8 million to the Hospital for Special Surgery in New York, where he was treated after he shattered his left elbow and lower arm in a skiing accident. Some of those grateful donors are researched and become major donors. But there is an ethical dilemma. Don't patients have a right to privacy regarding their medical records, including their hospital admissions?

People go to hospitals for all kinds of sensitive reasons and don't want the medical reason for their hospital stay to become available. As reported in *The New York Times* (October 6, 2000), one woman in a cancer hospital was upset when she got a solicitation asking her to put that hospital in her will. She wondered if the fundraisers had used her medical records and found her diagnosis was worse than she knew herself.

Congress mandated new federal laws governing the security and privacy of electronic medical records, but they won't take effect until 2003. Due to aggressive efforts by healthcare development staffs, the release of patient identification for fundraising and marketing purposes will be allowed.

Fundraisers must disclose the source of personal information and explain why those solicited were targeted. Patients will have the option of saying no to such solicitations—but only after they are contacted at least once. Many privacy consultants are not pleased with the regulations that put fundraising and marketing together. They feel patients should be able to opt out up front, not after the fact. For recent information on healthcare legislation, go to

http://www.go-ahp.org

Most fundraisers want only a patient's name, address, and telephone number. Information about the patient's illness or treatment is restricted and few disagree with that. Nonprofit researchers, if they know their job well, are aware of the abundant amount of information that can be found with just a person's name and address.

Evidence of potential medical privacy problems became clear when a hacker easily accessed thousands of medical records from the University of Washington Medical Center. The records contained patient names, medical conditions, home addresses, and Social Security numbers. Specialists say the act demonstrated the increasing vulnerability of confidential records in the healthcare system as files are computerized and made available via computer networks.

If the healthcare development office has access to records, even names and addresses, it provides another link that could be hacked if not secured by knowledgeable electronic security technicians. (*The Washington Post*, December 9, 2000)

Statements of ethics and privacy

The latest revision of the Association of Professional Researchers for Advancement APRA Statement of Ethics was adopted in September 1998.

APRA also endorses A Donor Bill of Rights as developed by the American Association of Fund-Raising Counsel (AAFRC), the Association for Healthcare Philanthropy (AHP), the Council for Advancement and Support of Education (CASE), and the National Society of Fund Raising Executives (NSFRE).

Both statements are available in the APRA member directory. Look for APRA's Statement of Ethics on this Web site or click on it from the home page.

http://www.APRAhome.org/apra_statement_of_ethics.htm
http://www.APRAhome.org

Another statement of ethics pertinent to researchers is from the National Society of Fund Raising Executives (NSFRE). Click on Ethics from the home page for The Code of Ethical Principles.

http://www.nsfre.org/

Up-to-date information on privacy in an electronic era is from the Electronic Privacy Information Center and the Electronic Freedom Foundation at these sites.

www.//epic.org/
http://www.eff.org/

⇒ 21 ⇐

Finding Jobs, Consultants, and Freelancers

Let him who knows how ring the bell.
—Spanish proverb

Now is a good time to be a nonprofit researcher or to look for a position as a researcher. Development research is beginning to enjoy a high profile in nonprofit organizations as their executives realize the need for the skills that researchers provide. Each year, professional research positions are being created in small organizations that previously had no researcher. Many colleges, universities, and large organizations are launching major fundraising campaigns requiring more researchers to assist in locating and profiling major donors.

Any job seeker wishing to apply for an advancement research position should look at the Skills Sets from the Association of Professional Researchers for Advancement (APRA). Available in the APRA Member Directory and from the APRA homepage, the Basic Skills Set lists minimal requirements for an entry-level research position. Mastering the Advanced Skills Set indicates a person has the experience and expertise necessary for a leadership research role.

Most researchers in nonprofit organizations have at least a bachelor's degree and many have master's degrees. Traditionally, a degree in information or library science has been useful to those applying for an advancement research position, but it is not normally required. More than 90 percent of persons in the nonprofit research profession are classified as exempt, professional-level staff within their offices.

Salaries for advancement researchers depend on a person's education, knowledge, experience, and job title as well as type of institution and geographical location. APRA's 2000 survey indicated more than 40 percent of development researchers earn salaries in the $30,000 - $39,999 range, and about 20 percent earn between $50,000 and $59,000. A small number make less than $25,000 and a few make more than $60,000. Contact APRA for a copy of the complete survey that includes salary range by education, gender, and position title.

With research jobs available in most regions of the country, job seekers have the opportunity to analyze their own abilities and interests, then look for the right match for themselves. That may mean leaving current employment and finding a similar position somewhere else or completely shifting gears and seeking a different type of position. The need to move on to something different comes to researchers as it does to those in other professions. It may come because you would welcome a new challenge, you think your skills have advanced to the next level in your profession, you are moving to another part of the country, your boss is driving you crazy, or you just want a change. Whatever the reason—go for it.

Looking for jobs in the nonprofit world is easier now than just a few years ago. Several Internet Web sites, print publications with job classified ads, and listservs are devoted to listing career advancing positions.

Sites listing research positions

A comprehensive listing of sites giving position openings for nonprofit researchers is given below. The first and best are the listserv PRSPCT-L and the APRA Web site.

PRSPCT-L. Throughout this book, I've recommended PRSPCT-L as the most useful listserv for researchers. Subscribing should be a requirement for anyone doing or hoping to do nonprofit research. Its postings of research positions (and, sometimes, other nonprofit development positions) give good job descriptions, detail requirements, and tell where to apply. These postings are from fellow researchers, sometimes from the person leaving the position, and include "insider" information about the job. Because PRSPCT-L postings may come out before print job listings, applicants can get a jump on the application process.

To subscribe to PRSPCT-L, e-mail to *PRSPCT-L-subscribe@ yahoogroups.com* or go to *http://groups.yahoo.com* and follow directions. After joining, to find archived job postings, go to that URL and login. Look on the left side of the screen to locate My Groups. Click PRSPCT-L. Under Most Recent Messages, find the Search Archive box. Fill in a search term and click Search Archive.

APRA. JobQuest at the APRA homepage offers a free service that allows employers to post job openings for members to view online or get by calling the APRA Westmont, IL, headquarters office (1-630-655-0177). Jobs are listed by location and job title.

http://www.APRAhome.org

Most regional APRA chapters include available positions in their newsletters and online at chapter Web sites.

For those with limited research experience, APRA's Mentor Program offers a one-on-one partnership with a veteran researcher in the same geographical region. The program provides the new researcher with encouragement and support in meeting the challenge of setting up and managing research operations. Call the APRA office for more details.

Jobs for advancement researchers are posted each year at the APRA international educational conference with opportunities for employment interviews. Those seeking positions can network with others and gain from those contacts.

OIA.MINES. This very useful site is for those searching for a job in advancement. It not only lists and links to sites with job postings, but also includes sample job descriptions for all varieties of advancement positions and even online application forms. Employers are advised to use the sample job descriptions to create their own job postings.

http://oia.mines.edu/advancement_resources/employment/

CharityChannel. This listserv maintains an extensive group of other listservs for the nonprofit community. All subscribers to any forum receive a CareerSearch Online Update each week with a partial listing of the latest nonprofit sector available positions on that online system. Each listing includes just position title, organization, location, and position number. Users are referred or linked to the CharityChannel URL for the full listing and for details on how nonprofit organizations and executive recruitment firms can post positions.

http://charitychannel.com/careersearch/

The Chronicle of Philanthropy. The *Chronicle's* print newspaper's classified employment listing has long been a favorite with job seekers for all kinds of philanthropy positions. Now it's also online in searchable format in the Career Network with job-market news and trends, salary surveys, and professional-development advice. Jobs from the current issue are available exclusively to subscribers, but job listings from previous issues are available to everyone. To find the entire Directory of Services, a list of consultants and their specialty, leave off the jobs designation on the URL.

http://philanthropy.com/jobs

The Chronicle of Higher Education **Career Network.** Besides checking for job postings, look at this site for employment articles and links to other job-seeking resources.

http://jobs.chronicle.com/free/jobs/admin/develop/links.htm

CASE Currents **Online Job Classified.** Jobs are listed, with daily updating, for development, fundraising, public relations, advancement services, alumni relations, and major gifts.

http://www.case.org/jobs

HigherEdJobs.com. Development and fundraising positions are included on the HigherEdJobs.com Web site from the Center for Internet Technology in Education. It gives college or university, state, application due date, and posting date. For more on a specific job, it links to further details.

http://higheredjobs.com

Career Center at Charity Village. Use this for all types of nonprofit jobs in Canada.

http://www.charityvillage.com/charityvillage/career/html

Charity Job. Fundraising and charity jobs in the United Kingdom are listed at this site.

http://www.charityjob.co.uk/

National Opportunity Nocs. Looking for a different position within the nonprofit sector? Or do you want to list, for a reasonable price, an available job within your organization? National Opportunity Nocs lists job openings with keyword searching access by state or type of job. Use this site for access to the many nonprofit listservs with information on their areas of interests. Most listservs give available positions.

http://www.opportunitynocs.org

Monster.com. Once in a while someone may decide to leave the nonprofit sector for the bigger world. For them, Monster.com has been online since 1994 and thus is one of the longest lasting online job listing sites. When I looked, it had 448,301 jobs ready for the taking. Experience as a researcher can lead to job opportunities in other related fields.

http://www.monster.com

CareerBuilder.com. CareerBuilder is a mega-route to the classified job ads from 75 sites around the country including some major newspapers from Chicago, the Bay area, Los Angeles, and *USA Today*. It gives advice on writing a resume and has a salary wizard.

http://www.careerbuilder.com

Hiring researchers

Sooner or later, you may need to interview and hire researchers in your nonprofit office. How can you test applicants to determine if they have the knowledge and skills necessary to perform researcher duties? Following an initial interview to narrow the applicant pool, most nonprofit officials use a research problem to show an applicant's familiarity with research resources and the ability to use the gathered information to produce a concise prospect profile.

Here are examples of tests used in hiring researchers to show level of knowledge, ability to work under stress, writing ability, and creativity. Answers should reflect the applicant's understanding of the use and value of research in the fundraising process.

1. Give the applicant a well-known name and ask him or her to find appropriate information on the Internet and write a one-page profile of that person. Either give the applicant time during an interview to complete the profile or ask the applicant to do the assignment before the second interview.
2. Give the applicant information, copied from a variety of print and electronic sources, on a person. Tell the applicant that the college president will be visiting the prospect and needs a one-page summary in order to ask for a donation.
3. Give the applicant a name and ask how a researcher would go about finding information, listing what resources could be used.
4. When they are called for an interview, give applicants the name of a

college trustee. They are asked to bring in a short profile of that person. During the interview have the applicant explain why certain details were included and others left out.

5. Prepare three fictitious profiles and ask the applicant to estimate which of the three will be most apt to make a large contribution. You can use some information from three of your donors, changing the names and details, but emphasizing differences between the three. For a fascinating example of this exercise used at the University of Vermont, see this Web site for a description of the exercise and the profiles of "Jack Sprat '92, Foghorn Leghorn, and Dagwood '73 and Blondie '74 Bumstead."

http://www.uvm.edu/~prospect/exercise.html

Hiring consultants

Occasionally, in many nonprofit organizations, it is time to consider hiring a consultant. It may be a worrisome thought. You are suggesting hiring someone from outside your organization to do what no one is currently doing, someone who has an area of expertise no one in your office has, or someone to set up a system and train your staff to continue it.

Whatever the reason for needing a consultant, you want to know how one is chosen and how you can be sure you will get your money's worth. As a first step, look within your institution to examine just what you want the consultant to do that will implement the long-range goals of the advancement office. Once need has been analyzed, it is time to go looking for a consultant.

Get listings of consultants in publications for nonprofits such as *The Chronicle of Philanthropy,* the *Non-Profit Times,* and *Contributions.* All include directory-type classified ads or an occasional special consultant directory. Of course, listings are paid advertising and not subject to any objective evaluation. Note the range of services each consultant or company offers, and pick what matches your need. You can ask the company for names of their customers, but be aware that they may give you only ones they know are satisfied.

With a list of possibilities in mind, you have a great chance to use the networking skills you developed at APRA local and national conferences. Look for satisfied customers of the consultants you are considering. Once you find others who have used a consultant, ask what they liked and didn't like about the service. Realize that each institution's needs and expectations are different.

Another way to find clients of potential consultants is to put a message on PRSPCT-L asking for former clients of a consultant to contact you. You will get those who are either very happy or very unhappy with their results, so you will need to digest what you hear and proceed on in your investigation. Check the PRSPCT-L archives for postings and general discussions about hiring a consultant and for the specific names of consultants and companies.

Be aware of recent mergers in companies working with nonprofits. Some have joined completely; others have sold off a portion of the company. Be sure you are dealing with up-to-date information. Many of these companies and consultants exhibit at APRA and fundraising conferences. Use those opportunities to gather information and talk to exhibitors to determine exactly how the consultants and their companies differ from each other. Look at the Web sites for each consultant you are considering.

Once you have decided on candidates for a major project, interview those who match your needs. For big jobs, expect an on-site presentation with your staff members who will be involved in the project. Listen to what the presenter says about other companies providing similar services. The presenter may raise issues about differences in service among the companies that you hadn't considered. But give the competitors a chance for rebuttal.

After the presentations, you may decide now is not a good time for the services offered. Perhaps you need to do more work to update your prospect/donor lists before, for example, a screening. Or you may need more staff to deal with results of the screening, but there are no funds for that in the current budget. Perhaps you will decide you cannot afford the services you desire. For whatever reason, don't be pressured into making a decision you may regret later.

To be a freelance researcher or to hire one

Circumstances or just interest may propel a person into the world as a freelance researcher. If you know how to do nonprofit prospect and donor research, you have attractive possibilities for freelance work. Some organizations with a short list of potential donors or an occasional need for a corporate or foundation grant may forego having a researcher or grant writer on staff. They may prefer to pay for research only when needed and to use a professional grant writer on occasion. In some institutions, a freelance prospect researcher may be hired to find wealthy prospects before a capital campaign. Paying a freelancer by the hour or by the profile may be less expensive than employing a staff member who expects customary benefits.

Enthusiastic freelancers cite several reasons they prefer their home-based business to a 9 to 5 office experience. Among them are: flexibility of working hours; the freedom to do what they want to do when they want to; staying home with the children; avoiding commute time; being their own boss; not being involved in office politics; having tax write-offs with a home office; choosing only clients they like and want to work with; being able to help small organizations with their research needs; and, maybe best of all, "working in pajamas."

The Internet offers hundreds of sites about organizing a freelance or other at-home business. Begin with the Web site from Nolo Press, a publisher of self-help legal books and software. Do a search for the word Freelance or Independent Contractor to find examples of contracts and ways to organize a home-based business.

http://www.nolo.com

Someone presenting himself or herself as a freelance researcher must have online access to the Internet and access to several databases. Gone are the days when that person can get everything needed from a visit to a library, checking indexes for newspapers and magazines, finding biographical and corporate information in directories, then feeding coins into a copy machine. From home, the researcher can subscribe to most of the same electronic resources found in a nonprofit research office. Using a book such as this one and postings on PRSPCT-L, a freelancer can ferret out titles of the most useful resources, investigate online subscription services, and then go looking for customers.

Ideally, a person will have had several years of research experience before launching a freelance career of providing research to nonprofit clients. He or she should have a thorough understanding of the purpose of prospect research as well as the organization for which the profiles will be prepared. Sometimes the freelancer will be asked to research wealthy persons living within a certain radius of the organization. Other times, the organization will supply the freelancer with specific names to be researched. In short, the freelance researcher will be asked for the same kind of profiles that are prepared in nonprofit offices with full-time researchers.

Before hanging up the shingle, the freelancer must survey her or his ability to find clients willing to pay for research services. They may be small independent schools, local hospitals, social service organizations, and small colleges. How well a person can network and get word out that he or she is available will determine success or failure. The best way is to spread the word around. Show up at APRA, Association of Fundraising Professionals (formerly NSFRE), and New England Development Research Association (NEDRA) meetings and get to know persons who may someday need research services. Another good way to get known as a freelancer is to answer questions on PRSPCT-L. That may take time, but it gives a good impression of a person's research talents.

What freelancers charge

The average rate to produce a prospect profile is between $40 and $75 an hour, plus online expenses and delivery costs. It depends on location and experience. Beginners may charge as little as $25—but it may take longer to do a profile. A top-notch researcher may charge up to $75 an hour, but can whip out an exceptional profile very quickly. If that rate sounds high, remember the expenses researchers must absorb: online subscriptions and online databases; telephone lines and Internet access; computers, office equipment, and supplies; travel, lodging, and attendance at professional meetings; business and health insurance; and self-employed Social Security tax. After all that, a freelancer may be lucky to end up with $10-15 an hour.

A freelancer must have the ability to cite the hourly rate and not flinch. The client should realize you are charging for not only the information gathered, but for experience, knowledge, and expertise. An alternative to the hourly rate method is charging for each profile, between $125 and $200 (assuming at least three hours per profile). The rate depends on who (the client or the freelancer) pays online and other expenses that average $25 per profile. Some experienced researchers who work very quickly prefer to charge by the profile, saying, "Why penalize myself for efficiency, by charging by the hour?" Sometimes, despite the best research skills, it is impossible to find any information on a name, but it still takes time to reach that conclusion. Consider charging two hours for such an attempt.

Most freelance researchers require a signed contract with their client before work begins. The freelancer should sign a statement of confidentiality to protect names and information on prospects. Information received in confidence from one client is not to be shared with another client. The researcher should understand the ethical considerations of prospect research and agree that information will be taken only from publicly available records.

Researchers may discuss with the client what information on the prospect already is available in the organization's database so as not to duplicate that information, and determine exactly what information is needed. The client can ask that a finished profile be returned in an agreed-upon format. Most freelancers submit their finished profiles electronically to clients.

Many resources are available on the Internet to facilitate the researcher's career options to find another research position, to advance within the development office, or to become a freelance researcher.

≫•≪

Epilogue

Beginning with the words "What hath God wrought?" sent over a long distance connection between Baltimore and Washington in 1844, electronic transmission of data has evolved to the phenomenon it is today. Technology's effect on the entire advancement research and fundraising process during the last decade is dramatic, but it will never take the place of human interaction. As technology develops further—as it surely will—the temptation may be to think of the researched prospect or donor as the goal of a technologically possible pursuit and to forget the human element.

Certainly, more and more personal and financial information on individuals will become available electronically. How this information is gathered and used in an advancement setting will remain an ethical and privacy issue. The goal of advancement research is to find not only persons with the ability to make a sizable donation, but also those with an interest in doing so and a commitment to the organization.

People helping others is the reason for philanthropy. It is the spirit behind most nonprofit organizations. Technological research for philanthropy is one element, but not the most significant one. The important end result of such research is that it offers persons the opportunity to make a significant contribution to an institution or organization. Philanthropy connects people with ideas that lead to achievement by the nonprofit that receives the gift. Ideally, those who give the gifts and those who receive them should be equally blessed.

The purpose of this book has been not only to describe the task required of advancement researchers, but also to offer assurance that the task is not an impossible one. It can be done, and I wish you great success doing it.

☞ Appendix A ☜

Where to Begin:
An Imaginary Research Scenario

You and every other development researcher have at some time been faced with the ultimate challenge. Your boss walks in and says, "Someone told me at lunch about a fellow whom he thinks graduated from our college and I hear he has a lot of money. His name is Edward Smith." (Not a real person.)

Your heart sinks, but you must appear confident. After all, he is the boss, and you want him to think you can find almost anything about anyone. You yearn for more information, if only a clue—like the child's quiz game of animal, vegetable or mineral.

"Hmm, do you know anything else about him? Like where he lives? Or how he made his money?"

"Nope," he said, "That's all." He leaves the office saying, "Can you get me everything on him by this afternoon." It seemed a statement, not a question.

You give him that smile that means "Sure we can do anything and we can do it fast."

Where to begin? If only his name was not Smith. Why not something like Kosmo Zablonski? You decide your first task is to determine, out of all the Edward Smiths in the world, which is the one you want. There are several routes to the same end.

Realizing you have had good relations with the staff in the alumni office, you call and ask someone to check their files for an Edward Smith. They have three. One died two years ago. You feel a bit relieved—he can't be the one. One graduated five years ago. You reason he probably hasn't had time to make a lot of money yet—but then, you never know in these days of the high-tech economy. What about the last one? Well, one Edward Smith graduated fifteen years ago and the last the alumni office heard of him was 10 years ago when he made a $100 gift to the alumni fund. His address was in the state's capital city.

It may be a wild goose chase but, crossing your fingers and hoping for the best, you go after *that* Edward Smith. Because you do not have elaborate fee-based services to use, you will have to begin with print resources.

He's not in your copy of *Who's Who in America*. Luckily, you have a copy of the print *Biography and Genealogy Master Index* published by Gale. You find someone with that name listed in another Marquis publication, *Who's Who in Finance and Industry*. You don't have a copy, but you know your public library does. You give them a call and find, to your extreme pleasure, the listed Edward Smith did indeed graduate from your college. His entry said he is an executive with a thriving electronic company, the XYZ Corporation. While the librarian reads the entry to you, you note his middle initial, his wife's maiden name, his current address, his age, his children's names, and a hint as to interests from his listed nonprofit board memberships. Eureka! You're halfway there. But is he very wealthy?

It's time to go to the Internet. You could have started there, but you would get thousands of hits if you had entered "Edward Smith" into a search engine. You know that as an executive or insider at his corporation, he is required to reveal his stock ownership there. You have his middle initial. That helps.

You go to a SEC Web site and search by Edward Smith's name and find the amount of his stock in his company. Using the daily newspaper, you can find the value of each share. The company's proxy statement should tell Smith's annual salary, bonuses, and perhaps pension plan details.

http://people.edgar-online.com/

Maybe the boss will be satisfied with the information you've found so far, but then again, may as well dazzle him with even more. Taking a clue from the *Who's Who* entry that indicated he was on the board of his city's art museum, you look for the museum's Web site and discover his name as a major donor. With his address, you can find what his house is worth using one of the Internet real estate services. That may give a clue to his wealth, or lack of it.

http:///www.domania.com
http://www.realestate.yahoo.com/realestate/homevalues

Knowing his wife's maiden name, you make another call to the alumni office and find his wife also graduated from your college. That's probably where they met. That should be a good enough reason to be thankful to the old alma mater and to consider a sizable gift, you reason.

You've bookmarked the ultimate reference resource that links almost everything. Use it to find an online newspaper for the city where Smith lives. Click on U.S.A. for a list of papers by state. Check the paper's archives for names.

http://www.refdesk.com

Ah, just what you need, an article about Smith's wife and her involvement with a charity art auction. Print a full-text copy from the Internet. It will cost a few dollars charged to a credit card, but well worth it.

You are a member of Foundation Center Associates so you use one of your allowed calls and ask if either Edward or his wife is involved as an officer or trustee of a foundation. No luck there.

You decide to check for political contributions. It may tell something about his view of life. After all, your college has a liberal reputation and you wonder if Smith shares those views—even if he did get rich. You go to the Web site from the Federal Elections Commission and type in Edward R. Smith and the state.

http://www.tray.com/fecinfo/_indiv.htm

It shows several contributions to liberal candidates for state office, with Smith's employer, his occupation, and his address listed, all required by law.

You wonder why he hasn't contributed anything to the college for the past 10 years? Perhaps the question has a simple answer. Maybe he was never asked. Let your boss worry why Smith wasn't discovered as a potential donor long before now.

This request was all too easy, you think to yourself. You're sorry your boss hadn't given you a really hard name to show your research skills. With a smug look on your face, carrying Internet printouts on Edward Smith, you head for the boss's office—and it's only two o'clock. He thanks you for the information, but doesn't seem to understand that from just a name, and a common one at that, you have given Edward Smith an identify and some hints that he may be interested in helping to finance the college's new art building. At least, you can hope.

You go back to your office and find a written research request. This one is for information on an elderly widow who graduated from your college 50 years ago. She "never worked outside the home," as they used to say, so if she has wealth it probably was inherited from her family or from her husband. Of course, she may have dabbled in the stock market from her kitchen. The officer requesting the search knew the maiden name because the donor signed her name Emma Sanborn Murphy (not a real person) on her check for a small gift with a note giving her graduation year. The check included her address.

You check the paper files and database entries by her last name. Nothing there. You call the alumni office. Nope. Apparently they didn't keep very good records 50 years ago, but you have a vague feeling you have heard that name before. Maybe it is that after doing research for a while, *every* name begins to sound familiar.

With a known address, you decide to check real estate assessment records for her neighborhood. Using the Internet sites you used earlier, you discover Emma's house has a fairly modest assessment compared to others in her neighborhood. That's no surprise, many elderly persons have lived in the same house for many years without making some of the improvements that raise the assessment. On the property assessment records you find the first name of Emma's deceased husband.

With that clue, you can pursue other options. Maybe there is an indication of "old money." Unfortunately, you don't have a copy of *Book of American Family Trees* from Waltman Associates, because there you would discover that Sanborn was a listed prominent family and perhaps Emma fits into that family tree, indicating possible inherited wealth.

With the name of Emma's husband, you can look for his obituary in an online newspaper archive for the city where they lived. You find the obit and get almost the whole story. His obit says he had married Emma of the Sanborn family that had started a chain of department stores in the Midwest. That tells where her wealth originated, but did the husband also have wealth? The obit listed no children—a significant fact for development purposes.

Remembering that the downtown public library keeps old biographical reference books, you call the librarian. You're happy the library employs some "fuddy duddy" librarians who don't believe information retrieval began with the Internet. You ask the librarian to check an old copy of *Who's Who in the Midwest*—perhaps one about 20 years ago. Emma's husband is listed there as a college professor, but the entry gives no clue that he might have achieved wealth. You decide that any wealth in the Murphy household came from her family.

You go back to where you started, your own files, and look under the name Sanborn and discover other members of the Sanborn family had made substantial gifts to the college. You check the Foundation Center one more time and get a lot of information about the Sanborn Foundation. Emma is listed as a trustee of the multimillion-dollar foundation! With a bit more time you're sure you will find more about Emma Sanborn Murphy, but maybe this is enough for today. So far, so good. You fill out the research report and fax it to the development officer who requested it.

Perhaps you will find absolutely nothing on the next name you research, but today you found enough information on both Edward Smith and Emma Sanborn Murphy to determine each has the capacity to make a significant gift—if they have the inclination to do so. You have played an important part in the development process. It's up to a development officer to take it from here. It's time to go home.

❧ Appendix B ❧

Company Addresses

Companies on this list provide one or more services described in the book. Including a company here is not an endorsement of that company, nor is exclusion of a company meant to be the opposite.

Access International
Enterprise/CS
432 Columbia Street
Cambridge, MA 02141
1-617-494-0066
http://accint.com

Advanced Solutions
International, Inc.
iMIS Fund Raising
901 North Pitt Street, Suite 200
Alexandria, VA 22314
1-800-727-8682
http://www.advsol.com

Alumni Data Services
2345 Route 52, Suite A
East Fishkill, NY 12533
1-800-935-4386 x 103
http://www.
    alumnidataservices.com

Anchor Computer, Inc.
1900 New Highway
Farmingdale, NY 11735
1-516-293-6100 or
    1-800-728-6262
http://www.anchor-
    computer.com/aci_ncoa.html

Ascend Technologies, Inc.
Ascend
2658 Crosspark Road, Suite 200
Coralville, IA 52241
1-800-624-4692
http://www.ascend-tech.com

Bentz Whaley Flessner
    7251 Ohms Lane
    Minneapolis, MN 55439
    1-952-921-0111

    5272 River Road, Suite 500
    Bethesda, MD 20816
    301-656-7823
    http://www.bwf.com

Blackbaud, Inc.
Raiser's Edge & Analytics
2000 Daniel Island Drive
Charleston, SC 29492-7541
1-800-443-9441
http://www.blackbaud.com

Boyd's City Dispatch
8 Holly Street - Pocket
  Knife Square
Lakeville, CR 06039
1-800-458-7664 or
  1-860-435-0861
http://www.li.com/boyds/

Business Credit Information
  Inc. (BCI)
251 Rhode Island, Suite 207
San Francisco, CA 94103
1-800-382-1735 or
  1-415-861-4224
http://www.alumnilocators.com

Business Systems Resources
(BSR)
1000 Winter Street, Suite 1200
Waltham, MA 02451
1-781-890-2105
http://www.sungardbsr.com or
  http://www.bsr.com

CAS, Inc.
616 So. 7th Street
Omaha, NE 68114
1-800-524-0908
http://cas-online.com

CDB Infotek (Subsidiary of
  Equifax)
6 Hutton Centre
Santa Ana, CA 92707
1-800-427-3747
http://www.cdb.com/

Campagne Associates
Giftmaker Pro & Alchemy
195 McGregor Street, Suite 410
Manchester, NH 03102
1-800-582-3489
http://www.campagne.com

Community Counselling
  Service Co., Inc.
350 Fifth Avenue, Suite 7210
New York, NY 10118
1-800-223-6733
http://www.ccsfundraising.com

Compulink Management
  Center, Inc.
LaserFiche Document
  Management/Imaging
20000 Mariner Avenue
Torrance, CA 90503
1-800-8533 or 1-310-793-1888
http://www.laserfiche.com

Datatel
Benefactor
4375 Fair Lakes Court
Fairfax, VA 22033
1-703-968-9000
http://www.datatel.com

DataQuick Information Systems
9620 Towne Centre Drive
San Diego, CA 92121
1-888-597-3100
http://www.dataquick.com

DocuWare
Document Management/
   Imaging
118 Bracken Road
Montgomery, NY 12549-2604
1-888-565-5907 or
   1-845-457-4027
http://www.docuware.com

Dun & Bradstreet
3 Sylvan Way
Parsippany, NJ 07054
1-800-526-0651
http://www.dnb.com

Dunhill International List Co.,
   Inc.
1951 NW 19th Street
Boca Raton, FL 33431
1-800-386-4455 or
   1-561-347-0200
http://www.dunhills.com

eTapestry.com
9201 Harrison Park Court
Indianapolis, IN 46216-1064
1-888-739-3827 or
   1-317-545-4170
http://www.etapestry.com

Executive Marketing Services,
   Inc.
184 Sherman Blvd., Suite 300
Naperville, IL 60563
1-800-527-3933
http://www.emsphone.com

Executive Data Systems, Inc.
1640 Powers Ferry Road,
Bldg.14
Marietta, GA 30067
1-800-272-3374
http://www.execdata.com

Experian Information Solutions
(formerly TRW)
(First American Title)
701 Experian Parkway
Allen, TX 75013
1-888-397-3742 or
   1-800-527-3933
http://www.experian.com

Executive Data Systems, Inc.
Donor Records
1640 Powers Ferry Road, Bldg.
27, Suite 300
Marietta, GA 30067
1-800-272-3374
http://www.execdata.com

The Foundation Center
79 Fifth Avenue
New York, NY 10003
1-800-877-4253
http://www.fdncenter.org

Grenzebach Glier & Associates
55 West Wacker Drive, Suite 1500
Chicago, IL 60601
1-312-372-4040
http://www.grenzebachglier.com

Harris Publishing Co.
3 Barker Avenue
White Plains, NY 10601
1-800-326-6600
http://www.bcharrispub.com

HEP Development Services
Executive ID, GIFTPLUS
43212 Lindsey Marie Ct.
Ashburn, VA 20147
1-800-681-4438
http://www.
  hepdevelopment.com

Heritage Design LLC
MatchMaker
5125 North 16th Street,
  Suite C-134
Phoenix, AZ 85016
1-800-752-3100
http://www.
  MatchMaker2000.com

Imaging Technology Group
Document Management/
Imaging
16 Technology #170
Irvine, CA 92618
1-949-727-2001
http://www.imagingtech.com

Info USA
PowerFinder PhoneDisc on
  CD-ROM
5711 S. 86th Circle
Omaha, NE 68127-0347
1-402-537-6702
http://www.infousa.com/

Institutional Memory, Inc.
GiftedMemory
559 Solon Road
Chagrin Falls, OH 44022-3334
1-440-247-2957
http://www.giftedmemory.com

iWave.com
Prospect Research Online (PRO)
53 Grafton Street
Charlottetown, PEI,
  Canada C1A 1K8
1-800-655-7729
http://www.iwave.com

JSI FundRaising Systems, Inc.
  Millennium
  4732 Longhill Road,
  Suite 2201
  Williamsburg, VA 23188
  1-800-574-5772
  http://www.jsifrs.com/
    millennium

Paradigm
44 Farnsworth St.
Boston, MA 02210
1-800-521-0132
http://www.jsi.com/frs

Kofile, Inc.
Document Management/
    Imaging
1225 Jefferson Road
Rochester, NY 14623
1-716-424-1950
http://www.kofile.com

LEXIS-NEXIS
*LEXIS-NEXIS Universe for
    Development Professionals*
4520 East-West Highway
Bethesda, MD 20814-3389
1-800-227-9597
http://www.lexis-nexis.com/
    cispubs

Lorton Data, Inc.
2125 E. Hennepin Ave.,
    Suite 200
Minneapolis, MN 55413-2717
1-612-362-0200
http://www.lortondata.com

MaGIC, Inc.
Major Gifts Identification/
    Consulting
133 Carnegie Way, Suite 1200
Atlanta, GA 30303
1-877-546-2442
http://magic.ahmp.com

Marquis Who's Who
Who's Who in America, etc.
121 Chanlon Road
New Providence, NJ 07974
1-908-771-8649
http://www.
    marquiswhoswho.com

Marts & Lundy, Inc.
Potential Plus & ES Solutions
1200 Wall Street West
Lyndhurst, NJ 07071
1-800-526-9005 or
    1-201-460-1660
http://www.martsandlundy.com

Metafile Information Systems, Inc.
Results/PLUS
2900 43rd Street NW
Rochester, MN 55901
1-800-638-2445
http://www.rp.metafile.com

Optika, Inc.
Document Management/
    Imaging
7450 Campus Drive
Colorado Springs, CO 80920
1-719-548-9800
http://www.optika.com

OTG Software, Inc.
Document Management/
    Imaging
6701 Democracy Blvd.
Bethesda, MD 20817
1-800-324-4222
http://www.otg.com

PeopleSoft Inc.
4460 Hacienda Drive
Pleasanton, CA 94588
1-888-773-8277
http://www.peoplesoft.com

PG Calc Inc.
GiftCalcs & GiftWrap
129 Mount Auburn Street
Cambridge, MA 02138
1-888-497-4970
http://www.pgcalc.com

Polk Company
City Directories
37001 Industrial Road
Livonia, MI 48150
1-800-275-7655
http://www.polk.com

Primark
Prospect Insight
5161 River Road
Bethesda, MD 20816
1-301-951-1300
http://www.primark.com/pfid

Prospect Information Network
P!N: Profile Builder
501 North Grandview Avenue,
Suite 203
Daytona Beach, FL 32118
1-888-557-1326
http://www.prospectinfo.com

RuffaloCODY
221 Third Avenue SE, Suite 10
Cedar Rapids, IA 52401
1-800-756-7483
http://www.ruffalocody.com

SCT Corporation
Banner 2000
4 Country View Road
Malvern, PA 19355
1-800-223-7036
http://www.sctcorp.com

SofterWare, Inc.
DonorPerfect
540 Pennsylvania Ave.
Ft. Washington, PA 19034
1-800-220-8111
http://www.donorperfect.com

SofTrek
PledgeMaker
2350 N. Forest Road, Suite 10A
Getzville, NY 14068
1-800-442-9211
http://www.pledgemaker.com

Software Alchemy, Inc.
Document Management
P.O. Box 5566
Aloha, OR 97006-0566
1-503-848-8104
http://www.alchemy.com

SunGard Asset Mngt. Systems
SunGard Non-Profit Solutions
104 Inverness Center Place,
    Suite 325
Birmingham, AL 35242
1-888-441-9935
http://www.asset.sungard.com

Systems Support Services
Donor2
8848-B Red Oak Blvd.
Charlotte, NC 28217-5518
1-800-548-6708 or
    1-704-522-8842
http://www.donor2.com

The Taft – Gale Group
27500 Drake Road
Farmington Hills, MI 48331
1-800-877-GALE
http://www.taftgroup.com

Target America
10560 Main Street,
    Suite LL 17-19
Fairfax, VA 22030
1-703-383-6905
http://www.tgtam.com

Target Software Inc.
Team Approach
1030 Massachusetts Avenue
Cambridge, MA 02138
1-617-583-8500
http://www.targetsite.com

Thomson Financial Wealth
Identification
(formerly CDA/Investnet)
1455 Research Boulevard
Rockville, MD 20850
1-800-933-4446
http://www.wealthid.com

Technology Resource Assistance
Center (TRAC)
Exceed!
610 Cowper Street
Palo Alto, CA 94301-1807
1-800-676-5831
http://www.tracworld.com

TransUnion
P.O. Box 2000
Chester, PA 19022
1-800-888-4213
http://www.transunion.com/

Viking Systems, Inc.
Viking
236 Huntington Avenue
Boston, MA 02115
1-800-23-VIKING
http://www.vikingsys.com

WealthEngine
410 First Street SE
Washington, DC 20003
1-202-484-2776
http://www.wealthengine.com/

Whelan Group
Datamagic
155 West 19th Street, 3rd Floor
New York, NY 10011
1-212-727-7332
http://www.whalengroup.com

≫ Appendix C ≪

Associations and Organizations

Within the nonprofit advancement and development world, many associations and organizations exist to offer assistance, networking opportunities, professional research studies, and support. Check on each Web site for additional information.

Alliance of Nonprofit Mailers
1211 Connecticut Ave. NW
Washington, DC 20036
1-202-462-5132
http://www.nonprofitmailers.org/

Nonprofit researchers are often involved in their organization's direct mailing. This group was established in 1980 to represent nonprofit clients in issues relating with postal rate changes, regulations, and policies dealing with the U.S. Postal Service. A newsletter, *The Alliance Report,* keeps members advised about mailing issues.

American Association of Fundraising Counsel (AAFRC)
25 West 43rd Street, Suite 1519
New York, NY 10036
1-212-354-5799
http://www.aafrc.org/

For over 65 years AAFRC member firms have served nonprofit clients for every size and virtually every type of nonprofit organization. Those clients have come to value the AAFRC's ethical practices and professional guidance. AAFRC is the founding publisher of *Giving USA,* the annual volume telling who gave, how much, and to whom? It includes an overview of the year's giving trends and is *the* reliable source of philanthropic statistics.

American Society of Association Executives (ASAE)
1575 I Street NW
Washington, DC 20005-1103
1-202-626-2723
http://www.asaenet.org/

This association of associations is an advocate for the nonprofit sector dedicated to advancing the value of voluntary associations and supporting the professionalism of association executives. ASAE represents about 10,000 trade, professional, and philanthropic associations and publishes *Association Management.*

Association for Healthcare Philanthropy (AHP)
313 Park Avenue, Suite 400
Falls Church, VA 22046
1-703-532-6243
http://www.go-ahp.org

AHP is an association of fundraising professionals dedicated to advancing healthcare philanthropy and resource development. It provides timely and accurate information with its member publications, *AHP Connect* and *AHP Journal.*

Association for Research on Nonprofit Organizations and Voluntary Action (ARNOVA)
550 West North Street, Suite 301
Indianapolis, IN 46202-3162
1-317-684-2120
http://www.arnova.org

Founded in 1971, ARNOVA is an international interdisciplinary membership organization. It offers an open forum committed to strengthening the research community in the emerging field of nonprofit and philanthropic studies. It provides research that nonprofit professionals can use to accomplish their missions. The association publishes the *Nonprofit and Voluntary Sector Quarterly.*

Association of Fundraising Professionals (AFP)
formerly The National Society of Fund-Raising Executives
1101 King Street, Suite 700
Alexandria, VA 22314

1-703-684-0410
http://www.nsfre.org

The new name of this association broadens its scope and reflects a greater inclusiveness. Local chapters offer classes on the fundamentals of fundraising, including how to win private donations. *Advancing Philanthropy* is the association journal.

Association of Independent Information Professionals (AIIP)
7044 So.13th Street
Oak Creek, WI 53154-1429
1-414-766-0421
http://www.aiip.org

AIIP's members are individuals and owners of firms that provide information-related services to clients. They are professionals who understand information systems and are skilled in retrieval methods. From an organization with just 26 founding members in 1987, AIIP now has over 750 members.

Association of Professional Researchers for Advancement (APRA)
414 Plaza Drive, Suite 209
Westmont, IL 60559
1-630- 655-0177
http://www.APRAhome.org

The best advice you will get as a nonprofit prospect researcher is to join this association of more than 1900 researchers. "APRA is the premier international association addressing the changing needs and wide scope of skills required of advancement researchers and advancement service professionals working within the nonprofit community." The annual membership fee is $125 for new members and $100 thereafter for individual and institutional memberships.

The APRA international educational conference each summer is the ultimate research workshop. If at all possible, plan to attend soon—and often. Conferences provide opportunities for researchers to improve skills through networking and with sessions on research techniques, management issues, and technology. In addition to these opportunities, vendor exhibits, a computer lab, and a model library allow attendees to gain first-hand experience with a variety of research resources. Members are eligible for discounted fees for some products.

Ask the APRA staff if there is a regional or local chapter in your area. Twenty-eight such chapters around this country (plus a new chapter forming in Canada) offer inexpensive training sessions and meetings that allow members to network with others from diverse research fields.

As an APRA member, you will receive its publications. *Connections* is a quarterly journal that tells of new research resources and includes articles about key issues in the profession. *The Electronic Bulletin* is published six times a year and distributed by e-mail. It gives regional chapter activities and member news.

The *APRA Resource Manual* is an annual directory of members, arranged alphabetically, by states, and by organization. Members may be listed by their area of expertise: office management, research techniques, and prospect management/tracking. The APRA directory includes a copy of the APRA Code of Ethics, the Donor Bill of Rights, and a list of member benefits. A buyer's guide lists directory advertisers and conference exhibitors with addresses and phone numbers for each.

Surveys done by APRA give a detailed sketch of the membership and tell what is happening throughout the profession. Compared with others, members can sometimes justify salary increases, adding additional staff members, and updating resource budgets.

Those new to advancement research may benefit from the APRA Mentor Program that links them to veteran researchers in similar shops and geographic areas on a one-to-one basis. For those seeking a research position, APRA provides Jobquest for job postings using a variety of search capabilities. Listing positions is free for employers and job seekers at http://www.APRAhome.org/job_postings.htm

CompassPoint Nonprofit Services
(formerly The Support Centers of America)
706 Mission Street, Fifth Floor,
San Francisco, CA 94103
1-415-541-9000
http://www.compasspoint.org

CompassPoint is based in San Francisco with an affiliate office in San Jose, CA. They provide nonprofits with consulting and training services.

CompuMentor/TechSoup.org
487 Third Street
San Francisco, CA 94107
1-415-512-7784
http://www.techsoup.org

CompuMentor was formed in 1986 by a group of computer experts. It receives grants from major corporations and foundations to provide information about technology for nonprofit organizations. As TechSoup, it offers nonprofits one-stop shopping for their technology needs—often at a discount. It publishes *By The Cup*, a monthly newsletter.

Council for Advancement and Support of Education (CASE)
1307 New York Avenue NW, Suite 1000
Washington, DC 20005-4701
1-202-328-5900
http://www.case.org

CASE offers conferences and classes on research techniques for beginning and advanced development researchers at various sites within the United States. Since 1998, CASE has offered "Prospect Research on the Internet," an online course. Beginning prospect researchers meet online for five weeks for live electronic chat and private coaching with the instructors. In 2000, CASE added a research course for Canadian fundraisers. Call for details or go online to http://www.case.org/training

CASE Currents articles cover a wide range of topics of interest not only to those in educational institutions, but also to those in most types of development offices. A five-year index is online at http://www.case.org/CURRIndex/main.html

Council on Foundations (COF)
1828 L Street NW
Washington, DC 20036-5168
1-202-466-6512
http://www.cof.org

Believing that foundations play an important role in our society by changing lives and communities, the COF works to support foundations by promoting knowledge, grown, and action in philanthropy. It is a nonprofit membership association of grantmaking foundations and corporations. It publishes *Foundation News & Commentary*.

Electronic Frontier Foundation (EFF)
454 Shotwell Street
San Francisco, CA 94110-1914
1-415-436-9333
http://www.eff.org/

EFF is a nonprofit, non-partisan organization working in the public interest to protect fundamental civil liberties, including privacy and freedom of expression in the arena of computers and the Internet. It was founded in 1990, just when electronic technology, such a positive force, was posing substantial challenges to basic human and legal rights because of the ease of transmitting information.

Electronic Privacy Information Center (EPIC)
1718 Connecticut Avenue NW, Suite 200
Washington, DC 20009
1-202-483-1140
http://www.epic.org

As a public interest research center, EPIC was established in 1994 to focus public attention on civil liberties issues and to protect privacy, the First Amendment, and constitutional values.

The Grantsmanship Center (TGCI)
1125 W. Sixth Street, Fifth Floor
P.O. Box 17220
Los Angeles, CA 90017
1-213-482-9860
http://www.tgci.com/tgci

Since 1972, The Grantsmanship Center has conducted workshops and training sessions on grantsmanship and proposal writing. Its publication, *The Grantsmanship Center Magazine,* goes to nonprofit and government agencies throughout the world. Its proposal writing guide, *Program Planning and Proposal Writing*, is very popular.

Independent Sector
1200 18th Street, NW, Suite 200
Washington, D.C. 20036
1-202-467-6100
http://www.independentsector.org

The Independent Sector is a coalition of corporations, foundations, and nonprofit groups that seeks to promote, strengthen, and advance the non-profit sector so that, according to its mission statement, "it may foster civic engagement through private initiative for the public good."

Irish Researchers Group
Christine Flanagan, Manager
Research and Administration
University of Limerick Foundation
University of Limerick
Limerick, Ireland
Tel: Intl +353 61 213 194
Christine.flanagan@ul.ie
http://www.ul.ie/~ulf

Researchers in nonprofit organizations in Ireland have organized to form this group.

IT Resource Center
29 E. Madison Street, 10th Floor
Chicago, IL 60602
1-312-372-4872
http://www.itresourcecenter.org/

The IT Resource Center enables member nonprofit organizations to achieve their goals through effective use of technology. This mission is accomplished through advocacy regarding the importance of technology, technology consulting, training, and problem solving. Its newsletters are *InterLink* and *Link~lite*.

The National Center for Nonprofit Boards (NCNB)
1828 L Street NW, Suite 900
Washington, D. C. 20036-5114
1-800-883-6262
http://www.ncnb.org

NCNB is dedicated to increasing the effectiveness of nonprofit organizations by increasing the effectiveness of their board of directors. It offers guidance on board formation and development with training programs, a clearinghouse of publications, workshops, and forums. The NCNB publishes *Board Member*.

National Council of Nonprofit Associations (NCNA)
1900 L Street NW, Suite 605
Washington, DC 20036-5024
1-202-467-6262
http://www.ncna.org

NCNA is a network of 39 state and regional associations with a collective membership of more than 20,000 community nonprofits. It provides services and peer-to-peer support for the nonprofit sector. It includes a grassroots advocacy system on issues affecting nonprofits.

New England Development Research Association (NEDRA)
389 Main Street, Suite 202
Malden, MA 02148
1-781-397-8870
http://www.nedra.org

NEDRA began in 1987 with members in the United States and Canada. It provides workshops and classes in the New England region, an annual conference, networking and information sharing events, and a mentor program for new researchers. It publishes the quarterly *NEDRA News.*

NewTithing Group
Four Embarcadero Center, Suite 3700
San Francisco, CA 94111-4107
1-415-274-2765
http://newtithing.org

This California-based organization is trying to encourage wealthy people to give more to charity. Founded by Claude Rosenberg, a philanthropist and retired investment manager, the group thinks Americans should double the amount given to charity each year.

Philanthropy Roundtable
1150 17th Street NW, Suite 503
Washington, DC 20036
1-202-822-8333
http://www.philanthropyroundtable.org

As a national association of individual donors, corporate giving representatives, foundation staff and trustees, and trust and estate officers, the Philanthropy Roundtable publishes *Philanthropy.* It holds workshops, an annual conference, and offers advice on starting and maintaining foundations.

The Points of Light Foundation
1400 I Street NW, Suite 800
Washington, DC 20005
1-202-729-8000
http://www.pointsoflight.org/

The Foundation is a nonpartisan nonprofit organization devoted to promoting volunteerism with a network of 500 Volunteer Centers across the United States. Founded in 1990, it believes bringing people together through volunteer service is a powerful way to combat disconnection and alleviating social problems.

RiF: Researchers in Fundraising
Samantha Tilling, Chair
Research Office
King's College, London
Tel: +44 20 7848 3336
Researchersinfundraising@yahoo.com

Advancement researchers in Great Britain have formed an organization similar to APRA.

Society for Nonprofit Organizations (SNPO)
6314 Odana Road
Madison, WI 53719
1-800-424-7367
http://danenet.wicip.org/snpo/

The Society serves as a resource for board members, staff, and volunteers who are involved in nonprofit organizations. It publishes *Nonprofit World,* a monthly magazine on relevant nonprofit issues, a monthly report on funding opportunities, and hosts satellite-based education for the nonprofit sector.

Society of Competitive Intelligence Professionals (SCIP)
1700 Diagonal Road, Suite 600
Alexandria, VA 22314
(703) 739-0696
http://www.scip.org

Advancement researchers have much in common with professional researchers in the corporate world. SCIP is the premiere online community for professionals in the area of competitive intelligence.

The Urban Institute
Center on Nonprofits & Philanthropy
2100 M Street NW
Washington, DC 20037
1-202-833-7200
http://www.urban.org/centers/cnp.html

The Center includes the National Center for Charitable Statistics (NCCS) which serves as the national repository of statistical information on the nonprofit sector from the IRS and other sources. These data enable researchers to develop a comprehensive picture of nonprofit sector trends and analyses of financial data. It in involved in providing scanned images of the Form 990 for online access.

Bibliography

Resources listed here are not necessarily recommended. Nor is the exclusion of a resource meant to discredit it. Publications mentioned in the text, but not in this bibliography, are available in many academic and public libraries.

Advancing Philanthropy. Association of Fund Raising Professionals,1101 King Street, Suite 700, Alexandria,VA 22314. Members receive one free subscription; non-members subscriptions are $50 for one year.

The American Almanac of Jobs and Salaries. Wright, John W., Ed. Harper Collins, 1000 Keystone Industrial Park, Scranton, PA 18512. 1-800-223-0690. $20.

American Bench. Forster-Long, Inc., 3280 Ramos Circle, Sacramento, CA 95827. 1-916-362-3277. $340, plus $5 shipping.

American Demographics Magazine. Intertec Publishing Co., 11 Riverbend Drive S., Stamford, CT 06907. 1-800-828-1133. $69 a year.

Annual Register of Grant Support. RR Bowker, 121 Chanlon Road, New Providence, RJ 07974. 1-800-521-8110. $210.

Association for Healthcare Philanthropy Journal. Association for Healthcare Philanthropy, 313 Park Avenue, Suite 400, Falls Church,VA 22046. 1-703-532-6243. Free with membership; non-members subscriptions are $40 a year.

Avenue magazine. 950 Third Avenue, 5th Floor, NewYork, NY 10022. 1-212-758-9516. Includes individuals in the Jewish community. Call for subscription price.

Bibliography: Resources for Prospect Development. BentzWhaley Flessner, 7251 Ohms Lane, Minneapolis, MN 55439. 1-952-921-0111. $35.

Biographpy & Genealogy Master Index (BGMI) 2001. The Gale Group, P.O. 9187, Farmington Hills, MI 48333-9187. Call 1-800-877-GALE. $260. Also available on CD-ROM and in a five-year cumulation in four volumes.

242 | Where the Money Is

Black Enterprise Magazine. Earl G. Graves Publishing Co., Inc., 130 Fifth Avenue, 10th Floor, New York, NY 10011-4399. 1-800-886-9618. $19.95 a year.

Book of American Family Trees. Bergquist, Inez, ed. Waltman Associates, 7800 Metro Parkway, Suite 300, Minneapolis, MN 55425. 1-612-338-0772. $295.

Book of Minnesota Family Trees. Bergquist, Inez, Ed., Waltman Associates, 7800 Metro Parkway, Suite 300, Minneapolis, MN 55425. 1-612-338-0772. $149.

Boston Business Journal. Boston Business Journal, 200 High Street, 4B, Boston, MA 02110. 1-617-330-1000. $89 a year.

Broadcasting & Cable Yearbook. RR Bowker, 121 Chanlon Road, New Providence, NJ 07974. 1-888-269-5372. $179.95, plus shipping.

Brooks, David. *Bobos in Paradise: The New Upper Class and How they Got There.* 2000. Simon & Schuster. $25.

Burke's Peerage and Baronetage, 2 vol. 2000. Distributed by Fitzroy Dearborn, Chicago. (Available on Amazon.com.) $395.

Business First (Buffalo). Business First, 472 Delaware Avenue, Buffalo, NY 14202. 1-716-882-6200. $76 a year.

Business Journal Book of Lists. American Business Journal, 120 West Morehead Street, Suite 100, Charlotte, NC 28202. 1-800-486-3289. Call for prices.

Business Week. McGraw-Hill, Inc. P.O. Box 645, Hightstown, NJ 08520. 1-800-635-1200. $54.94 a year.

Canadian Directory of Foundations. Canadian Centre for Philanthropy, 425 University Avenue, Suite 7oo, Toronto, Ontario M5G 1T6. 1-416-597-2993. $195 Canadian for members; $295 Canadian for non-members, plus $10 shipping.

CASE Currents. Council for Advancement and Support of Education (CASE) 1307 New York Avenue NW, Suite 1000, Washington, DC 20005-4701. 1-800-554-8536. $95 a year.

CCH Capital Changes Reporter. 7 volumes. Weekly update subscription service at approximately $1425-$1800 annually. Commerce Clearing House Inc., 4025 W. Peterson Avenue, Chicago, IL 60646-6085. 1-800-TELL-CCH.

Chicago Magazine. Chicago Publishing, Inc., P.O. Box 57285, Boulder, CO 80322. 1-800-999-0879. $19.90 a year.

The Chronicle of Higher Education. 1255 23rd St. NW, Suite 700, Washington, DC 20037. 1-800-842-7817. $75 a year.

The Chronicle of Philanthropy. 1255 23rd St. NW, Suite 700, Washington, DC 20037. 1-800-287-6072. $67.50 a year.

The Chronicle's Nonprofit Handbook. More than one thousand resources are listed in the easy-to use, fully searchable database from *The Chronicle of Philanthropy.* Available free to subscribers at http://philanthropy.com/handbook

City Directories. The Polk Company, 37001 Industrial Road, Livonia, MI 48150. 1-800-275-7655. Prices vary.

Complete Marquis Who's Who on CD-ROM. RR Bowker, 121 Chanlon Road, New Providence, NJ 07974. 1-800-521-8110. $1995 for a one year subscription with semi-annual updates. Includes back volumes.

Congressional Staff Directory. CQ Staff Directories, 1414 22nd Street NW, 6th Floor, Washington, DC 20036. 1-800-638-1710. $169 for a single edition; $279 for spring, summer, and fall issues.

Connections. Association of Professional Researchers for Advancement (APRA), 414 Plaza Drive, Suite 209, Westmont, IL 60559. 1-630-655-0177. Free to members.

Contemporary Black Biography. Gale Research, Inc. P.O. 33477, Detroit, MI 48232-5477. 1-800-877-GALE. $60 each volume.

Contributions. Contributions, P.O. Box 338, Medfield, MA 02052-0338. 1-508-359-2703. $40 a year.

The Corporate Directory of U.S. Public Companies. Walker's Research, 1650 Borel Place, Suite 130, San Mateo, CA 94402. 1-800-258-5737 $360 in hardcover; $595 on CD-ROM, plus $8 shipping.

Corporate Foundation Profiles. The Foundation Center, 79 Fifth Avenue, New York, NY 10003-3076. 1-800-424-9836. $155.

Corporate Giving Directory. The Taft Group, P.O. Box 9187, Farmington Hills, MI 48333. 1-800-877-TAFT. $485.

Corporate Philanthropy Report. Aspen Publishers, 7201 McKinney Circle, Frederick, MD 21704. 1-800-655-5597. $229 a year.

Corporate Yellow Book: Who's Who at the Leading U.S. Companies. Leadership Directories, Inc., 104 Fifth Avenue, 2nd Floor, New York, NY 10011. 1-212-627-4140. Quarterly for $290 a year.

Crain's Business. Crain Detroit Business, 1400 Woodbridge Avenue, Detroit, MI 48207-3187. 1-800-678-9595. $89 for Chicago annual subscription; $53 for Cleveland annual subscription; and $53 for Detroit annual subscription.

Cumulative List of Organizations. (IRS Publication 78) Internal Revenue Service, Superintendent Of Documents, P.O. Box 371954, Pittsburgh, PA 15250-7954. 1-202-512-1800. $91 with supplements.

Debrett's Peerage & Baronetage. Published every 5 years. Debrett's Peerage Limited, 73-77 Britannia Road, London, SW6 2JY, England. 44 (0) 171 916 9633. $375. (Use at a library.)

Directory of American Firms Operating in Foreign Countries. Uniworld Business Publications, 257 Central Park West, Suite 10A, New York, NY 10024. 1-212-752-0329. $325 for print version; $975 for CD-ROM subscription.

Directory of Computer and High Technology Grants. Research Grant Guides Inc., P.O. Box 1214, Loxahatchee, FL 33470. 1-561-795-6129. $59.50.

Directory of Corporate Affiliations. National Register Publishing Company, 121 Chanlon Road, New Providence, NJ 07974. 1-800-521-8110. $1059. Also available on CD-ROM.

Directory of Directors in the City of Boston and Vicinity. The Bankers Service Company, Boston, MA 1-617-742-5786. $320.

Directory of Directors in the City of New York and Tri-State Area. Directory of Directors Company, P.O. Box 462. Southport, CT. 06490. 1-203-255-8525. Book $265 plus shipping; CD-ROM $400..

Directory of Operating Grants. Research Grant Guides, Inc., P.O. Box 1214, Loxahatchee, FL 33470. 1-561-795-6129. $59.50.

Directory of Public Libraries Offering Information and Referral Services. American Library Association, Order Fulfillment Dept., 155 N. Wacker Drive, Chicago, IL 60606-1719. 1-800-545-2433 x 2153. $28.

Donor Series. National Connections. Bergquist, Inez, Ed. Waltman Associates, 7800 Metro Parkway, Suite 300, Minneapolis, MN 55425. 1-612-338-0772. CD-ROMs for several geographical areas. Call for details.

Dun and Bradstreet Regional Business Directories. Dun and Bradstreet Information Services, Three Sylvan Way, Parsippany, NJ 07054-3896. 1-800-526-0651 Lists top 20,000 companies ranked by sales in various regions. Call for prices.

Dun & Bradstreet Million Dollar Disc and *Dun & Bradstreet Million Dollar Plus.* Dun & Bradstreet Information Services, Three Sylvan Way, Parsippany, NJ 07054-3896. 1-800-526-0651. Call for prices.

Ebony—100 Most Influential Black Americans Issue. May issue. Johnson Publishing Company, Inc., 820 S. Michigan Avenue, Chicago, IL 60605. 1-312-322-9200. $14.95 a year.

Ethics in Nonprofit Management. 1998. O'Neill, Michael. Institute for Nonprofit Organization Management. 2130 Fulton Street, San Francisco, CA 04117-1080. 1-415-422-2336. $25.

FC Search: The Foundation Center's Database on CD-ROM. The Foundation Center, 79 Fifth Avenue, New York, NY 10003-3076. 1-800-424-9836. $1,195.

Financial Yellow Book: Who's Who at the Leading U.S. Financial Institutions. Leadership Directories, Inc., 104 Fifth Avenue, 2nd Floor, New York, NY 10011. 1-212-627-4140. $223.

Forbes. Forbes, P.O. Box 10048, Des Moines, IA 50340-0048. 1-800-888-9896. $59.95 a year.

Fortune. Time Customer Service Inc., P.O. Box 60001, Tampa, FL 33660-0001. 1-800-233-9003. $59.95 a year.

The Foundation Center's Guide to Grantseeking on the Web. 2000. The Foundation Center. 79 Fifth Avenue, New York, NY 10003. 1-800-424-9836. $19.95.

The Foundation Center's Guide to Proposal Writing. 2001. The Foundation Center, 79 Fifth Avenue, New York, NY 10003. 1-800-424-9836. $34.95.

The Foundation Directory. The Foundation Center, 79 Fifth Avenue, New York, NY 10003-3076. 1-800-424-9836. Available in hardcopy, on CD-ROM, and online. Call for pricing and check the Web site: www.fdncenter.org.

Foundation Reporter. The Taft Group. P.O. Box 9187, Farmington Hills, MI 48333. 1-800-877-TAFT. $425.

Fund Raising Management Magazine. Hoke Communications, Inc., 224 Seventh Street, Garden City, NY 11530. 1-516-746-6700. $58 a year.

Giving USA. 2001. American Association of Fundraising Counsel Trust for Philanthropy, P.O. Box 1020, Sewickley, PA 15143-1020, 1-888-544-8464. Computer disk is $135, plus $9 shipping. Print copies are $65, plus $6 shipping.

Government Assistance Almanac. Dumouchel, J. Robert, ed. Omnigraphics, 615 Griswold Street, Detroit, MI 48226. 1-800-234-1340. $195.

Grants on Disc. Annual subscription to CD-ROM with quarterly updates. $695. The Taft Group, P.O. Box 9187, Farmington Hills, MI 48333. 1-800-877-TAFT.

GrantScape: Electronic Fundraising Database on CD-ROM. Aspen Publishers, 7201 McKinney Circle, Frederick, MD 21705 1-800-655-5597. $595.

Guide to Greater Washington D.C. Grantmakers on CD-ROM. The Foundation Center, 79 Fifth Avenue, New York, NY 10003. 1-800-424-9836. $75.

Haines Criss+Cross Directory. 7957 Fernham Drive, Forestville, MD 20747. 1-301-736-2720. Call for pricing.

Hispanic Business. Hispanic Business. 425 Pine Avenue, Goleta, CA 93117-3709. 1-805-964-4554. $12 a year.

Hoover's Handbook of Private Companies. Hoover's Inc. 1033 La Posada Drive, Suite 250, Austin, TX 78752. 1-800-486-8666. $139.95.

Hoover's Master List of Major U.S. Companies. Hoover's Inc., 1033 La Posada Drive, Suite 250, Austin, TX 78752. 1-800-486-8666. $99.95.

How to Locate Anyone Who's Ever Been in the Military. 1999-2000. MIE Publishing, P.O. Box 17118, Spartanburg, SC 29301. 1-800-937-2133. $19.95.

Index to Who's Who Publications. RR Bowker, 121 Chanlon Road, New Providence, NJ 07974. 1-800-521-8110. $103.50. Indexes latest editions.

The Industry Standard. 1-800-395-1977. $37.97 a year. http://www.thestandard.com

International Directory of Company Histories. Distributed by Gale Group, 27500 Drake Road, Farmington Hills, MI. 48331-3535. 1-800-877-GALE. 33 volume set. $180 each volume. (Use at a large public or academic library.)

Judicial Yellow Book: Who's Who in Federal and State Courts. Leadership Directories, Inc., 104 Fifth Avenue, 2nd Floor, New York, NY 10011. 1-212-627-4140. $235.

Lilith: The Independent Jewish Women's Magazine. Lilith Publications, Inc., 250 W.57th St., Suite 2432, New York, NY 10107. 1-800-783-4903. $18 a year.

National Connections Directory. Bergquist, Inez, ed. Waltman Associates, 7800 Metro Parkway, Suite 300, Minneapolis, MN 55425. 1-612-338-0772. $195.

National Cyclopedia of American Biography, 1898 to the last 1980s. (Use at a large public or academic library.)

National Directory of Corporate Giving. The Foundation Center, 79 Fifth Avenue, New York, NY 10003. 1-800-424-9836. $195.

National Directory of Minority-Owned Business Firms. Gale Research, Inc., P.O. Box 34777, Detroit, MI 48232-5477. 1-800-877-GALE. $285.

National Directory of Women-Owned Business Firms. Gale Research, Inc., P.O. Box 34777, Detroit, MI 48331-3535. 1-800-877-8238. $275.

NEDRA News. New England Development Research Association, 389 Main Street, Suite 202, Malden, MA 02148. 1-781-397-8870. $50 for individuals in non-profits; $80 for individuals and consultants for profit. Free with NEDRA membership.

New York Times Index, 1913 to present. (Use at a large public or academic library.)

Nonprofit Sector Yellow Book. Leadership Directories, Inc., 104 Fifth Avenue, New York, NY 10011. 1-212-627-4140. $223.

The Nonprofit Times. 240 Cedar Knolls Road, Suite 318, Cedar Knolls, NJ 07927. 1-973-734-1700. $59 a year; free for nonprofits.

Notable Black American Men. The Gale Group, 27500 Drake Road, Farmington Hills, MI 48331-3535. 1-800-877-8238. $99.

Notable Black American Women. Gale Research, Inc., P.O. Box 33477, Detroit, MI 48232-5477. 1-800-877-GALE. 2 volumes, each $99.

Notable Hispanic American Women. Gale Research, Inc., P.O. 33477, Detroit, MI 48232-5477. 1-800-877-GALE. $85.

The Philanthropy News Network Online. The Philanthropy News Network, 5 West Hargett Street, Suite 805, Raleigh, NC 27601. 1-919-832-2325. $60 a year.

Potomac Tech Journal. 1555 Wilson Blvd., Suite 400, Arlington, VA 22209. 1-703-741-3716. $75 a year. http://www.potomactechjournal.com

Privacy Journal. P.O. Box 28577, Providence, RI 02908. 1-401-274-7861. $118 a year.

Prospector's Choice on CD-ROM. The Gale Group. P.O. Box 9187, Farmington Hills, MI 48333-9187. 1-800-877-4253. $849.

Readers' Guide to Periodical Literature. 1905- present. H.W. Wilson Company, New York. (Use at a library.)

The Rich Register (2000 individuals worth over $100 million). *The Junior Rich Register* (1800 individuals worth between $25 million and $100 million). *Mini Rich Register* (for individual states). Published by The Rich Register, 7520 Stonecliff Drive, Austin, TX 78731. Call 1-512-477-8871 for prices.

The Social List of Washington (The Green Book). Thomas J. Murray, P.O. Box 29, Kensington, MD 20895. Call 1-301-949-7544 for price.

Social Register. Annual. Copies available with written request to the Social Register Association, 381 Park Avenue South, New York, NY 10016. 1-800-221-5277 or 1-212-685-2634. $105. (Several other cities have Social Registers, including Los Angeles, Cincinnati, Denver, and Seattle. Check a local library there.)

The Sourcebook of Zip Code Demographics. CACI, 1100 N. Glebe Road, Arlington, Va. 22201. 1-703-841-4400. $495 for zip code edition; $395 for country edition.

Standard and Poor's Register of Corporations, Directors and Executives. Standard and Poor's, 65 Broadway, 8th Floor, New York, NY 10006. 1-800-221-5277. $849 for 3-volume set; $1095 for CD-ROM.

Stanley, Thomas J. and William D. Danko. *The Millionaire Next Door.* Pocket Books. $7.99.

Stanley, Thomas J. *The Millionaire Mind.* 2000. Andrew McMeel. $26.95.

Successful Fund Raising. Stevenson Consultants, Inc., 417 Eton Court, Sioux City, IA 51104. 1-712-239-3010. $120 a year.

Thomas Register. Thomas Publishing Company. 1-800-222-7900. This national directory of 152,000 manufacturers is available free on the Internet at http://www.thomasregister.com

Town and Country magazine. Published at 1700 Broadway, New York, NY 10019. 1-212-903-5000. Subscribe to P.O. Box 7182, Red Oak, IA 51591. 1-800-289-8696. $24 a year.

Town and Country Magazine Personal Name Index. Waltman Associates, 7800 Metro Parkway, Suite 300, Minneapolis, MN 55425. 1-612-338-0772. $95.

Wall Street Journal newspaper. Dow Jones Publishing Co., 84 Second Avenue, Chicopee, MA 01020. 1-800-568-7625. $175 a year.

Washington Technology. 8500 Leesburg Pike, Suite 7500, Vienna, VA 22182-2496. 1-703-848-2800. Free to some. http://www. washingtontechnology. com

Weiss, Michael J. *The Clustered World: How We Live, What We Buy, and What it Means About Who We Are.* 2000. 2000. Little Brown. $27.50. Little, Brown.

Who Was Who in America. Marquis Who's Who, 121 Chanlon Road, New Providence, NJ 07974. 1-800-521-8110. An index volume covers 1607-1996. $135. (Use other volumes at a library.)

Who's Wealthy in America 2000. 2 volume set. The Taft Group. P.O. Box 9187, Farmington Hills, MI 48333. 1-800-877-TAFT. $479.

Who's Who (British). A. & C Black Ltd., Howard Road, Eaton Socon, Huntington, Cambridgeshire, England, UK PE19 3EZ. 44 1480 212666. 105 pounds sterling.

Who's Who Among African Americans. The Taft Group, P.O. Box 9187, Farmington Hills, MI 48333. 1-800-877-TAFT. $175.

Who's Who Among Asian Americans. 1994. The Taft Group, P.O. Box 9187, Farmington Hills, MI 48333. 1-800-877-TAFT. $99

Who's Who Among Hispanic Americans. 1994. The Taft Group, P.O. Box 9187, Farmington Hills, MI 48333. 1-800-877-TAFT. $125.

Who's Who in America. $575 for 3 volumes. *Complete Marquis Who's Who on CD-ROM.* $995. *The Index to Marquis Who's Who Publications.* Marquis Who's Who, 121 Chanlon Road, New Providence, NJ 07974. Call 1-

800-521-8110 for a complete listing of regional and professional directories.

Who's Who of American Women. Marquis Who's Who, 121 Chanlon Road, New Providence, NJ 07974. 1-800-521-8110. $259.

Women's Philanthropy Institute News. Women's Philanthropy Institute. 6314 Odana Road, Suite 1, Madison, WI 53719. 1-608-270-5205. $50 a year.

Working Woman. Lang Communications, 135 W. 50th Street, 16th Floor, New York, NY 10020. 1-800-234-9675. Subscribe to P.O. Box 3274, Harlan, IA 51537. $11 a year.

Worth magazine. Capital Publishing, 575 Lexington Avenue, New York, NY 10022. 1-800-777-1851. $18 a year.

➤•◄

➤ Index ❖

For listings of companies that provide research services, see pages 191–194 and Appendix B, pages, 223-229. For individual Web sites not indexed here, please refer to the chapter titles.

Order Form

Where the Money Is: Advancement Research for Nonprofit Organizations by Helen Bergan   ISBN: 0-9615277-7-3

Number of copies _____ x $45.00   _____
Shipping/Handling $5.00 first copy   _____
$1.00 each additional copy   _____
Non tax-exempt Virginians only
Add 4.5 % sales tax ($2.03 per copy)   _____
Total   _____

Payment:

_____   Check enclosed (payable to BioGuide Press)

_____   Credit Card   _____ Visa   _____ Master Card

Card number _____

Expiration Date (Month/Year) _____/ _____

Name, as it appears on card _____

Signature _____

Ship book(s) to:

Name _____

Title _____

Organization _____

Address _____

_____

City/State/Zip _____

Telephone (_____) _____

Send order to: BioGuide Press
P.O. 42005
Arlington, VA 22204

Telephone orders with credit card: (703) 820-9045